An American National Standard

IEEE Standards for Local Area Networks:

Token-Passing Bus Access Method and Physical Layer Specifications

Published by
The Institute of Electrical and Electronics Engineers, Inc

Distributed in cooperation with
Wiley-Interscience, a division of John Wiley & Sons, Inc

IEEE Standards documents are developed within the Technical Committees of the IEEE Societies and the Standards Coordinating Committees of the IEEE Standards Board. Members of the committees serve voluntarily and without compensation. They are not necessarily members of the Institute. The standards developed within IEEE represent a consensus of the broad expertise on the subject within the Institute as well as those activities outside of IEEE which have expressed an interest in participating in the development of the standard.

Use of an IEEE Standard is wholly voluntary. The existence of an IEEE Standard does not imply that there are no other ways to produce, test, measure, purchase, market, or provide other goods and services related to the scope of the IEEE Standard. Furthermore, the viewpoint expressed at the time a standard is approved and issued is subject to change brought about through developments in the state of the art and comments received from users of the standard. Every IEEE Standard is subjected to review at least once every five years for revision or reaffirmation. When a document is more than five years old, and has not been reaffirmed, it is reasonable to conclude that its contents, although still of some value, do not wholly reflect the present state of the art. Users are cautioned to check to determine that they have the latest edition of any IEEE Standard.

Comments for revision of IEEE Standards are welcome from any interested party, regardless of membership affiliation with IEEE. Suggestions for changes in documents should be in the form of a proposed change of text, together with appropriate supporting comments.

Interpretations: Occasionally questions may arise regarding the meaning of portions of standards as they relate to specific applications. When the need for interpretations is brought to the attention of IEEE, the Institute will initiate action to prepare appropriate responses. Since IEEE Standards represent a consensus of all concerned interests, it is important to ensure that any interpretation has also received the concurrence of a balance of interests. For this reason IEEE and the members of its technical committees are not able to provide an instant response to interpretation requests except in those cases where the matter has previously received formal consideration.

Comments on standards and requests for interpretations should be addressed to:

> Secretary, IEEE Standards Board
> 345 East 47th Street
> New York, NY 10017
> USA

ANSI/IEEE Std 802.4-1985
ISO Draft
International
Standard 8802/4

An American National Standard

IEEE Standards for Local Area Networks:

Token-Passing Bus Access Method and Physical Layer Specifications

Sponsor

**Technical Committee on Computer Communications
of the
IEEE Computer Society**

Approved June 13, 1984
IEEE Standards Board

Approved December 17, 1984
American National Standards Institute

ISBN 0-471-82750-9

Library of Congress Catalog Number 84-43094

© Copyright 1985 by

**The Institute of Electrical and Electronics Engineers, Inc
345 East 47th Street, New York, NY 10017, USA**

*No part of this publication may be reproduced in any form,
in an electronic system or otherwise,
without the prior written permission of the publisher.*

February 25, 1985

Foreword

(This Foreword is not a part of IEEE Std 802.4-1985, IEEE Standard Token-Passing Bus Access Method and Physical Layer Specifications.)

This standard is part of a family of standards for Local Area Networks (LANs). The relationship between this standard and other members of the family is shown below. (The numbers in the figure refer to IEEE Standard numbers.)

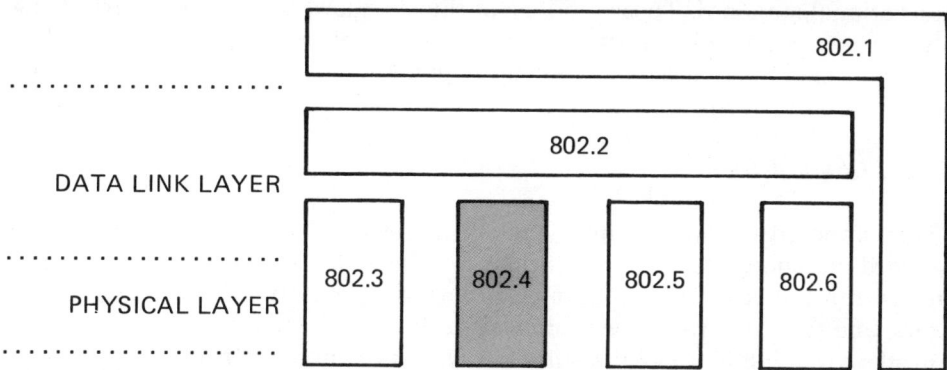

This family of standards deals with the physical and data link layers as defined by the ISO Open System Interconnection Reference Model. The access standards define three types of medium access technologies and associated physical media, each appropriate for particular applications or system objectives. The standards defining these technologies are

(1) IEEE Std 802.3-1985 (ISO DIS 8802/3), a bus utilizing CSMA/CD as the access method

(2) IEEE Std 802.4-1985 (ISO DIS 8802/4), a bus utilizing token passing as the access method

(3) IEEE Std 802.5[1], a ring utilizing token passing as the access method

Other access methods (for example, metropolitan area networks) are under investigation.

IEEE Std 802.2[2] (ISO DIS 8802/2), IEEE Standard Logical Link Control protocol, is used in conjunction with the medium access standards.

A companion document, IEEE 802.1[3], (ISO 8802/1), describes the relationship among these standards and their relationship to the ISO Open Systems Interconnection Reference Model in more detail. This companion document also explains the relation of the standards to higher layer protocols, and discusses internetworking and network management issues.

The reader of this standard is urged to become familiar with the complete family of standards.

Portions of the text of this standard are the ISO DIS 8802/4 standard supported by the ISO, International Organization for Standardization.

---

[1] Approval and publication anticipated for early 1985.

[2] This standard has been approved and publication is anticipated for early 1985.

[3] In preparation.

Some portions of the text of this standard are peculiar to IEEE Std 802.4-1985, specifically areas relating to
(1) References to national standards
(2) Recommended frequency allocations for North American CATV systems (see 14.9.4)
(3) Recommendations and guidelines related to safety concerns

To avoid duplications of standards the ISO has not developed a separate international standard. Those sections of this standard that are not part of the International Standard are prefaced with a note enclosed in braces '{...}'.

At the time of publication of this document, ISO Standard 8802/4 is a Draft International Standard (DIS).

IEEE Std 802.4-1985

This standard contains state-of-the-art material. The area covered by this standard is undergoing rapid evolution. Revisions are anticipated to this standard within the next few years, to clarify existing material, to correct possible errors, and to incorporate new related material.

Readers wishing to know the state of revisions should contact the
Secretary
IEEE Standards Board
Institute of Electrical and Electronics Engineers, Inc
345 East 47th Street
New York, NY 10017, USA

The parts of this standard relating to the immediate response mechanism are for Trial Use. This mechanism has not received as widespread review as the rest of this standard and had not been commercially implemented at the time the revised standard was approved.

The Trial Use parts of this standard are in italic type.

When the IEEE Standards Board approved this standard on June 13, 1984, it had the following membership:

James H. Beall, *Chairman*   **John E. May,** *Vice Chairman*

Sava I. Sherr, *Secretary*

J. J. Archambault	Jay Forster	Donald T. Michael[*]
J. T. Boettger	Daniel L. Goldberg	John P. Riganati
J. V. Bonucchi	Donald N. Heirman	Frank L. Rose
Rene Castenschiold	Irvin N. Howell, Jr	Robert W. Seelbach
Edward Chelotti	Jack Kinn	Jay A. Stewart
Edward J. Cohen	Joseph L. Koepfinger[*]	Clifford O. Swanson
Len S. Corey	Irving Kolodny	W. B. Wilkens
Donald C. Fleckenstein	George Konomos	Charles J. Wylie

[*]Member emeritus

The following members were participants in the Token-Bus Access Method effort of the IEEE Project 802 Working Group. Those names followed by an asterisk were voting members of the 802.4 Token-Bus Subcommittee at the time of approval of this standard.

Bob Douglas*, *Chairman* **Laurie Lindsey***, *Secretary*

Om Agrawal	Maris Graube	Juan Pimentel
Phil Arneth	Ed Harada	Lavern Pope
Jeff Bobzin	Lo Hsieh	Dave Potter
Mark Bauer*	Karen Hsing	Dennis Quy
Le Biu	Kevin Hughes	John Rance
Clyde Boenke*	Marco Hurtado	Dan Ratner*
Bob Bowen	Bob Husak*	Richard Read
Bob Bridge	Dittmar Janetzky*	Ted Rebenko
Chuck Brill	Ross Jaibaji	John Ricketson
Wayne Brodd	George Jelatis*	Edouard Rocher
Werner Bux	Gabor Kardos	Rob Rosenthal
Jim Campbell	Peggy Karp	Chip Schnarel
Tony Capel	Kristin Kocan	Walter Schreuer*
Dave Carlson	Zak Kong	Gerard Segarra
Ron Cates	Sy Korowitz*	Dennis Sosnoski
Rao Cherukuri	George Koshy*	Robert C. Smith
Po Chen*	Don Kotas	Mark Stahlman
Jade Chien	Tony Kozlik	Steve Stearns*
Mike Clader	Mike Kryskow	Garry Stephens
Jerry Clancy	Dave Laffitte	Mark Steiglitz*
Rich Collins*	Terry Lawell	Kathleen Sturgis*
Steve Cooper	Ron Leuchs	Bob Stover
Bob Crowder*	Peter Lin	Bart Stuck
Kirit Davé	Jim Lindgren	Dave Sweeton
John Davidson	Bill Livingston*	Dan Sze
Em Delahostria	Then Tang Liu	Vic Tarassov
Jan Dolphin	Don C. Loughry	Angus Telfer*
Bob Donnan	Don J. Loughry*	Dave Thompson
Bill Durrenberger	Bruce Loyer*	Fouad Tobagi
Rich Fabbri	Jerry Lurtz*	Jean-Marie Tourret
Eldon Feist*	Bill Miller	Bo Viklund
Jim Field	Ken Miller	Bruce Watson
Larry Foltzer	Lou Mitta	Don Weir
Ron Floyd	Bob Moles	Dan Wendling
Darrell Furlong	Jim Mollenauer	Walter Wheeler
Mel Gable*	Ware Myers	Hugh White
Mike Garvey	Gene Nines	Steve Whiteside
Bud Glick	Bill Northup	Earl Whitaker
Arie Goldberg	Brian O'Neil	Ping Wu
Pat Gonia*	Kul Padda	Esin Ulug
Gordon Griffiths	Mahendra Patel	Hiroshi Yoshida
Bob Grow	Tom Phinney*	Hank Zannini

Special thanks are due to J. Michael Kryskow, G. J. (Jerry) Clancy, and Thomas L. Phinney for their technical contributions.

Contents

SECTION	PAGE

1. Introduction and Overview 15
   1.1 Scope... 15
   1.2 Definitions... 16
   1.3 References.. 16
   1.4 Compliance 17
   1.5 Overview of the Token Method 19
   1.6 MAC Layer Internal Structure........................ 20
   1.7 Physical Layer and Media 22
   1.8 Access Method Characteristics........................ 25
   1.9 Standard Organization............................... 26
2. LLC-MAC Interface Service Specification 27
   2.1 Overview of the LLC-MAC Service 28
   2.2 Detailed Interactions with the LLC Entity.............. 29
3. Station Management—MAC Interface Service Specification 32
   3.1 Overview of the Station Management—MAC Service......... 32
   3.2 Detailed Interactions with the Station Management Entity..... 34
4. Frame Formats.. 42
   4.1 Frame Components 43
   4.2 Enumeration of Frame Types......................... 50
   4.3 Appendix—Recommendation for a Hierarchical Structure for Locally-Administered Addresses 52
5. Elements of MAC Sublayer Operation......................... 54
   5.1 Basic Operation.................................... 55
   5.2 Access Control Machine (ACM) States 63
   5.3 Interface Machine Description......................... 69
   5.4 Receive Machine Description 70
   5.5 Transmit Machine Description......................... 74
   5.6 Regenerative Repeater Machine Description 74
6. MAC Sublayer Definitions and Requirements 75
   6.1 MAC Definitions 75
   6.2 Transmission Order................................. 78
   6.3 Delay Labeling 78
   6.4 Miscellaneous Requirements 78
   6.5 Use of Address Bits in Contention Algorithms............ 81
   6.6 Options Within MAC Sublayer 82
   6.7 Delegation of Right to Transmit 83
7. Access Control Machine (ACM) Formal Description............. 83
   7.1 Variables and Functions.............................. 83
   7.2 Access Control Machine Formal Description.............. 93
8. MAC—Physical Layer Interface Service Specification 130
   8.1 Overview of the LAN Physical Layer Service............. 130
   8.2 Detailed Specifications of Interactions with the Physical Layer Entity 131

SECTION	PAGE

9. Generic Station Management—Physical Layer Interface Service Specification 135
   9.1 Overview of the LAN Physical Layer Management Service 136
   9.2 Detailed Specifications of Interactions with the Station Management Entity... 137
10. Single-Channel Phase-Continuous-FSK Bus Physical Layer Specification 141
   10.1 Nomenclature 142
   10.2 Object 143
   10.3 Compatibility Considerations............................. 144
   10.4 Overview of the Single-Channel Phase-Continuous-FSK Bus Medium.. 144
   10.5 Overview of the Phase-Continuous-FSK Bus Physical Layer 144
   10.6 Detailed Application of Section 9, Generic Station Management to Physical Layer Interface Service Specification 146
   10.7 Single-Channel Phase-Continuous-FSK Physical Layer Functional, Electrical, and Mechanical Specifications.......... 146
   10.8 Environmental Specifications............................. 150
   10.9 Labeling 151
11. Single-Channel Phase-Continuous-FSK Bus Medium "Layer" Specification..................................... 152
   11.1 Nomenclature 153
   11.2 Object 154
   11.3 Compatibility Considerations............................. 155
   11.4 Overview of the Phase-Continuous-FSK Bus Medium "Layer" ... 155
   11.5 Bibliography 156
   11.6 Single-Channel Phase-Continuous-FSK Bus Medium "Layer" Functional, Electrical, and Mechanical Specifications.......... 156
   11.7 Environmental Specifications............................. 158
   11.8 Transmission Path Delay Considerations 160
   11.9 Documentation.. 160
   11.10 Network Sizing 161
   11.11 Appendix—Guidelines for Configuring the Medium of a Single-Channel Phase-Continuous-FSK Bus LAN 161
12. Single-Channel Phase-Coherent-FSK Bus Physical Layer Specification 164
   12.1 Nomenclature 164
   12.2 Object 166
   12.3 Compatibility Considerations............................. 166
   12.4 Operational Overview of the Single-Channel Phase-Coherent-FSK Bus Medium......................... 166
   12.5 Overview of the Phase-Coherent-FSK Bus Physical Layer 167
   12.6 Detailed Application of Section 9, Gerneric Station Management to Physical Layer Interface Service Specification 168
   12.7 Single-Channel Phase-Coherent-FSK Bus Physical Layer Functional, Electrical, and Mechanical Specifications.......... 168
   12.8 Environmental Specifications............................. 173
   12.9 Labeling 174

SECTION	PAGE

13.	Single-Channel Phase-Coherent-FSK Bus Medium "Layer" Specification	174
13.1	Nomenclature	176
13.2	Object	177
13.3	Compatibility Considerations	177
13.4	Overview of the Phase-Coherent-FSK Bus Medium "Layer"	178
13.5	Bibliography	179
13.6	Single-Channel Phase-Coherent-FSK Bus Medium "Layer" Functional, Electrical, and Mechanical Specifications	180
13.7	Environmental Specifications	182
13.8	Transmission Path Delay Considerations	184
13.9	Documentation	184
13.10	Network Sizing	185
13.11	Appendix—Guidelines for Configuring the Medium of a Single-Channel Phase-Coherent-FSK Bus Local Area Network	185
14.	Broadband Bus Physical Layer Specification	188
14.1	Nomenclature	190
14.2	Object	191
14.3	Compatibility Considerations	191
14.4	Operational Overview of a Single-Cable Broadband Bus Medium	191
14.5	Operational Overview of a Dual-Cable Broadband Bus Medium	192
14.6	Overview of the Broadband Bus Physical Layer	192
14.7	Bibliography	194
14.8	Detailed Application of Section 9, Generic Station Management to Physical Layer Interface Service Specification	195
14.9	Broadband Bus Physical Layer Functional, Electrical, and Mechanical Specifications	195
14.10	Environmental Specifications	211
14.11	Labeling	212
14.12	Appendix—Provisions for Two MAC-symbol/Bd and Four MAC-symbol/Bd Signaling	213
14.13	Appendix—Detailed Scrambling and Descrambling Process	221
15.	Broadband Bus Medium "Layer" Specification	222
15.1	Nomenclature	222
15.2	Object	225
15.3	Compatibility Considerations	225
15.4	Overview of the Broadband Bus Medium "Layer"	226
15.5	Bibliography	228
15.6	Broadband Bus Medium "Layer" Functional, Electrical, and Mechanical Specifications	228
15.7	Environmental Specifications	233
15.8	Transmission Path Delay Considerations	235
15.9	Documentation	235
15.10	Network Sizing	235

FIGURES

		PAGE
Fig 1-1	Relationship of Adjacent Protocol Layers	15
Fig 1-2	Logical Ring on Physical Bus	19
Fig 1-3	MAC Layer Functional Partitioning	20
Fig 2-1	Relation to LAN Model	28
Fig 3-1	Relation to LAN Model	32
Fig 5-1	Relation to LAN Model	54
Fig 5-2	Token Rotation Time "Priority" Example	61
Fig 5-3	MAC Finite State Machine Diagram	64
Fig 5-4	Receive Machine	71
Fig 5-5	sil/act Detector Finite State Machine	72
Fig 5-6	SD Detector Finite State Machine	72
Fig 5-7	ED Detector Finite State Machine	73
Fig 5-8	noise—burst/bus—quiet (NB/BQ) Detector Finite State Machine	73
Fig 5-9	Bus Repeater	74
Fig 6-1	MAC Protocol_data_unit Transmission Order	77
Fig 6-2	Logical Token-Passing Ring	80
Fig 8-1	Relation to LAN Model	130
Fig 9-1	Relation to LAN Model	135
Fig 10-1	Relation to LAN Model	142
Fig 10-2	Physical Hardware Partitioning Token-Passing Bus Local Area Network	143
Fig 11-1	Relation to LAN Model	152
Fig 11-2	Physical Hardware Partitioning, Token-Passing Bus Local Area Network	153
Fig 12-1	Relation to LAN Model	164
Fig 12-2	Physical Hardware Partitioning, Token-Passing Bus Local Area Network	165
Fig 13-1	Relation to LAN Model	175
Fig 13-2	Physical Hardware Partitioning, Token-Passing Bus Local Area Network	176
Fig 13-3	Limits for Group-Delay Distortion	181
Fig 14-1	Relation to LAN Model	189
Fig 14-2	Physical Hardware Partitioning, Token-Passing Broadband Bus Local Area Network	189
Fig 14-3	Limits for Amplitude Distortion	203
Fig 14-4	Transmit Spectrum Mask	205
Fig 14-5	$1+X^{-6}+X^{-7}$ Scrambler	221
Fig 14-6	Examplary Scrambler / Descrambler Circuitry	221
Fig 15-1	Relation to LAN Model	222
Fig 15-2	Physical Hardware Partitioning, Token-Passing Broadband Bus Local Area Network	223
Fig 15-3	Limits for Amplitude Distortion	230
Fig 15-4	Limits for Group-Delay Distortion	231

TABLES

Table 12-1	Data Rate Versus Signaling Frequencies	170
Table 14-1	Baseband Pulse Coding Rules	198
Table 14-2	Usual North American 6 MHz Mid-split Channels Nomenclature and Pairing	200
Table 14-3	Required Transmit Level Range	201
Table 14-4	Breakpoints of Amplitude Distortion Limits	204
Table 14-5	Required Noise Floor and In-band Signal Level	206
Table 14-6	Minimum Length of Pad_idle Preamble	207
Table 14-7	Desired Head-end Received Signal Levels	209
Table 15-1	Delivered In-band Signal Level	229

APPENDIX

Appendix A   A Model used for the Service Specification 237

APPENDIX FIGURES

Fig A1 Service Hierarchy Relationships. 237
Fig A2 Service Primitive Interactions 238

An American National Standard

IEEE Standards for Local Area Networks:

Token-Passing Bus Access Method and Physical Layer Specifications

1. Introduction and Overview

This portion of the LAN standards deals with all elements of the token-passing bus access method and its associated physical signaling and media technologies. The access function coordinates the use of the shared medium among the attached stations and has the relationship to the other protocol functions given by Fig 1-1.

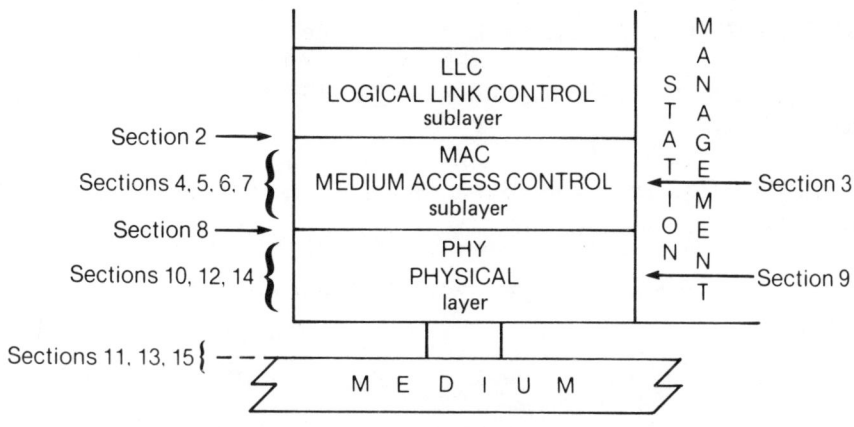

**Fig 1-1
Relationship of Adjacent Protocol Layers**

1.1 Scope. For the purpose of compatible interconnection of stations by way of a Local Area Network using the Token-Passing Bus access method this standard
  (1) Specifies the electrical and physical characteristics of the transmission medium
  (2) Specifies the electrical signaling method used
  (3) Specifies the frame formats transmitted
  (4) Specifies the actions of a station upon receipt of a data frame
  (5) Specifies the services provided at the conceptual interface between the

Medium Access Control (MAC) sublayer and the Logical Link Control (LLC) sublayer above it.

Within this standard the operation of a station is specified in terms of the layered model shown in Fig 1-1, see ISO/DIS 7498, Data Processing—Open System Intercommunication Basic Reference Model, Feb. 4, 1982.

The figure also shows which sections of the standard specify interfaces between layers and which sections specify the operation of the layers themselves.

1.2 Definitions. Terms that are used in a specific or specialized manner in one section of this standard are defined at the beginning of that section.[4]

1.3 References. When the following standards referred to in this standard are superseded by an approved revision the latest revision shall apply.

References to ANSI, EIA, IEEE, ISA, MIL, and NFPA standards are not a part of the equivalent ISO standard.

[1] Reserved for future use[5]

[2] ANSI/MIL STD 1851A-1983, Ada® Programming Language.[6,7]

[3] ANSI/NFPA 70-1984, National Electrical Code.[8]

[4] ANSI/UL 94-1979, Tests for Flammability of Plastic Materials for Parts in Devices and Appliances.[9]

[5] ANSI/UL 114-1982, Safety Standard for Office Appliances and Business Equipment.

[6] ANSI/UL 478-1979, Safety Standard for Electronic Data-Processing Units and Systems.

---

[4] Specialized terms used in this standard are defined in IEEE Std 802.1 (ISO 8802/1), Glossary. See footnote 5.

[5] When the following document is completed, approved, and published it will become a part of this reference section.
[1] IEEE Std 802.1 (ISO 8802/1), Local Area Network Standard - Overview, Interworking, and Management.

[6] Ada is a registered trademark of the United States government, Ada Joint Program Office.

[7] ANSI documents are available from the Sales Department, American National Standards Institute, 1430 Broadway, New York, NY 10018, USA.

[8] The National Electrical Code is published by the National Fire Protection Association, Batterymarch Park, Quincy, MA 02269, USA. Copies are also available from the Sales Department, American National Standards Institute, 1430 Broadway, New York, NY 10018, USA.

[9] UL documents are available from Underwriters Laboratories, Inc, 1285 Walt Whitman Road, Melville, LI, New York 11747, USA.

[7] *Cable Television Rules and Regulations, Title 47,* Code of Federal Regulations, Part 70-79. Revised Oct 1, 1983. Part 76, Subpart K, Cable Radiation Specification.[10]

[8] CSA Standard C22.2 No 154-M 1983, Data Processing Equipment.[11]

[9] EIA CB8-1981, Components Bulletin (Cat 4) List of Approved Agencies, US and Other Countries, Impacting Electronic Components and Equipment (August).[12]

[10] FCC Docket 20780-1980 {Part 15}, Technical Standards for Computing Equipment. Amendment of Part 15 to redefine and clarify the rules governing restricted radiation devices and low-power communication devices. Reconsidered First Report and Order, April 1980.[13]

[11] IEC 716-1983, Expression of the Properties of Signal Generators. (This document supersedes IEC 435-1, Safety of Data Processing Equipment, 1978.)[14]

[12] IEEE Std 472-1974 (R 1979), IEEE Guide for Surge Withstand Capability (SWC) Tests.[15]

[13] IEEE Std 802.2-1985 (ISO DIS 8802/2), Local Area Network Standard - Logical Link Control.

[14] ISO/DIS 7498 Data Processing - Open System Intercommunication Basic Reference Model, Feb 4, 1982.[16]

---

[10] This document is available from the US Government Printing Office, Washington, DC 20402, USA.

[11] In the US, CSA documents are available from the Sales Department, American National Standards Institute, 1430 Broadway, New York, NY 10018, USA. In Canada the documents are available at the Canadian Standards Association (Standards Sales), 178 Rexdale Blvd, Rexdale, Ontario, Canada M9W 1R3.

[12] EIA documents are available from Electronic Industries Association, 2001 Eye Street, NW Washington, DC 20006, USA.

[13] FCC documents are available from the Federal Communications Commission, Washington, DC 20402, USA.

[14] IEC documents are available in the US from the Sales Department, American National Standards Institute, 1430 Broadway, New York, NY 10018, USA. The IEC documents are also available from International Electrotechnical Commission, 3, rue de Varembé, Case postale 131, 1211—Genève 20, Switzerland/Suisse.

[15] IEEE documents are available from IEEE Service Center, 445 Hoes Lane, Piscataway, NJ 08554, USA.

[16] ISO documents are available in the US from the Sales Department, American National Standards Institute, 1430 Broadway, New York, NY 10018, USA. ISO documents also available from the ISO Office, 1, rue de Varembé, Case postale 56, CH-1211, Genéve 20, Switzerland/Suisse.

[15] ISA-dS72.01, PROWAY-LAN (Local Network) An Industrial Data Highway.[17]

[16] The Yellow Book, Data Communication over the Telephone Network, *CCITT Recommendations of the V Series*, vol 8, Fascicle 8.1, ITU, Geneva, Nov 1980 (esp V35–V37).[18]

[17] The Yellow Book, Data Communication Network Transmission, Signaling and Switching, Network Aspects, Maintenance, Administrative Arrangements, CCITT Recommendation X.150, vol 8, Fascicle 8.3, ITU, Geneva, Nov 1980.

[18] The Yellow Book, Line Transmission of Non-telephone Signals, *CCITT Recommendations of the H Series*, vol III, Fascicle III.4, ITU, Geneva, 1980 (esp H14).

[19] The Yellow Book, Impedance Matching Between Repeaters and Coaxial Pair in Television Transmission, Annex A of Recommendation J.73, vol III, Fascicle III.4, ITU, Geneva, 1980.

1.4 Compliance. Implementations that claim compliance with this standard shall

(1) Offer the mandatory LLC - MAC interface and services specified in this standard

(2) Offer the mandatory station management interface and services specified in this standard

(3) Support the medium access protocol specified in this standard

(4) Support at least one of the specified physical layers and their associated media

(5) Support at least one of the data rates specified for the selected physical layer.

A number of options are specified in this standard. An implementation should indicate which, if any, of these options are supported.

---

[17] ISA documents are available from Instrument Society of America, 67 Alexander Drive, PO Box 12277, Research Triangle Park, NC 27709, USA.

[18] CCITT documents are available in the US from National Technical Information Service, Department of Commerce, 5285 Port Royal Road, Springfield, VA 22161, USA.

1.5 Overview of the Token Method
1.5.1 The Essence of the Token Access Method

(1) A token controls the right of access to the physical medium; the station which holds (possesses) the token has momentary control over the medium.

(2) The token is passed by stations residing on the medium. As the token is passed from station to station a logical ring is formed.

(3) Steady state operation consists of a data transfer phase and a token transfer phase.

(4) Ring maintenance functions within the stations provide for ring initialization, lost token recovery, new station addition to the logical ring, and general housekeeping of the logical ring. The ring maintenance functions are replicated among all the token using stations on the network.

Shared media generally can be categorized into two major types. These types are broadcast and sequential. This standard deals exclusively with the broadcast type. On a broadcast medium, every station may receive all signals transmitted. Media of the broadcast type are usually configured as a physical bus.

In Fig 1-2, note that the token medium access method is always sequential in a logical sense. That is, during normal, steady state operation, the right to access the medium passes from station to station. Furthermore, note that the physical connectivity has little impact on the order of the logical ring and that stations can respond to a query from the token holder even without being part of the logical ring. (For example, stations H and F can receive frames but cannot initiate a transmission since they will never be sent the token.)

The medium access control (MAC) sublayer provides sequential access to the shared bus medium by passing control of the medium from station to station in a logically circular fashion. The MAC sublayer determines when the station has the right to access the shared medium by recognizing and accepting the token from the predecessor station, and it determines when the token shall be passed to the successor station.

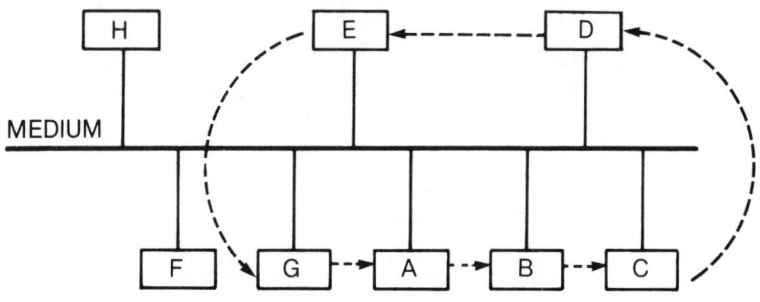

**Fig 1-2
Logical Ring on Physical Bus**

1.5.2 General Sublayer Functions
(1) Lost token timer
(2) Distributed initialization
(3) Token holding timer (for multiple classes of service)
(4) Limited data buffering
(5) Node address recognition
(6) Frame encapsulation (including token preparation)
(7) FCS generation and checking
(8) Valid token recognition
(9) New ring member addition
(10) Node failure error recovery

1.6 MAC Layer Internal Structure. The MAC layer performs several functions which are loosely coupled. The descriptions and specifications of the MAC layer in this standard are organized in terms of one of several possible partitionings of these functions. The partitioning used here is illustrated in Fig 1-3, which shows five asynchronous logical "machines", each of which handles some of the MAC functions, as discussed in 1.6.1 through 1.6.5.

1.6.1 Interface Machine (IFM). This machine acts as an interface and buffer between the LLC and MAC layers and between Station Management and MAC layers. It interprets all incoming MA_DATA and other service primitives,

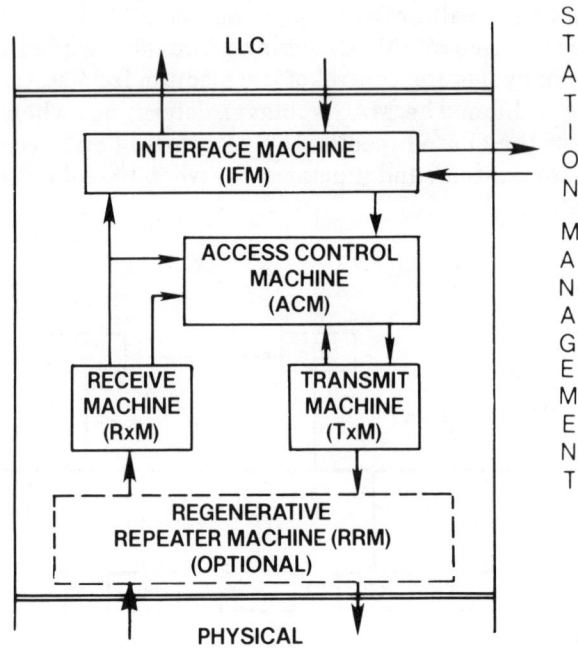

Fig 1-3
MAC Layer Functional Partitioning

and generates appropriate outgoing service primitives. This machine handles the mapping of "quality of service" parameters from the LLC view to the MAC view, where this is necessary. It handles queuing of service requests, for example, requests to send an LLC protocol data unit (pdu). Finally, it performs the "address recognition" function on received LLC frames, accepting only those addressed to this station.

1.6.2 Access Control Machine (ACM). This machine cooperates with the ACMs of all other stations on the bus in handling the token to control transmission access to the shared bus. The ACM may (optionally) manage multiple MAC access_ classes so as to provide different levels of "quality of service" to the LLC layer. The ACM is also responsible for initialization and maintenance of the logical ring, including the admission of new stations. Finally, it has responsibility for the detection of, and, where possible, recovery from faults and failures in the token-bus network.

1.6.3 Receive Machine (RxM). This machine accepts atomic_symbol inputs from the physical layer, assembles them into frames which it validates and passes to the IFM and ACM. The RxM accomplishes this by recognizing the frame start and the frame end delimiters (SD and ED), checking the frame check sequence (FCS) and validating the frame's structure. The RxM also identifies and indicates the reception of noise_bursts and the bus_quiet condition.

1.6.4 Transmit Machine (TxM). This machine generally accepts a data frame from the ACM and transmits it, as a sequence of atomic_symbols in the proper format, to the physical layer. The TxM builds a MAC protocol-data-unit by prefacing each frame with the required preamble and SD, and appending the FCS and ED. When operating with a Regenerative Repeater Machine, its operation may be somewhat different.

1.6.5 Regenerative Repeater Machine (RRM). This machine is an optional MAC component which is present only in special "repeater" stations, for example, a broadband or head-end remodulator. In such repeater stations, the RRM, when appropriate, repeats the incoming atomic_symbol stream, from the physical layer, back to the physical layer for retransmission; in such cases the physical layer is understood to be connected to at least two different segments of a single bus. The RxM and TxM may cooperate with the RRM in such repeating operations.

Of these five machines, the ACM is the most critical and most complex; it is the key control mechanism for the token-bus access method, and it shall cooperate closely with ACMs in other stations given only limited information regarding the state of the network. Because of its importance, and because much of its operation is not easily inferred from its functional requirements, the explanation and specification of the ACM are the major concerns of Sections 5, 6, and 7 of this standard.

The IFM and RxM participate heavily in the operation of the MAC layer protocol. They are however discussed only in sufficient detail so that the reader will understand their role in the MAC layer, in support of the ACM. The level of discussion was chosen to avoid any ambiguities which might compromise the coexistence of complying stations on a single bus.

1.7 Physical Layer and Media. The broad outlines for the physical layer sections of this standard and also an introduction to the various physical signaling techniques and media defined for local area networks using the token-passing medium access protocol are given here.

Three bus media and corresponding physical layer entities are specified for use with the token-passing medium access protocol.

Each physical layer entity and corresponding bus medium is described in a pair of consecutive sections (that is, Sections 10 and 11, Sections 12 and 13, and Sections 14 and 15), consisting of

(1) A section specifying a specific physical layer entity, including how the generic interface service specification (Section 9) between that physical layer entity and the station's Station Management functions is particularized, and

(2) A section specifying the medium appropriate to that physical layer entity.

Three different physical layer entities with corresponding media suitable for use with the token-bus medium access protocol are specified in this standard. They are distinguished primarily by the different forms of signaling specified for each type of physical layer entity. The remainder of this subsection outlines the salient points of each type of physical layer entity and corresponding medium.

1.7.1 Summary of Phase Continuous FSK (Frequency Shift Keying)

Topology. Omnidirectional bus

Trunk Cable. 75 Ω coaxial cable, such as types RG-6, RG-11, and semirigid

Drop Cable. 35 Ω to 50 Ω coaxial cable stub, less than 350 mm long

Connector at Station. 50 Ω male BNC-series

Recommended Cable Configuration. Long unbranched trunk cable with very short "stub" drop cables

Trunk Connection Unit. 75 Ω tee connector

Repeaters. Active regenerative repeaters used for branching and extension of the system beyond the basic signal loss budget

Transmit Level. +54 dB to +60 dB (1 mV, 37.5 Ω)

Receiver Sensitivity. +24 dB (1 mV, 37.5 Ω)

Data Rate. 1 Mb/s

Signaling. Manchester encoding of data and non_data symbols
The symbol representations are
    {HL}   = zero—initial high, final low level
    {LH}   = one—initial low, final high level
    {LL HH} = pairs of non_data symbols
            —initial pair of low level followed by
              a final pair of high level

Modulation. Phase continuous FSK (a form of Frequency Modulation), with Manchester representation:

(1) Frequency of high level = 6.25 MHz ± 0.08 MHz
(2) Frequency of low level = 3.75 MHz ± 0.08 MHz

Pad-idle. Alternating <u>one</u> and <u>zero</u> symbols

Clock Recovery. From transitions generated by the Manchester encoding

1.7.2 Summary of Phase Coherent FSK

Topology. Omnidirectional bus

Cable. 75 Ω coaxial cable, such as types RG-6 and semirigid

Connector at Station. 75 Ω female F-series

Recommended Cable Configuration. CATV-like semirigid trunk and flexible drop cable

Trunk Connection Unit. 75 Ω nondirectional passive impedance-matching tap

Repeaters. Active regenerative repeaters used for high-fanout branching and extension of the system beyond the basic signal loss budget

Transmit Level. +60 dB to +63 dB (1 mV, 75 Ω) [dBmV]

Receiver Sensitivity. −15 dB (1 mV, 75 Ω) [dBmV]

Data Rates. 5 Mb/s and 10 Mb/s

Signaling. Direct encoding of <u>data</u> and <u>non_data</u> symbols, each as an integral number of cycles of constant frequency, with frequency changes only at the zero crossings of the waveforms. Two frequencies are used:
(1) The lower is 1 Hz/(b/s) (that is, 5 MHz at 5 Mb/s, 10 MHz at 10 Mb/s)
(2) The higher is 2 Hz/(b/s) (that is, 10 MHz at 5 Mb/s, 20 MHz at 10 Mb/s)
The symbol representations are
 <u>zero</u>—two full cycles of the higher frequency
 <u>one</u>—one full cycle of the lower frequency
 pairs of <u>non_data</u> — one full cycle of the higher frequency, one full cycle of the lower frequency, and another one full cycle of the higher frequency

Pad-idle. Consecutive one symbols

Clock Recovery. From zero crossings in the received signaling

Transmit Data Timing. Phase locked to transmit frequencies. All ports of a regenerative repeater shall use the same transmit data timing and hence exactly the same transmit frequencies.

1.7.3 Summary of Multilevel Duobinary AM/PSK

Topology. Directional bus with active head-end repeater

Cable. 75 Ω coaxial cable, such as types RG-6 and semirigid

Connector at Station. 75 Ω female F-series

Recommended Cable Configuration. CATV-like semirigid trunk and flexible drop cable

Trunk Connection Unit. 75 Ω directional passive impedance-matching tap

Repeaters. Head-end regenerative repeater used as system data-rate clock source, as central assessor of contention and noise, and to retransmit all signaling received on the directional medium

Amplifiers. Standard CATV bidirectional mid-split or sub-split or high-split (or unidirectional for dual-cable configuration) broadband amplifiers used for extension of the system beyond the basic signal loss budget

Channel Bandwidths. 1.5 MHz, 6 MHz, and 12 MHz

Transmit Level.
In 1.5 MHz bandwidth, +24 dB to +44 dB (1 mV, 75 Ω) [dBmV], adjustable
In 6 MHz bandwidth, +30 dB to +50 dB (1 mV, 75 Ω) [dBmV], adjustable
In 12 MHz bandwidth, +33 dB to +53 dB (1 mV, 75 Ω) [dBmV], adjustable

Receiver Sensitivity.
In 1.5 MHz, −16 dB to +4 dB (1 mV, 75 Ω) [dBmV]
In 6 MHz, −10 dB to +10 dB (1 mV, 75 Ω) [dBmV]
In 12 MHz, −7 dB to +13 dB (1 mV, 75 Ω) [dBmV]

Data Rates. 1 Mb/s in 1.5 MHz, 5 Mb/s in 6 MHz, 10 Mb/s in 12 MHz

{NOTE: The following channel assignments are not part of the ISO Standard.}

Recommended North American Channel Assignments.

For 10 Mb/s, channels 3' and 4' (59.75 MHz - 71.75 MHz) and P and Q (252 MHz - 264 MHz)

For 5 Mb/s, channels 3' (59.75 MHz - 65.75 MHz) and P (252 MHz - 258 MHz), or 4' (65.75 MHz - 71.75 MHz) and Q (258 MHz - 264 MHz)

For 1 Mb/s, any of the eight equally spaced 1.5 MHz subchannels of reverse channels 3' and 4', paired with the corresponding forward channels P and Q

Scrambler. A self-sync scrambler with a generator polynomial of $1+X^{-6}+X^{-7}$ is applied to all framed data prior to encoding for transmission, both to increase the average number of transitions within a transmission and to randomize spectral components of the transmitted modulation.

Signaling. data and non_data symbols are encoded so as to specify the amplitude of the eventual modulation. A single form is defined in this standard one MAC-symbol per baud "three-symbol" ({0}, {2}, {4}) signaling together with compatibility considerations for three additional forms; the additional forms are described in 14.12.

In all of these forms of signaling, the middle level is used only to signal the non_data symbols found in frame delimiters and reported "silence", and as a "kicker" to break up long sequences of a single other signaling level. Such long sequences are unlikely since a scrambler is applied to framed data before it is encoded for transmission.

TOKEN-PASSING BUS

For one MAC-symbol per baud signaling, the symbol representations at the receiver are:

{0} = zero—zero amplitude
{4} = one—"maximum" amplitude
{2} = non_data symbols or "kickers", always occurring in pairs with a "median" amplitude of one-half the "maximum"

Modulation. Multilevel duobinary AM/PSK

Pad-idle. Alternating {4} and {0} symbols, starting with {4}

Reported Silence. The repeated sequence of symbols transmitted by the head-end to report that it is not receiving any signaling. The sequence has a period of four symbols and the repetition may break off after any symbol of the sequence. Listening modems can set their AGC, and can determine the signaling mode of the system by the sequence used.

For one MAC-symbol per baud signaling, the sequence is

{2} {2} {0} {4}

For possible future two and four MAC-symbols per baud signaling modes, the following sequences are reserved:

{2} {2} {4} {0}
{2} {0} {4}
{2} {4} {0}

Implementations which detect any of these reserved repeating sequences should either switch to the corresponding mode of operation or inhibit transmission.

Clock Recovery. From level transitions within the received signaling

Transmit Data Timing. Sourced by head-end remodulator; frequency locked to received data timing at all other stations.

1.7.4 Alternate Physical Layer and Medium for Industrial Control. Alternate physical layers and media for industrial control are specified in [15].[19] These alternate physical layers and media are compatible at the MAC-Physical interface.

1.8 Access Method Characteristics. An understanding of the basic characteristics of the token-passing access method is useful, so as to better understand where and when a token-passing bus is an appropriate LAN technology.

Some of the important features of this medium access method are as follows:

(1) The method is efficient in the sense that under high offered load the coordination of the stations requires only a small percentage of the medium's capacity.

(2) The method is fair in the sense that it offers each station an equal share of the medium's capacity. It does not however require any station to use its full share.

---

[19] The numbers in brackets correspond with those of the references in 1.3

(3) The method permits multiple classes of service.

(4) The method coordinates the stations' transmissions so that they minimize and control their interference with each other.

(5) The method imposes no additional requirements on the media and the modem capabilities over those necessary for transmission and reception of multibit, multiframe sequences at the specified mean bit error rate.

(6) In the absence of system noise, the method provides computable, deterministic, worst-case bounds on access delay, for the highest priority class of service, for any given network and loading configuration.

(7) Periods of controlled interference are distinguishable; system noise measurements are possible during the remaining periods.

(8) The method places minimal constraints on how a station which momentarily controls the medium may use its share of the medium's capacity. In particular, the access method does not prohibit any station from using other specialized access methods (such as poll/response for example) during that station's access periods, provided only that those specialized methods do not confuse the other stations on the network as to the (distributed) state of the overall access mechanism.

(9) The method permits the presence of large numbers of low-cost reduced-function stations in the network, together with one or more full-function stations. (It is assumed that at least one full-function station is needed to make the system operational, for example, initialize.) An example of a reduced function station is one that can "receive only" and therefore does not contain access control logic.

1.9 Standard Organization. This standard is organized in 15 sections, which are summarized as follows:

Section 1 begins with a general discussion of the token-passing bus access method. The MAC layer functional partitioning used in subsequent discussions is introduced here. The Physical Layer and Media options are also surveyed. Finally, features of the token-passing bus access method are reviewed.

Section 2 details the interfaces between the LLC and MAC layers, and the services and command interfaces (such as sending a frame) provided to the LLC layer.

Section 3 details the interface between the station management entity and the MAC layer. It describes the initialization services (such as setting timer values) provided by the station management.

Section 4 details the MAC general frame structure including delimiters, addressing, and the FCS. All of the frame formats which MAC handles, including MAC control frames, are enumerated.

Section 5 discusses the basic concepts of the access protocols and provides an informal description of the actions in each state of the access control machine. The other state machines of the MAC sublayer are also described in Section 5.

Section 6 contains definitions of essential MAC terms and components and specifies those mandatory compliance requirements for the MAC sublayer protocols which are not covered elsewhere.

Section 7 specifies the MAC access control machine by means of a state machine model. This is the definitive specification of the token-passing bus MAC operation. Section 7 also describes the MAC layer variables, functions, and procedures used in the state machine.

Section 8 details the interface between the medium access control sublayer and the physical layer. Included here are descriptions of the interface symbols, requests, and responses.

Section 9 describes the generic interfaces between the station management entity and the various token-passing bus physical layers.

Sections 10 and 11 detail the physical layer and medium, respectively, for a single-channel (that is, omnidirectional) Phase Continuous FSK coaxial cable bus at 1 Mb/s.

Sections 12 and 13 detail the physical layer and medium, respectively, for a single-channel (that is, omnidirectional) Phase Coherent FSK coaxial cable bus at 5 Mb/s or 10 Mb/s.

Sections 14 and 15 detail the physical layer and medium, respectively, for a dual-channel (that is, head-ended) broadband Duobinary AM/PSK coaxial cable bus at 1 Mb/s, 5 Mb/s, or 10 Mb/s.

2. LLC - MAC Interface Service Specification

This section specifies the services provided to the logical link control (LLC) sublayer, and to the alternative sublayer specified in Ref [15], at the boundary between the logical link control functions and the medium access sublayer of the data link layer of the reference model. This standard specifies these services in an abstract way. It does not specify or constrain the implementation entities and interfaces within a computer system. The relationship of this section to other sections of this standard and to LAN specifications is illustrated in Fig 2-1.

NOTE: The exact relationship of the layers described in this standard to the layers defined by the OSI Reference Model is for future study.

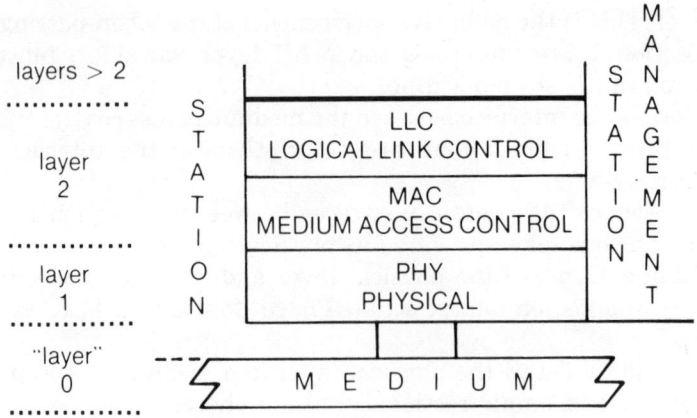

**Fig 2-1
Relation to LAN Model**

2.1 Overview of the LLC - MAC Service

2.1.1 General Description of Services Provided. This section describes informally the services provided to the logical link control sublayer by the token-passing medium access control sublayer, both of the data link layer. These services only provide connectionless data transfer services between peer LLC entities. They provide the means by which logical link control entities can exchange MAC service data units (m_sdu) without the establishment of an underlying point-to-point connection. The data transfer can be point-to-point or multipoint, unacknowledged *or acknowledged*.

2.1.2 Model Used for the Service Specification. The model and descriptive method are detailed in Appendix A.

2.1.3 Overview of Interactions. The primitives associated with this connectionless data transfer service are

(1) MA_DATA.request
(2) MA_DATA.indication
(3) MA_DATA.confirmation

An MA_DATA.request primitive is passed to the MAC sublayer to request that an m_sdu be sent. (All m_sdus are sent using connectionless procedures.) An MA_DATA.indication primitive is passed from the MAC sublayer to indicate the arrival of an m_sdu. An MA_DATA.confirmation primitive is passed from the MAC sublayer to convey the local results of the previous associated MA_DATA.request primitive.

2.1.4 Basic Services and Options. All services are mandatory and are required in all implementations.

2.2 Detailed Interactions with the LLC Entity. This subsection describes in detail the primitives and parameters associated with the LLC connectionless data transfer services. Note that the parameters are specified in an abstract sense. The parameters specify the information that shall be available to the receiving entity. A specific implementation is not constrained in the method of making this information available. For example, the m_sdu parameter associated with some of the data transfer service primitives may be provided by actually passing the MAC service data unit, by passing a descriptor, or by other means. The values of some selection parameters may be implied by an implementation. The MAC sublayer may also provide local confirmation mechanisms for all request type primitives.

2.2.1 MA_DATA.request

2.2.1.1 Function. This primitive is the service request primitive for the LLC connectionless data transfer service.

2.2.1.2 Semantics. The primitive shall provide parameters as follows:

MA_DATA.request
(destination_address,
  m_sdu,
  desired_quality)

destination_address specifies either an individual or a group MAC-entity address.

m_sdu specifies the MAC service data unit to be transmitted by the MAC sublayer entity for the requesting LLC sublayer entity.

desired_quality specifies the desired quality of service. The semantics of this parameter include both MAC-level priority, with a range of 0 (lowest) to 7 (highest) (see 6.6.1.2), and MAC-level delivery confirmation service, with values of request_with_no_response, *request_with_response, and response.*

2.2.1.3 When Generated. This primitive is passed from a LLC sublayer entity to the MAC sublayer entity to request that the MAC sublayer entity compose and transmit the specified frame at the desired quality of service on the local area network (LAN).

2.2.1.4 Effect on Receipt. Receipt of this primitive causes the MAC entity to attempt to compose and transmit the specified frame.

2.2.1.5 *Additional Comments.* *A value of request_with_response for the delivery-confirmation component of the quality parameter indicates that the next MA_DATA.indication should itself have a quality parameter specifying response, in which case that next MA_DATA.indication shall be associated with this MA_DATA.request.*

A value of response for the delivery-confirmation component of the quality parameter indicates that the immediately-prior MA_DATA.indication shall itself have had a quality parameter specyifying request_with_response.

A group destination_address should not be used when specifying request_with_response.

2.2.2 MA_DATA.indication

2.2.2.1 Function. This primitive is the service indication primitive for the LLC connectionless data transfer service.

2.2.2.2 Semantics. The primitive shall provide parameters as follows:

MA_DATA.indication
  (destination_address,
    source_address,
    m_sdu,
    quality)

destination_address and source_address parameters specify the DA and SA fields of a frame (see Section 4) as received by the local MAC entity, and thus the MAC-entities involved in the transmission.

m_sdu specifies the MAC service data unit as received by the local MAC sublayer entity.

quality specifies the delivered quality of service. The semantics of this parameter include both MAC-level priority, with a range of 0 (lowest) to 7 (highest) (see 6.6.1.2), and MAC-level delivery confirmation service, with values of request_with_no_response, *request_with_response, and response.*

2.2.2.3 When Generated. This primitive is passed from the MAC sublayer entity to the LLC sublayer entity to indicate the arrival of a frame from the physical layer entity. Such frames are reported only when they are free of detected errors and their (individual or group) destination address designates the local MAC entity.

2.2.2.4 Effect on Receipt. The effect of receipt of this primitive by the LLC entity is specified in Ref [13].

2.2.2.5 Additional Comments. In the absence of errors, the contents of the m_sdu parameter are logically complete and unchanged relative to the m_sdu parameter in the associated MA_DATA.request at the sending station.

NOTE: This is a guarantee of transparency.

A value of request_with_response for the delivery-confirmation component of the quality parameter indicates that the receiving MAC-user entity should immediately respond with an MA_DATA.request which itself has a quality parameter specifying response.

A value of response for the delivery-confirmation component of the quality parameter indicates that this MA_DATA.indication may be associated with a prior MA_DATA.request which itself had a quality parameter specifying request_with_response, and which was issued by the same MAC-user entity.

2.2.3 MA_DATA.confirmation

2.2.3.1 Function. This primitive is the service confirmation primitive for the LLC connectionless data transfer service.

2.2.3.2 Semantics. The primitive shall provide parameters as follows:

MA_DATA.confirmation
  (quality,
    status)

quality specifies the quality of service actually provided. The semantics of this parameter (for example, priority, MAC-level delivery confirmation) are left for further study.

status indicates the local success or failure of the corresponding previous MA_DATA.request.

2.2.3.3 When Generated. This primitive is passed from the MAC sublayer entity to the LLC sublayer entity to confirm the success or failure of the service provided for the previous associated LLC data transfer request.

When the quality parameter of that request specifies request_with_no_response or response, the MA_DATA.confirmation is passed immediately after the transmission of the corresponding frame.

When the quality parameter of that request specifies request_with_response, the MA_DATA.confirmation is passed when the requested response frame is received, or when the allowed number of retries has occurred, or upon local failure.

2.2.3.4 Effect on Receipt. The effect of receipt of this primitive by the LLC sublayer entity is specified in [13].

2.2.3.5 Additional Comments. Success of this request indicates that the previously specified m_sdu has been transmitted correctly to the best of the local MAC entity's knowledge. *In the case that the corresponding MA_DATA.request had a quality parameter specifying request_with_response, the MA_DATA.confirmation is associated with the MA_DATA.indication conveying the response, if any such occurred.* Also, it is assumed that sufficient information is available to the LLC sublayer entity to associate the confirmation with the corresponding request.

3. Station Management - MAC Interface Service Specification

This section specifies the services provided to and by the station management functions by and to the token-passing MAC sublayer of this standard. This standard specifies these services in an abstract way. The standard does not specify or constrain the implementation entities and interfaces within a computer system. The relationship of this section to other sections of this standard and to other LAN specifications is illustrated in Fig 3-1.

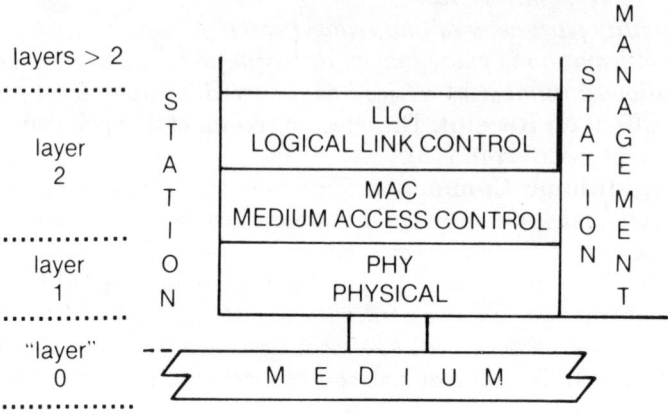

Fig 3-1
Relation to LAN Model

3.1 Overview of the Station Management - MAC Service

3.1.1 General Description of Services Provided. This subsection describes informally the services provided to and by the station management functions by and to the token-passing medium access control sublayer of the data link layer. These services are local administrative services between the MAC sublayer and its manager. They provide the means and method of

(1) Resetting the MAC entity, selecting the MAC entity's MAC address (and implicitly the length of all MAC addresses on the network) and the token-passing protocol appropriate for the network (for example, token bus, token-bus repeater), and confirming that the MAC entity can implement that protocol.

(2) Specifying the values of timer and counter preset constants appropriate for the network (for example, a bus slot_time).

(3) Determining whether the MAC entity should be a member of the token-passing ring, and whether its address appears to be unique to the local network.

TOKEN-PASSING BUS

IEEE
Std 802.4-1985

(4) Reading the current values of some of the MAC-entity's parameters.

(5) Notifying the station management entity of relevant changes in the MAC-entity's parameters.

(6) Specifying the set of group addresses which the MAC entity recognizes.

(7) Providing the means by which station management peer entities can exchange MAC service data units (m_sdus) without the establishment of an underlying point_to_point connection.

3.1.2 Model Used for the Service Specification. The model and descriptive method are detailed in Appendix A.

3.1.3 Overview of Interactions. The primitives associated with local administrative services are

MA_INITIALIZE_PROTOCOL.request
MA_INITIALIZE_PROTOCOL.confirmation

MA_SET_VALUE.request
MA_SET_VALUE.confirmation

MA_READ_VALUE.request
MA_READ_VALUE.confirmation

MA_EVENT.indication

MA_FAULT_REPORT.indication

MA_GROUP_ADDRESS.request
MA_GROUP_ADDRESS.confirmation

MA_CDATA.request
MA_CDATA.indication
MA_CDATA.confirmation

3.1.3.1 MA_INITIALIZE_PROTOCOL. The MA_INITIALIZE_PROTOCOL.request primitive is passed to the MAC sublayer to reset the entire MAC sublayer and to select the MAC entity's MAC address (and implicitly the length of all MAC addresses on the network), the token-passing protocol appropriate for the network (that is, token_bus) and the station's role in that network (for example, originate_only or originate_and_repeat). It elicits an immediate MA_INITIALIZE_PROTOCOL.confirmation specifying whether the desired protocol is available.

3.1.3.2 MA_SET_VALUE. The MA_SET_VALUE.request primitive is passed to the MAC sublayer from the station management entity to set the value of a MAC variable. The MA_SET_VALUE.confirmation returns a success or failure indication for the associated primitive.

3.1.3.3 MA_READ_VALUE. The MA_READ_VALUE.request primitive is passed to the MAC sublayer from the station management entity to request the value of a MAC variable. The MA_READ_VALUE.confirmation returns the value of the requested MAC variable.

3.1.3.4 MA_EVENT. The MA_EVENT.indication primitive is passed to the station management entity to indicate that the value of a significant MAC variable has changed or some other significant event has occurred.

33

3.1.3.5 MA_FAULT_REPORT. The MA_FAULT_REPORT.indication primitive is passed to the station management entity to indicate that an error has been inferred by the MAC entity.

3.1.3.6 MA_GROUP_ADDRESS. The MA_GROUP_ADDRESS.request primitive is passed to the MAC sublayer to specify the set of MAC-level group addresses which the MAC entity should recognize, so that valid MAC-level frames with these destination addresses will be passed to a MAC-user entity by way of the appropriate indicate primitive. The MA_GROUP_ADDRESS. confirmation primitive returns a success or failure indication for the associated request primitive.

3.1.3.7 MA_CDATA. The MA_CDATA.request primitive is passed to the MAC sublayer to request that a station management m_sdu be sent. (All m_sdus in station management frames are sent using connectionless procedures. See 4.2.3 for frame format.) An MA_CDATA.indication primitive is passed from the MAC sublayer to indicate the arrival of a station management m_sdu. An MA_CDATA.confirmation primitive is passed from the MAC sublayer to convey the local results of the previous associated MA_CDATA.request primitive.

3.1.4 Basic Services and Options. All services are mandatory, and are required in all implementations.

3.2 Detailed Interactions with the Station Management Entity. The primitives and parameters associated with the MAC administrative services are described in detail here. Note that the parameters are specified in an abstract sense. The parameters specify the information that shall be available to the receiving entity. A specific implementation is not constrained in the method of making this information available. For example, the station address (TS) or set-of-group-addresses parameters associated with some of the administrative service primitives may be provided by actually passing MAC addresses, by passing descriptors, or by other means. The values of some selection parameters may be implied by an implementation. The MAC sublayer may also provide local confirmation mechanisms for all request type primitives.

3.2.1 MA_INITIALIZE_PROTOCOL.request

3.2.1.1 Function. This primitive is the service request primitive for the protocol initialization service. It also functions as a RESET service request primitive for the entire MAC sublayer.

3.2.1.2 Semantics. This primitive shall provide parameters as follows:

MA_INITIALIZE_PROTOCOL.request
(desired_protocol)

desired_protocol specifies the token-passing protocol which the MAC entity should implement: simple token_bus or token_bus_repeater (for example, a head-end station on a broadband medium).

3.2.1.3 When Generated. This primitive is passed from the station management entity to the MAC sublayer entity to request that the MAC sublayer entity reset itself and reconfigure itself as specified by the parameters.

TOKEN-PASSING BUS

IEEE
Std 802.4-1985

3.2.1.4 Effect of Receipt. Receipt of this primitive causes the MAC entity to reset itself exactly as at power-on, select the desired protocol, and generate a MA_INITIALIZE_PROTOCOL.confirmation to indicate the availability of the desired protocol.

3.2.1.5 Additional Comments. This primitive causes the MAC entity to be a nonmember of the token-passing ring.

3.2.2 MA_INITIALIZE_PROTOCOL.confirmation

3.2.2.1 Function. This primitive is the service confirmation primitive for the protocol initialization service.

3.2.2.2 Semantics. This primitive shall provide parameters as follows:

MA_INITIALIZE_PROTOCOL.confirmation
(status)

status indicates the success or failure of the initialization request.

3.2.2.3 When Generated. This primitive is passed from the MAC sublayer entity to the station management entity to indicate the success or failure of the previous associated protocol initialization request.

3.2.2.4 Effect of Receipt. The effect of receipt of this primitive is unspecified.

3.2.3 MA_SET_VALUE.request

3.2.3.1 Function. This primitive is the service request primitive for the setting of values of MAC sublayer variables.

3.2.3.2 Semantics. This primitive shall provide parameters as follows:

MA_SET_VALUE.request
(variable_name,
  desired_value)

variable_name indicates which MAC sublayer variables is to be assigned the specified desired_value.

The following variables shall be settable by way of this primitive:

(1) TS (station address, see 7.1.1)
(2) slot_time
(3) hi_pri_token_hold_time
(4) max_ac_4_rotation_time   (if priority option is implemented)
(5) max_ac_2_rotation_time   (if priority option is implemented)
(6) max_ac_0_rotation_time   (if priority option is implemented)
(7) max_ring_maintenance_rotation_time
(8) ring_maintenance_timer_initial_value
(9) max_inter_solicit_count
(10) min_post_silence_preamble_length   (see 4.1.1)
(11) in_ring_desired
(12) event_enable_mask   (see 3.2.7)
(13) max_retry_limit

Other MAC variables are for future study.

The range of desired_value is the range defined in Section 7 for the specified MAC variable.

3.2.3.3 When Generated. This primitive is passed from the station management entity to the MAC sublayer entity to request that the MAC sublayer entity change the value of the specified variable.

3.2.3.4 Effect of Receipt. The receipt of this primitive causes the variable value to be changed and to generate the associated MA_SET_VALUE. confirmation primitive.

3.2.4 MA_SET_VALUE.confirmation

3.2.4.1 Function. This primitive is the service confirmation primitive for the MAC sublayer set value service.

3.2.4.2 Semantics. This primitive shall provide parameters as follows:

MA_SET_VALUE.confirmation
(status)

status indicates the success or failure of the set value request. If the MAC variable of the MA_SET_VALUE.request is not implemented, status shall be returned as failure.

3.2.4.3 When Generated. This primitive is passed from the MAC sublayer entity to the station management entity to indicate the success or failure of the previous associated MA_SET_VALUE.request.

3.2.4.4 Effect of Receipt. The effect of receipt of this primitive is unspecified.

3.2.5 MA_READ_VALUE.request

3.2.5.1 Function. This primitive is the service request primitive for the reading of values of MAC sublayer variables.

3.2.5.2 Semantics. This primitive shall provide parameters as follows:

MA_READ_VALUE.request
(variable_name)

variable_name indicates which of the MAC sublayer variables is to be read. Readable MAC sublayer variables are
(1) Address of successor, NS (see Section 4)
(2) Address of predecessor, PS (see Section 4)
(3) *Number of retries on request_with_response frames*
A partial list of variables under study are:
(a) Number of stations in ring
(b) Measured token rotation time
(c) Number of valid received frames
(d) Number of received frames with FCS errors

3.2.5.3 When Generated. This primitive is passed from the station management entity to the MAC sublayer entity to request that the MAC sublayer entity return the value of the specified variable.

3.2.5.4 Effect of Receipt. The receipt of this primitive causes the value of the specified variable to be returned by way of the associated MA_READ _VALUE.confirmation primitive.

3.2.6 MA_READ_VALUE.confirmation

3.2.6.1 Function. This primitive is the service confirmation primitive for the read value service.

3.2.6.2 Semantics. This primitive shall provide parameters as follows:

MA_READ_VALUE.confirmation
  (current_value,
    status)

If status equals success, current_value has taken on the current value of the MAC variable specified in the associated read value primitive. If status equals failure, the MAC variable is not readable or not implemented and the value of current_value is not specified.

3.2.6.3 When Generated. This primitive is passed from the MAC sublayer entity to the station management entity to indicate the success or failure of the previous associated MA_READ_VALUE.request.

3.2.6.4 Effect of Receipt. The effect of receipt of this primitive is unspecified.

3.2.7 MA_EVENT.indication

3.2.7.1 Function. This primitive is the service indication primitive by which station management is informed of significant events within the MAC sublayer.

3.2.7.2 Semantics. This primitive shall provide parameters as follows:

MA_EVENT.indication
  (event)

event identifies the event that has occurred within the MAC sublayer. The events that cause an MA_EVENT.indication are

(1) Change of successor address
(2) Change of successor address to null

Additional events are for future study.

3.2.7.3 When Generated. This primitive is passed from the MAC sublayer entity to the station management entity to indicate the occurrence of an enabled significant event within the MAC sublayer. It is enabled when an MA_SET_VALUE.request has set the event_enable_mask to a non-zero value.

3.2.7.4 Effect of Receipt. The effect of receipt of this primitive is unspecified.

3.2.8 MA_FAULT_REPORT.indication

3.2.8.1 Function. This primitive is the service indication primitive for MAC failure indications.

3.2.8.2 Semantics. This primitive shall provide parameters, as follows:

MA_FAULT_REPORT.indication
  (fault_type)

fault_type identifies the particular fault condition the MAC sublayer has detected

(1) Duplicate_address
(2) Faulty_transmitter

The duplicate_address fault is indicated when the MAC sublayer entity has inferred that there is another MAC entity on the network which has the same MAC address as the current value of the variable TS.

The faulty_transmitter fault is indicated when the MAC sublayer entity has inferred evidence that the station's transmissions are not being received correctly by other stations in the network.

3.2.8.3 When Generated. This primitive is passed from the MAC sublayer entity to the station management entity to indicate that the MAC entity has detected a failure condition within the protocol. The indication is passed when the access control machine transitions to the OFFLINE state.

The situations in which an MA_FAULT_REPORT.indication is passed are defined in Section 7 in the ACM state tables.

3.2.8.4 Effect of Receipt. The effect of receipt of this primitive is unspecified.

3.2.8.5 Additional Comments. This primitive is generated in response to detection of a network administration or hardware fault which may be due to failure of circuitry in either the detecting station or another station.

3.2.9 MA_GROUP_ADDRESS.request

3.2.9.1 Function. This primitive is the service request primitive for the protocol's group address activation service.

3.2.9.2 Semantics. This primitive shall provide parameters as follows:

MA_GROUP_ADDRESS.request
  (set of group-addresses)

set of group-addresses specifies zero or more group MAC-entity addresses.

3.2.9.3 When Generated. This primitive is passed from the station management entity to the MAC sublayer entity to request that the MAC sublayer entity recognize the specified set of group addresses, so that valid MAC-level frames with these destination addresses will be passed to a MAC-user entity by way of the appropriate indicate primitive.

3.2.9.4 Effect of Receipt. Receipt of this primitive causes the MAC sublayer entity to load the desired set of group addresses for comparison with the destination address of MAC-user frames and to return a MA_GROUP_ADDRESS.confirmation primitive. The last set of group addresses loaded are the only ones recognized. Loading zero (no) group addresses deactivates the group address recognition service.

3.2.9.5 Additional Comments. The predefined broadcast group address (of all one bits) is always recognized and cannot be disabled.

3.2.10 MA_GROUP_ADDRESS.confirmation

3.2.10.1 Function. This primitive is the confirmation primitive for the protocol's group address activation service.

3.2.10.2 Semantics. This primitive shall provide parameters as follows:

MA_GROUP_ADDRESS.confirmation
  (status)

status indicates the success or failure of the request.

TOKEN-PASSING BUS

IEEE
Std 802.4-1985

3.2.10.3. When Generated. This primitive is passed from the MAC sublayer entity to the station management entity to indicate the success or failure of the previous associated MA_GROUP_ADDRESS.request.

3.2.10.4 Effect of Receipt. The effect of receipt of this primitive is unspecified.

NOTE: To provide a basis for network monitoring and analysis, an implementation also may support
  (1) Reception of all MAC-user frames, independent of destination address
  (2) Reception of all frames, including MAC_control frames, as specified in 4.1.3

3.2.11 MA_CDATA.request

3.2.11.1 Function. This primitive is the service request primitive for the station management connectionless data transfer service.

3.2.11.2 Semantics. This primitive shall provide parameters as follows:

MA_CDATA.request
  (destination_address,
    m_sdu,
    desired_quality)

destination_address specifies either an individual or a group MAC-entity address.

m_sdu specifies the MAC service data unit to be transmitted by the MAC sublayer entity for the requesting station management entity.

desired_quality specifies the desired quality of service. The semantics of this parameter include both MAC-level priority, with a range of 0 (lowest) to 7 (highest) (see 6.6.1.2), and MAC-level delivery confirmation service, with values of request_with_no_response, *request_with_response, and response.*

3.2.11.3 When Generated. This primitive is passed from the station management entity to the MAC sublayer entity to request that the MAC sublayer entity compose and transmit the specified frame at the desired quality of service on the local area network.

3.2.11.4 Effect of Receipt. Receipt of this primitive causes the MAC entity to attempt to compose and transmit the specified frame.

3.2.11.5 *Additional Comments.* *A value of request_with_response for the delivery-confirmation component of the quality parameter indicates that the next MA_CDATA.indication should itself have a quality parameter specifying response, in which case that next MA_CDATA.indication shall be associated with this MA_CDATA.request.*

A value of response for the delivery-confirmation component of the quality parameter indicates that the immediately-prior MA_CDATA.indication shall itself have had a quality parameter specyifying request_with_response.

A group destination_address should not be used when specifying request_with_response.

3.2.12 MA_CDATA.indication

3.2.12.1 Function. This primitive is the service indication primitive for the station management connectionless data transfer service.

3.2.12.2 Semantics. This primitive shall provide parameters as follows:

MA_CDATA.indication
  (destination_address,
    source_address,
    m_sdu,
    quality)

destination_address and source_address parameters specify the DA and SA fields of a frame (see Section 4) as received by the local MAC entity, and thus the MAC-entities involved in the transmission.

m_sdu specifies the MAC service data unit as received by the local MAC sublayer entity.

quality specifies the delivered quality of service. The semantics of this parameter include both MAC-level priority, with a range of 0 (lowest) to 7 (highest) (see 6.6.1.2), and MAC-level delivery confirmation service, with values of request_with_no_response, *request_with_response, and response.*

3.2.12.3 When Generated. This primitive is passed from the MAC sublayer entity to the station management entity to indicate the arrival of a frame from the local area network communications medium. Such frames are reported only when they are free of detected errors and their (individual or group) destination address designates the local MAC entity.

3.2.12.4 Effect of Receipt. The effect of receipt of this primitive is unspecified.

3.2.12.5 Additional Comments. In the absence of errors, the contents of the m_sdu parameter are logically complete and unchanged relative to the m_sdu parameter in the associated MA_CDATA.request at the sending station.

NOTE: This is a guarantee of transparency.

A value of request_with_response for the delivery-confirmation component of the quality parameter indicates that the receiving MAC-user entity should immediately respond with an MA_CDATA.request which itself has a quality parameter specifying response.

A value of response for the delivery-confirmation component of the quality parameter indicates that this MA_CDATA.indication may be associated with a prior MA_CDATA.request which itself had a quality parameter specifying request_with_response, and which was issued by the same MAC-user entity.

3.2.13 MA_CDATA.confirmation

3.2.13.1 Function. This primitive is the service confirmation primitive for the station management connectionless data transfer service.

3.2.13.2 Semantics. This primitive shall provide parameters as follows:

MA_CDATA.confirmation
  (quality,
    status)

quality specifies the quality of service actually provided. The semantics of this parameter are identical to those of 3.2.11.2.

status indicates the local success or failure of the corresponding previous MA_CDATA.request.

3.2.13.3 When Generated. This primitive is passed from the MAC sublayer entity to the station management entity to confirm the success or failure of the service provided for the previous associated station management data transfer request.

When the quality parameter of that request specifies request_with_no_response or response, the MA_CDATA.confirmation is passed immediately after the transmission of the corresponding frame.

When the quality parameter of that request specifies request_with_response, the MA_CDATA.confirmation is passed when the requested response frame is received, or when the allowed number of retries has occurred, or upon local failure.

3.2.13.4 Effect of Receipt. The effect of receipt of this primitive is unspecified.

3.2.13.5 Additional Comments. Success of this request indicates that the previously requested m_sdu has been transmitted correctly to the best of the local MAC entity's knowledge. *In the case that the corresponding MA_CDATA.request had a quality parameter specifying request_with_response, the MA_CDATA.confirmation is associated with the MA_CDATA.indication conveying the response, if any such occurred.* Also, it is assumed that sufficient information is available to the station management entity to associate the confirmation with the corresponding request.

4. Frame Formats

This section defines the required MAC frame formats. This includes all allowed frame formats and the arrangement of all frame subfields. The term frame as used here refers to the protocol_data_units exchanged by MAC sublayer entities. The MAC_service_data_units received from the LLC sublayer are contained within these MAC frames.

The frame components and formats used by medium access control are also described in this section.

The MAC level transmit frames and abort sequences are described in the following subsections. First the components of the frames are discussed, followed by the definition of the valid frame formats. All frames sent or received by the MAC sublayer shall conform to the following general format:

| PREAMBLE | SD | FC | DA | SA | DATA_UNIT ... | FCS | ED |

```
where
   PREAMBLE = pattern sent to set receiver's modem
              clock and level (1 or more octets)
         SD = start delimiter (1 octet)
         FC = frame control (1 octet)
         DA = destination address (2 or 6 octets)
         SA = source address (2 or 6 octets)
  DATA_UNIT = information (0 or more octets)
        FCS = frame check sequence (4 octets)
         ED = end delimiter (1 octet)
```

The number of octets between SD and ED, exclusive, shall be 8191 or fewer. The abort sequence shall conform to the following format:

| SD | ED |

```
where
   SD = start delimiter (1 octet)
   ED = end delimiter (1 octet)
```

Within this section the following acronyms are used for the addresses of the station under discussion, its successor and its predecessor in the logical ring:

   TS - this station's address
   NS - next station's address
   PS - previous station's address

4.1 Frame Components. This subsection describes the frame components which are shown in the previous illustrations in greater detail.

4.1.1 Preamble. The preamble pattern precedes every transmitted frame. Preamble is sent by MAC as an appropriate number of pad_idle symbols. Preamble may be decoded by the receiver as arbitrary data symbols that occur outside frame delimiters. Preamble is primarily used by the receiving modem to acquire signal level and phase lock by using a known pattern. The preamble pattern is chosen for each modulation scheme and data rate for this purpose. The parameter min_post_silence_preamble_length specifies the minimum amount of preamble on the first frame transmitted after a period of "transmitted" silence. See 7.1.1 for use of the parameter within the MAC sublayer. See 10.6, 12.6, and 14.8 for the specification of the different physical layers.

A secondary purpose for the preamble is to guarantee a minimum ED to SD time period to allow stations to process the frame previously received. The minimum amount of preamble transmitted is a function of both the data rate and the modulation scheme. The standard requires that the duration of the preamble shall be at least 2 μs, regardless of data rate, and that an integral number of octets shall be sent. Thus at a data rate of 1 Mb/s one octet of preamble is required to meet the interal number of octets requirement, and at a data rate of 10 Mb/s three octets are required to meet the minimum time requirement.

The maximum amount of preamble is constrained by the "jabber" control in the physical layer. Additionally, for claim_token frames, all stations shall use the minimum number of preamble octets to ensure that all frames are of uniform specified length.

4.1.2 Start Delimiter. The frame structure requires a start delimiter, which begins the frame. The start delimiter consists of signaling patterns that are always distinguishable from data.

The start delimiter is coded as follows: (See 10.7, 12.7, 14.9, and 14.12 for representations of the symbol coding as present on the medium.)

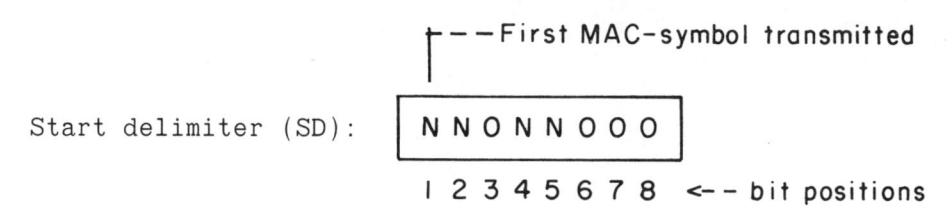

```
                          ┌ ─ ─ First MAC-symbol transmitted
                          │
                         ┌─────────────────┐
Start delimiter (SD):    │ N N O N N O O O │
                         └─────────────────┘
                           1 2 3 4 5 6 7 8    <-- bit positions
```

where
    N = non_data MAC-symbol
    O = zero MAC-symbol

4.1.3 Frame Control Field. The frame control octet (FC) determines what class of frame is being sent among the following general categories:
(1) MAC control
(2) LLC data
(3) Station management data
(4) Special purpose data—reserved for future use

The frame formats for each of these categories is illustrated below.

4.1.3.1 MAC control frame

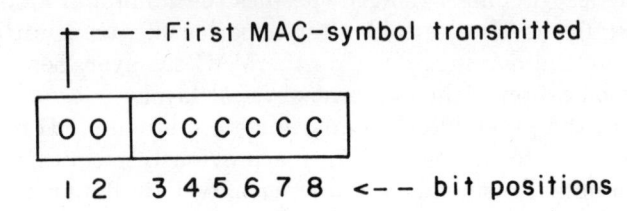

```
            ┌────First MAC-symbol transmitted
            │
           ┌──┬──────┐
           │00│CCCCCC│
           └──┴──────┘
            1 2  3 4 5 6 7 8  <-- bit positions
```

where
           CCCCCC = type of MAC_control frame as follows:

```
C C C C C C
-----------
3 4 5 6 7 8    <---- bit positions
-----------
0 0 0 0 0 0    claim_token
0 0 0 0 0 1    solicit_successor_1 (has 1 response window)
0 0 0 0 1 0    solicit_successor_2 (has 2 response windows)
0 0 0 0 1 1    who_follows (has 3 response windows)
0 0 0 1 0 0    resolve_contention (has 4 response windows)
0 0 1 0 0 0    token
0 0 1 1 0 0    set_successor
```

4.1.3.2 Data frames

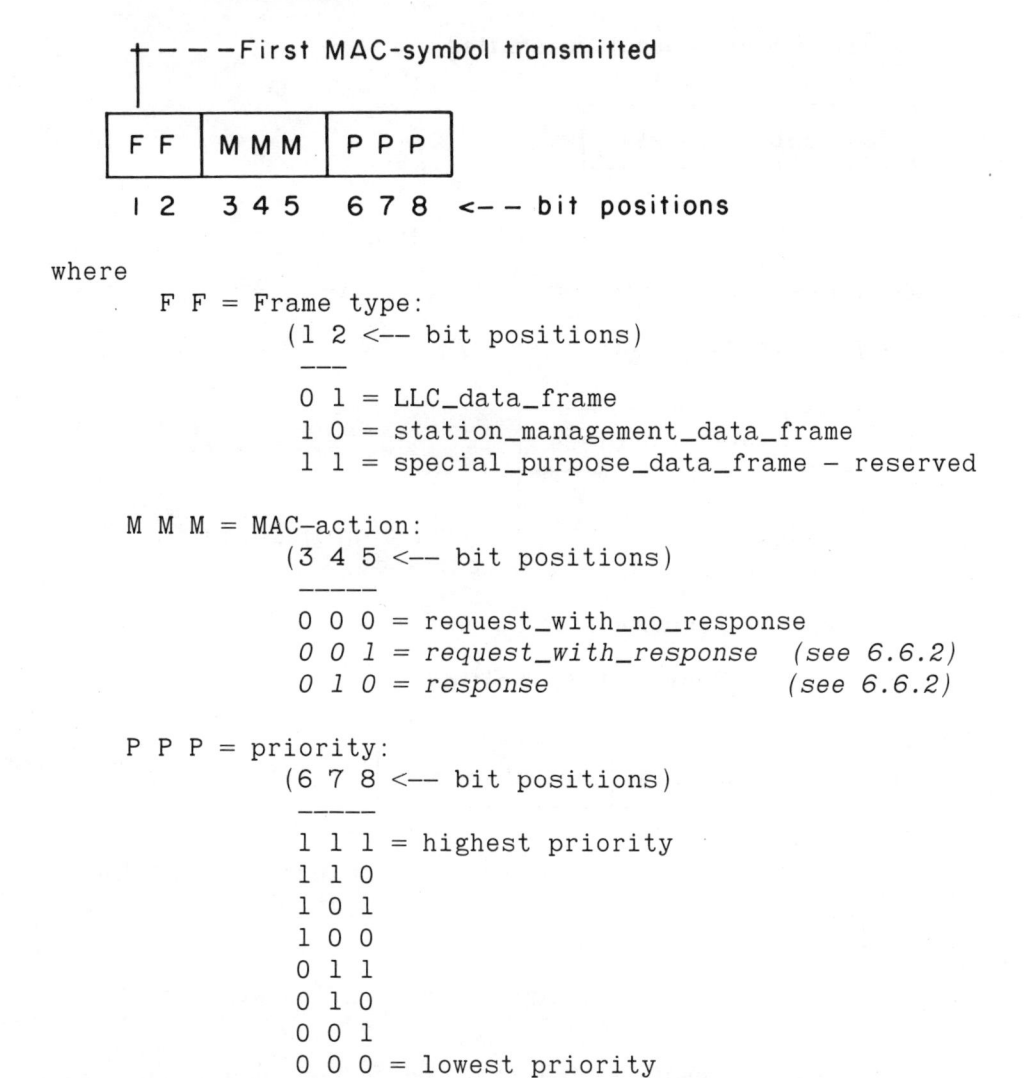

```
  +---First MAC-symbol transmitted
  |
+----+-----+-----+
| F F| M M M| P P P|
+----+-----+-----+
  1 2  3 4 5  6 7 8   <-- bit positions
```

where
    F F = Frame type:
        (1 2 <-- bit positions)
        0 1 = LLC_data_frame
        1 0 = station_management_data_frame
        1 1 = special_purpose_data_frame - reserved

    M M M = MAC-action:
        (3 4 5 <-- bit positions)
        0 0 0 = request_with_no_response
        0 0 1 = request_with_response (see 6.6.2)
        0 1 0 = response (see 6.6.2)

    P P P = priority:
        (6 7 8 <-- bit positions)
        1 1 1 = highest priority
        1 1 0
        1 0 1
        1 0 0
        0 1 1
        0 1 0
        0 0 1
        0 0 0 = lowest priority

Other bit patterns in the frame control octet are reserved for future study. The action of a station upon receiving an FC value not defined in this standard is not specified.

4.1.4 Address Fields. Each frame shall contain two address fields: the destination address field and the source address field, in that order. Addresses shall be either 16 bits or 48 bits in length. All addresses on a given LAN shall be of the same length.

4.1.4.1 Destination Address Field. The following illustration shows the possible representations of destination addresses:

(1) 16-bit address form

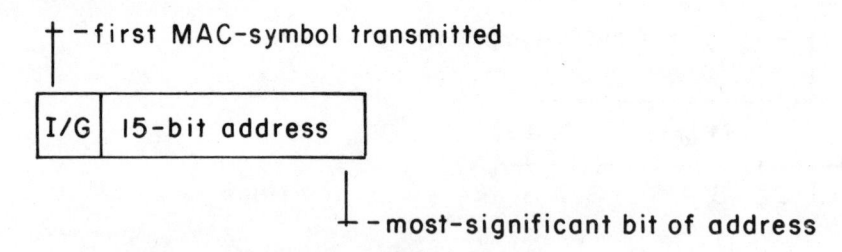

```
+-first MAC-symbol transmitted
|
+-----+---------------+
| I/G | 15-bit address|
+-----+---------------+
            |
            +--most-significant bit of address
```

(2) 48-bit locally administered form

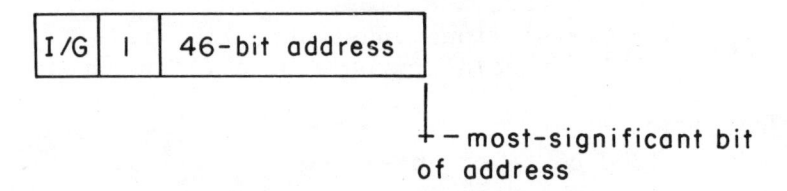

```
+-first MAC-symbol transmitted
|
+-----+---+---------------+
| I/G | 1 | 46-bit address|
+-----+---+---------------+
              |
              +--most-significant bit
                 of address
```

(3) 48-bit globally administered or universal form

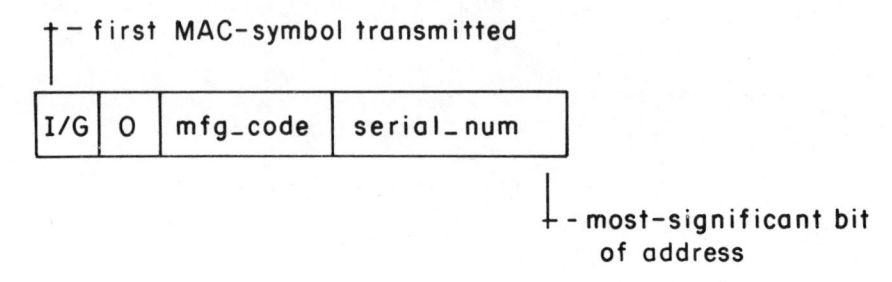

```
+-first MAC-symbol transmitted
|
+-----+---+----------+------------+
| I/G | 0 | mfg_code | serial_num |
+-----+---+----------+------------+
                          |
                          +--most-significant bit
                             of address
```

where
    I/G = individual/group address indication bit

The first MAC-symbol transmitted of the destination address (the I/G bit) distinguishes individual addresses from group addresses

    0 = individual address
    1 = group address

For 48-bit addresses, the second MAC-symbol transmitted of source or destination addresses (the local/universal or L/U bit) distinguishes locally administered addresses from globally administered, universally unique addresses.

NOTE: mfg_code and serial_num merely demonstrate a way of partitioning and assigning 48-bit globally administered addresses, which was employed at the time this standard was drafted. This already-existing practice dictated the numeric interpretation of addresses used in the protocol's address comparison operations.

Individual Addresses. An individual address identifies a particular station on the LAN and shall be distinct from all other individual station addresses on the same LAN.

Group Addresses. A group address is used to address a frame to multiple destination stations. Group addresses may be associated with zero, one, or more stations on a given LAN. In particular, a group address is an address associated by convention with a group of logically related stations.

Broadcast Addresses. The group address consisting of all ones (that is, 16 or 48 ones for two- or six-octet addressing, respectively) shall constitute a broadcast address, denoting the set of all stations on the given LAN.

NOTE: For some of the frame types used by the token bus MAC procedures, the contents of the destination address field is irrelevant. In such cases, the originating station's own address or any other properly formed address can be sent in this field.

Address Administration (48-bit addresses only). There are two methods of administering the set of 48-bit station addresses: locally or through a global authority. The second bit transmitted of the destination address indicates whether the address has been assigned by a global or local administrator.

```
0 = globally administered
1 = locally administered
```

Global Administration. With this method, all individual addresses are distinct from the individual addresses of all other LAN stations on a global basis. The procedure for administration of these addresses is not specified in this standard.

Local Administration. Individual station addresses are administered by a local (to the LAN) authority. (This is the only method allowed for 16-bit addresses.)

4.1.4.2 Source Address Field. The source address identifies the station originating the frame and has the same format and length as the destination address in a given frame, except that the individual/group bit shall be set to 0; the significance of it being set to 1 is a subject for future study.

NOTE: 4.3 contains a suggested method for hierarchical structuring of locally administered addresses.

4.1.4.3 Numerical Interpretation of Addresses. Strictly speaking, addresses are bit strings which serve as unique station identifiers or group identifiers. For the purpose of the MAC address comparison within the token bus MAC sublayer, as used in ordering the logical ring and as expressed in the formal access control machine of 7.2.4, each MAC-address bit string is interpreted as if it were an unsigned integer value sent least-significant bit first, and thus as if the last bit transmitted had the highest numeric significance.

NOTE: This interpretation does not extend beyond the logical ring ordering operations of the token bus MAC sublayer.

Additionally the address bits are used in determining delays in the contention process and transmission lengths in the token claiming process. These processes start with the most significant address bits, under the above interpretation, using two bits at a time. Thus the internal processing order is reversed from the serial transmission order on the medium.

4.1.5 MAC Data Unit Field. Depending on the bit pattern specified in the frame's frame control octet, the MAC data unit field can contain either

(1) An LLC protocol data unit as specified in Ref [13], which is used to exchange LLC information between LLC entities.

(2) A MAC management data frame which is used to exchange MAC management information between MAC management entities.

(3) A value specific to one of the MAC control frames.

Each octet of the MAC data unit field shall be transmitted low-order bit first.

4.1.6 Frame Check Sequence (FCS) Field. The FCS is a 32-bit frame checking sequence, based upon the following standard generator polynomial of degree 32:

$$X^{32} + X^{26} + X^{23} + X^{22} + X^{16} + X^{12} + X^{11} + X^{10}$$
$$+ X^8 + X^7 + X^5 + X^4 + X^2 + X + 1$$

The FCS is the one's complement of the sum (modulo 2) of
(1) The remainder of

$$X^K * (X^{31} + X^{30} + X^{29} + ... + X^2 + X + 1),$$

divided (modulo 2) by the standard 32-bit generating polynomial, where K is the number of bits in the Frame Control, address (SA and DA), and MAC Data_Unit fields, and

(2) The remainder of the division (modulo 2) by the standard generator polynomial of the product of X^{32} by the content of the Frame Control, address (SA and DA), and MAC Data_Unit fields.

The FCS is transmitted commencing with the coefficient of the highest degree term.

As a typical implementation, at the transmitter, the initial content of the register of the device computing the remainder of the division is preset to all ones and is then modified by the generator polynomial (as described above) on the frame control, address, and information fields. The one's complement of the resulting remainder is transmitted as the 32-bit FCS sequence.

At the receiver, the initial content of the register of the device computing the remainder is preset to all ones. The serial incoming protected bits and the FCS, when divided by the generator polynomial, result, in the absence of transmission errors, in a unique nonzero remainder value. The unique remainder value for the 32-bit FCS is the polynomial:

$$X^{31} + X^{30} + X^{26} + X^{25} + X^{24} + X^{18} + X^{15} + X^{14} + X^{12}$$
$$+ X^{11} + X^{10} + X^8 + X^6 + X^5 + X^4 + X^3 + X + 1$$

NOTE: To test the FCS generation and checking logic in a station, an implementation should provide a means of bypassing the FCS generation circuitry and providing an FCS from an external source. The ability to pass frames that have FCS errors along with the received FCS value and an error indication, to higher levels of the protocol, is another desirable testability feature.

4.1.7 End Delimiter. The frame structure requires an end delimiter (ED), which ends the frame and determines the position of the frame check sequence. The data between the SD and the ED shall be an integral number of octets. All bits between the start and end delimiters are covered by the frame check sequence.

The end delimiter consists of signaling patterns that are always distinguishable from data. The end delimiter also contains bits of information that are not error checked.

The end delimiter is coded as follows:

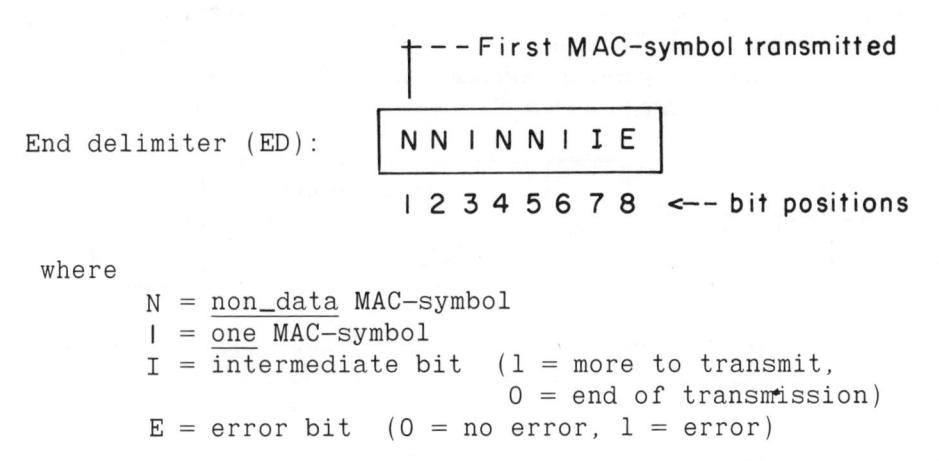

```
                        ┌--First MAC-symbol transmitted
                        │
End delimiter (ED):    │N N I N N I I E│
                        1 2 3 4 5 6 7 8   <-- bit positions
```

where
- N = non_data MAC-symbol
- I = one MAC-symbol
- I = intermediate bit (1 = more to transmit, 0 = end of transmission)
- E = error bit (0 = no error, 1 = error)

The seventh ED MAC-symbol is called the intermediate bit. If <u>one</u>, it indicates that more transmissions from the station follow. If <u>zero</u>, it indicates that this is the last frame transmitted by the station and silence follows the ED. The I bit assists a repeater in determining what follows the ED.

The eighth ED MAC-symbol is called the error bit. When set to <u>one</u> by a repeater, the error bit indicates that the immediately preceding frame had an FCS error within the frame, and thus that the error did not occur on the communication path between that prior repeating station and this receiving station. When the error bit is set, the receiving station may treat the frame as an invalid frame.

4.1.8 Abort Sequence. This pattern prematurely terminates the transmission of a frame. The abort sequence is sent by a station that does not wish to continue to send a frame it has already begun. An abort sequence is inserted by a repeater upon receiving an invalid coding sequence. When a repeater originates an abort sequence upon receiving an invalid coding sequence, it shall be originated on an octet boundary. An abort sequence consists of the following pattern:

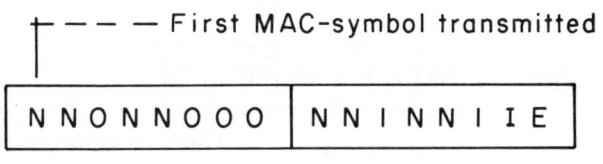

```
       ┌---- First MAC-symbol transmitted
       │
   │N N O N N O O O│N N I N N I I E│
```

where
```
        N = non_data MAC-symbol
        0 = zero MAC-symbol
        I = one MAC-symbol
```

4.2 Enumeration Of Frame Types. This subsection shows how the components of the frames are arranged in the various frame types transmitted by the MAC sublayer. Section 5 discusses the frames and terminology used here.

4.2.1 MAC Control Frame Formats. The following frames are sent and received by the MAC sublayer and are not passed to higher layers.

4.2.1.1 Claim_token. The frame has a data_unit whose value is arbitrary and whose length in octets (between addresses and FCS exclusive) is 0, 2, 4, or 6 times the system's slot_time also measured in octets.

| PREAMBLE | SD | 00000000 | DA | SA | arbitrary value, length = (0, 2, 4, 6) * slot_time octets | FCS | ED |

4.2.1.2 Solicit_successor_1. The frame has a DA = the contents of the station's NS register and a null data unit. One response window always follows this frame.

| PREAMBLE | SD | 00000001 | DA | SA | FCS | ED | |

one response window

4.2.1.3 Solicit_successor_2. The frame has DA = the contents of the station's NS or TS register and a null data unit. Two response windows always follow this frame.

| PREAMBLE | SD | 00000010 | DA | SA | FCS | ED | | |

two response windows

4.2.1.4 Who_follows. The frame has a data_unit = the value of the station's NS register. The format and length of the data_unit is the same as a source address. Three response windows always follow this frame. (This gives receivers two extra slot_times to make a comparison with an address other than TS.)

| PREAMBLE | SD | 00000011 | DA | SA | value NS | FCS | ED | | | |

three response windows

4.2.1.5 Resolve_contention. The frame has a null data_unit. Four response windows always follow this frame.

| PREAMBLE | SD | 00000100 | DA | SA | FCS | ED |

four response windows

4.2.1.6 Token. The frame has DA = the contents of the station's NS register, and has a null data_unit.

| PREAMBLE | SD | 00001000 | DA | SA | FCS | ED |

4.2.1.7 Set_Successor. The frame has DA = the SA of the last frame received, and data_unit = the value of the station's NS or TS register. The format and length of the data_unit is the same as that of a source address.

| PREAMBLE | SD | 00001100 | DA | SA | new value of NS | FCS | ED |

4.2.2 LLC Data Frame Format. LLC data frames have a DA and data-unit specified by a station's LLC sublayer. A frame of this type with a nonnull data unit shall be passed to the receiving station's LLC sublayer (see 4.1.3.2).

| PREAMBLE | SD | 01MMMPPP | DA | SA | LLC_data_unit | FCS | ED |

4.2.3 Station Management Data Frame Format. Station management data frames have a DA and data-unit specified by a station's station management entity. A frame of this type with a nonnull data-unit shall be passed to the receiving station's station management sublayer (see 4.1.3.2).

| PREAMBLE | SD | 10MMMPPP | DA | SA | station_mgmt_data_unit | FCS | ED |

4.2.4 Special Purpose Data Frame Format. Special purpose data frames have a DA and data-unit specified by a special purpose sublayer within a station. A frame of this type with a nonnull data-unit shall be passed to the corresponding special purpose sublayer within the receiving station, if such exists (see 4.1.3.2).

| PREAMBLE | SD | 11MMMPPP | DA | SA | special_purpose_data_unit | FCS | ED |

4.2.5 Invalid Frames. An invalid frame is defined as one which meets at least one of the following conditions:

(1) It is identified as such by the physical layer (For example, it contains non_data or invalid symbols.)

(2) It is not an integral number of octets in length

(3) It does not consist of a start delimiter, one frame control field, two properly formed address fields, one data unit field of appropriate length (dependent on the bit pattern specified in the frame control field), one FCS field, and an end delimiter, in that order

(4) The FCS computation, when applied to all octets between the SD and the ED, fails to yield the unique remainder specified in 4.1.6.

An implementation may also include any of the following additional conditions for an invalid frame:

(5) The frame control field contains an undefined bit pattern

(6) The error bit within the end delimiter immediately following the frame is asserted.

Invalid frames shall be treated as noise. Their existence, as noise bursts, is relevant at some points in the token bus elements of procedure.

Appendix

(This Appendix is not a part of this standard but is included for information only.)

4.3 Appendix. Recommendation for a Hierarchical Structure for Locally-Administered Addresses.

The concepts introduced in this Appendix are under study for inclusion in a future revision of this standard.

This Appendix describes an addressing structure for a bus network divided into multiple logical segments, with one or more MAC-level relay stations interconnecting the segments. Structuring MAC addresses in an hierarchical fashion can facilitate the operation of these relay stations.

A logical segment is defined as the collection of all stations of a LAN which have the same segment address and which can exchange frames without any intermediary MAC-level relay entity. Stations of a segment can communicate with stations with different segment addresses only through a MAC-level relay or some other intermediary. For example, for a token bus implementation, the stations of a logical segment share a single token forming a single logical ring distinct from other logical segments.

An hierarchical address permits a MAC-level relay station to recognize frames which require forwarding to other logical segments by applying an algorithm similar to that used in the recognition of group addresses.

The source and destination address partitioning recommended for this purpose is:

(1) 16-bit hierarchical form

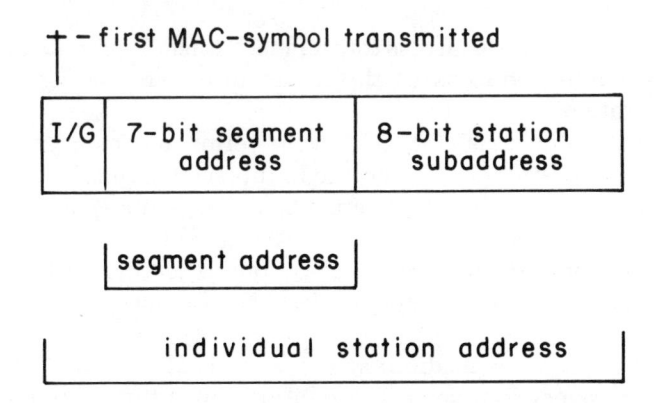

```
┬ — first MAC-symbol transmitted
│
┌───┬──────────────────┬──────────────────┐
│I/G│  7-bit segment   │   8-bit station  │
│   │     address      │    subaddress    │
└───┴──────────────────┴──────────────────┘
    ┌──────────────────┐
    │ segment address  │
    └──────────────────┘
    ┌─────────────────────────────────────┐
    │    individual station address       │
    └─────────────────────────────────────┘
```

(2) 48-bit locally administered hierarchical form

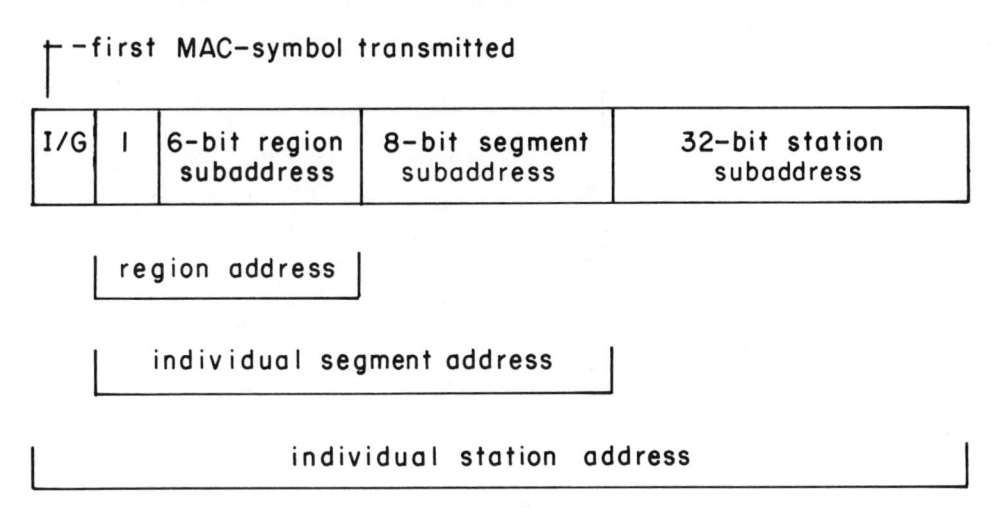

```
┬ — first MAC-symbol transmitted
│
┌───┬─┬──────────────┬──────────────┬──────────────────┐
│I/G│1│ 6-bit region │ 8-bit segment│   32-bit station │
│   │ │  subaddress  │  subaddress  │    subaddress    │
└───┴─┴──────────────┴──────────────┴──────────────────┘
      ┌──────────────┐
      │region address│
      └──────────────┘
      ┌─────────────────────────────┐
      │  individual segment address │
      └─────────────────────────────┘
  ┌───────────────────────────────────────────────────┐
  │            individual station address             │
  └───────────────────────────────────────────────────┘
```

The 8-bit or 32-bit station subaddress distinguishes stations on a single logical segment. The 8-bit segment subaddress distinguishes logical segments within a single region defined by the 7-bit region address.

5. Elements of MAC Sublayer Operation

A description of the token bus medium access control mechanism is provided in this section. This section is intended to assist the reader in understanding the MAC sublayer and its operation.

Section 6 contains precise definitions of MAC-specific terms and mandatory aspects of the mechanism. Where statements included in this section conflict with those in Section 6 or are incomplete, those in Section 6 shall take precedence.

Section 7 describes the required behavior of the access-control machine of the MAC sublayer. Where statements in this section or Section 6 conflict with the formal description in Section 7 or are incomplete, the formal description shall take precedence.

This section describes the token bus medium access control (MAC) sublayer's operational and exception recovery functions. The relationship of this section to other sections of this standard and to LAN specifications is illustrated in Fig 6-1.

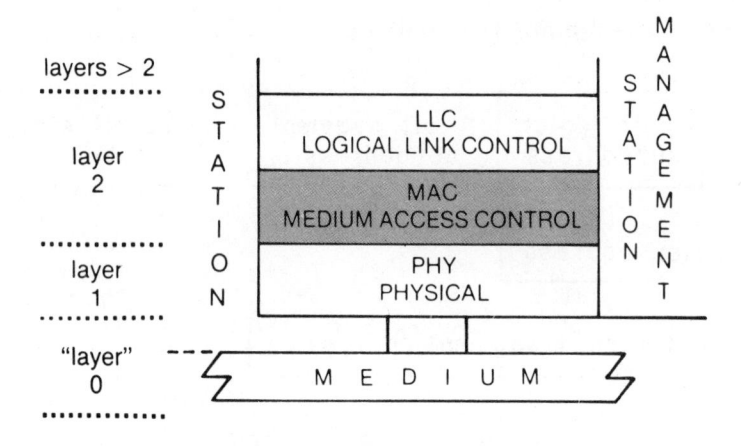

Fig 5-1
Relation to LAN Model

Specific responsibilities of the medium access control sublayer for a broadcast medium involve managing ordered access to the medium, providing a means for admission and deletion of stations (adjustment of logical ring membership), and handling fault recovery.

The faults considered here are those caused by communications errors or station failures. These faults include
  (1) Multiple tokens
  (2) Lost token
  (3) Token-pass failure
  (4) "Deaf" station (that is, a station with an inoperative receiver)
  (5) Duplicate station addresses

TOKEN-PASSING BUS

IEEE
Std 802.4-1985

This medium access protocol is intended to be robust, in the sense that it should tolerate and survive multiple concurrent errors.

Some basic observations are useful in understanding the operation of tokens on a broadcast medium.

(1) Stations are connected in parallel to the medium. Thus, when a station transmits, its signal is received (or "heard") by all stations on the medium. Other stations can interfere with the first station's transmission but cannot predictably alter its contents.

(2) When a station transmits, it may assume that all other stations hear something (though not necessarily what was transmitted).

(3) When a station receives a valid frame (properly formed and delimited and containing a correct frame check sequence), it may infer that some station transmitted the frame and therefore that all stations heard something.

(4) When a station receives something other than a valid frame (that is, noise), it may make no inference regarding what the other stations on the medium might have heard.

(5) Not all stations need be involved in token passing (only those which desire to initiate transmissions).

(6) Multiple tokens and lost tokens may be detected by any station. There are no special "monitor" stations that perform token recovery functions.

(7) Due to spatial separation, stations cannot be guaranteed to have a common perception of the system state at any instant. (The medium access protocol described herein accounts for this.)

5.1 Basic Operation. Steady state operation (the network condition where a logical ring has been established and no error conditions are present) simply requires the sending of the token to a specific successor station as each station is finished transmitting (see Fig 1-2).

Other essential and more difficult tasks are establishment of the logical ring (at initialization or re-establishing it in the case of a catastrophic error) and maintenance of the logical ring (allowing stations to enter and leave the logical ring without disrupting the other stations in the network).

The right to transmit, the token, passes among all stations in the logical ring. Each participating station knows the address of its predecessor (the station that transmitted the token to it), referred to as Previous Station or PS. It knows its successor (which station the token should be sent to next), referred to as Next Station or NS. It knows its own address, referred to as This Station or TS. These predecessor and successor addresses are dynamically determined and maintained by the algorithms described. Whenever a station changes its successor (NS), an indication of this change is passed to station management (if enabled).

The following subsections introduce major elements and features of the token bus access protocol.

NOTE: For the purpose of description, all state machines are presumed to be instantaneous with respect to external events.

5.1.1 Slot Time. In describing the access operations, the term slot_time is used to refer to the maximum time any station need wait for an immediate medium access level response from another station. Slot_time is precisely defined in 6.1.9.

The slot_time (along with the station's address and several other station management parameters) shall be known to the station before it attempts to transmit on the network. If all stations in a network are not using the same value for slot_time, the medium access protocol may not operate properly. The method of setting these parameters in each station is outside the scope of this standard.

5.1.2 Right To Transmit. The token (right to transmit) is passed from station to station in descending numerical order of station-address. When a station hears a token frame addressed to itself, it "has the token" and may transmit data frames. When a station has completed transmitting data frames it passes the token to the next station in the logical ring, as discussed in 5.1.3.

When a station has the token it may temporarily delegate its right to transmit to another station *by sending a request_with_response data frame. When a station hears a request_with_response data frame addressed to itself it shall respond with a response data frame, if the request with response option is implemented. The response data frame causes the right to transmit to revert back to the station which sent the request_with_response data frame.*

5.1.3 Token Passing. After each station has completed transmitting any data frames it may have, and has completed other maintenance functions (described in 5.1.4), the station passes the token to its successor by sending a "token" MAC_control frame.

After sending the token frame the station listens for evidence that its successor has heard the token frame and is active. If the sender hears a valid frame following the token, it assumes that its successor has the token and is transmitting. If the token sender does not hear a valid frame following its token pass, it shall attempt to assess the state of the network.

If the token sending station hears a noise_burst or frame with an incorrect FCS, it cannot be sure from the source address which station sent the frame. The medium access protocol treats this condition in a way which minimizes the chance of the station causing a serious error. If a noise_burst is heard, the token sending station sets an internal indicator and continues to listen in the check _token_pass state for up to four more slot times. If nothing more is heard, the station assumes that it heard its own token that had been garbled and so repeats the token transmission. If anything is heard during the following four slot time delay, the station assumes its successor has the token.

If the token holder does not hear a valid frame after sending the token the first time, it repeats the token pass operation once, performing the same monitoring as during the first attempt.

If the successor does not transmit after a second token frame, the sender assumes that its successor has failed. The sender then sends a who_follows frame with its successor's address in the data field of the frame. All stations compare the value of the data field of a who_follows frame with the address of their predecessor (the station that normally sends them the token). The station whose predecessor is the successor of the sending station responds to the who_follows frame by sending its address in a set_successor frame. The station holding the token thus establishes a new successor, bridging the failed station out of the logical ring.

If the sending station hears no response to a who_follows frame, it repeats the frame a second time. If there is still no response, the station tries another strategy to reestablish the logical ring. The station now sends a solicit_successor_2 frame with its own address as both DA and SA, asking any station in the system to respond to it. Any operational station that hears the request and needs to be part of the logical ring responds, and the logical ring is reestablished using the response window process discussed next.

If all attempts at soliciting a successor fail, the station assumes that a fault may have occurred; either all other stations have failed, all stations have left the logical_ring, the medium has broken, or the station's own receiver has failed so that it cannot hear other stations who have been responding to its requests. Under such conditions the station quits attempting to maintain the logical ring. If the station has no frames to send, it listens for some indication of activity from other stations. If the station has data frames to send, it sends its remaining data frames and then repeats the token pass process. Once the station has sent its frames and still cannot locate a successor it becomes silent and listens for another station's transmissions.

In summary, the token is normally passed from station to station using a short token pass frame. If a station fails to pick up the token, the sending station uses a series of recovery procedures that grow increasingly more drastic as the station repeatedly fails to find a successor station.

5.1.4 Response Windows. New stations are added to the logical ring through a controlled contention process using "response windows". A response window is a controlled interval of time (equal to one slot time) after transmission of a MAC_control frame in which the station sending the frame pauses and listens for a response. If the station hears a transmission start during the response window, the station continues to listen to the transmission, even after the response window time expires, until the transmission is complete. Thus the response windows define the time interval during which a station will hear the beginning of a response from another station.

The two frame types, solicit_successor_1 and solicit_successor_2, indicate the opening of response windows for stations wishing to enter the logical ring. The solicit_successor frame specifies a range of station addresses between the frame source and destination addresses. Stations whose addresses fall within this range and who wish to enter the logical ring respond to the frame.

The sender of a solicit_successor frame transmits the frame and then waits, listening for a response in the response window following the frame. Responding stations send the frame sender their requests to become the next station in the logical ring. If the frame sender hears a valid request, it allows the new station to enter the logical ring by changing the address of its successor to the new station and passing its new successor the token.

In any response window there exists the possibility that more than one station simultaneously will desire logical ring entry. To minimize contention when this happens, the token pass sequence is limited by requiring that a station only request admission when a window is opened for an address range that spans its address.

There are two solicit_successor frames. Solicit_successor_1 has one response window following. Solicit_successor_2 has two response windows. Solicit_successor_1 is sent when the station's successor's address is less than the station's address. This is the normal case when the token is being passed from higher to lower addressed stations. Solicit_successor_1 allows only stations whose address is in the range between the token sender and the token destination to respond, thus limiting the possible contenders and preserving the descending order of the logical ring.

Exactly one station in the logical ring has its station's address below that of its successor (that is, the unique station having the lowest address which shall send the token to the "top" of the address ordered logical ring). When soliciting successors this station shall open two response windows, one for those stations with addresses below its own, and one for stations with addresses above its successor. The station with the lowest address sends a solicit_successor_2 frame when opening response windows. Stations having an address below the sender respond in the first response window; while stations having an address higher than the sender's successor, respond in the second response window.

In any response window, when the soliciting station hears a valid set_successor frame, it has found a new successor. When multiple stations simultaneously respond, only unrecognizable noise may be heard during the response period. The soliciting station then sequences through an arbitration algorithm to identify a single responder, by sending a resolve_contention frame. The stations which had responded to the earlier solicit_successor frame and which have not yet been eliminated by the iterative resolve responders algorithm, choose a two-bit value (usually from the station's address) and listen for 0, 1, 2, or 3 slot_times as determined by that listen delay value. (This listen delay value is further described later.) If these contending stations hear anything (that is, non-silence) while listening, they eliminate themselves from the arbitration. If they hear only silence, they continue to respond to further resolve_contention requests from the soliciting station.

5.1.5 Bound on Token Rotation Time.
The worst-case token rotation time determines the maximum delay a station experiences in gaining access to the network. A very long token rotation occurs if many stations attempt to add new stations to the logical ring by performing the solicit successor procedure on the same rotation of the token.

The maximum token rotation time is bounded by deferring the solicit successor procedure whenever the token rotation time is longer than a defined maximum. The ring_maintenance timer in each station measures the rotation time of the token. If the time exceeds a value set by station management (max_ring _maintenance_rotation_time), the station does not perform the solicit successor procedure. On the next token rotation the station determines if the token now is rotating fast enough to perform the solicit successor procedure.

In conjunction with the priority option (see 5.1.7), the value of max_ring _maintenance_rotation_time determines the maximum token rotation time.

5.1.6 Initialization. Initialization is primarily a special case of adding new stations; it is triggered by the exhaustion of an inactivity timer (bus_idle) in one station. If the inactivity timer expires, the station sends a claim_token frame. As in the response window algorithm, the initialization algorithm assumes that more than one station can try to initialize the network at a given instant. This is resolved by address sorting the initializers.

Each potential initializer sends a claim_token frame having an information field length that is a multiple of the system slot_time (the multiple being 0, 2, 4, or 6 based on selected bits of the station address). Each initializing station then waits one slot time for its own transmission, and those of other stations that chose the same frame length, to pass. The station then samples the state of the medium.

If a station senses non-silence, it knows that some other station(s) sent a longer length transmission. The station defers to those stations with the longer transmission and reenters the idle state.

If silence was detected, and unused bits remain in the address string, the station attempting initialization repeats the process using the next two bits of its address to derive the length of the next transmitted frame. If all bits have been used and silence is still sensed, the station has "won" the initialization contest and now holds the token.

Once there is a unique token in the network, the logical ring builds by way of the response window process previously described.

NOTE: A random pair of bits is used at the end of the address sort algorithm to ensure that two stations with the same address (which is a fault condition) will not permanently bring down an entire system. If the two stations don't separate (random choices identical), they both attempt to form a logical ring, and at most one of them will succeed. If they do separate (random choices are different), one will get in. In the latter case, the station which doesn't get in will hear a transmission from a station with an identical address and so will discover the error condition.

A station can remove itself from the logical ring at any time by simply choosing not to respond to a token passed to it, allowing the fault recovery mechanisms in the medium access protocol to patch it out. A more efficient method is: when the station has the token and desires to exit the logical ring, the station sends a set_successor frame to its predecessor (the station that transmitted the token to it) containing the address of its successor. The exiting station then simply sends the token as usual to its successor, knowing the token will not be received again. Re-admission to the logical ring requires one of the sequences described in 5.1.4 and 5.1.6.

5.1.7 Priority Option. The token passing access method provides an optional priority mechanism by which higher layer data frames awaiting transmission are assigned to different "service classes", ranked or ordered by their desired transmission priority. This priority mechanism allows the MAC sublayer to provide eight service classes to the LLC sublayer, and higher level protocols. The priority of each frame is determined by the "service class" requested in the MA_DATA.request command.

The token bus access method distinguishes only four levels of priority, called "access classes". Thus there are four request queues to store frames pending transmission. The access classes are named 0, 2, 4, and 6, with 6 being the highest priority and 0 the lowest.

MAC maps the service class requested by the LLC layer into a three bit priority value, which is included in the frame format field. The priority value is then mapped into the MAC access class by ignoring the least significant bit of the priority field. Thus service classes 0 and 1 correspond to access class 0, service classes 2 and 3 to access class 2, service classes 4 and 5 to access class 4, and service classes 6 and 7 to access class 6.

Any station not using the optional priority feature shall transmit every data frame with an access class of 6 (the highest priority). The service class value in the MA_DATA.request shall still be carried in the FC octet. For all stations, the rule governing the transmission of these highest priority frames is that a station shall not transmit consecutive frames for more than some maximum time set by station management. This time, called the hi_pri_token_hold_time, prevents any single station from monopolizing the network. If a station has more access class 6 data frames to send than it can transmit in one hi_pri_token_hold_time period, it is prohibited from sending additional frames after that time has expired and shall pass the token. When a station, which is using the optional priority feature, has lower access class frames to send and has time available, it shall send these frames subject to the priority system rules described in these paragraphs.

The object of the priority system is to allocate network bandwidth to the higher priority frames and only send lower priority frames when there is sufficient bandwidth. The network bandwidth is allocated by timing the rotation of the token around the logical ring. Each access class is assigned a "target" token rotation time. For each access class the station measures the time it takes the token to circulate around the logical ring. If the token returns to a station in less than the target rotation time, the station can send frames of that access class until the target rotation time has expired. If the token returns after the target rotation time has been reached, the station cannot send frames of that priority on this pass of the token.

Each station using the optional priority scheme shall have three rotation timers for the three lower access classes. Each access class has a queue of frames to be transmitted. When a station receives the token it first services the highest access class queue, which uses the hi_pri_token_hold_time to control its operation. After having sent any frames of the highest priority, the station begins to service the rotation timers and queues working from higher to lower access class.

Each access_class acts as a virtual substation in that the token is passed, internally, from the highest access_class downward, through all access_classes, before being passed to the station's successor.

The access class service algorithm consists of loading the residual value from a token rotation timer into a "token hold timer" and reloading the same rotation timer with the target rotation time for that access class. (Thus frames sent by a station, for this access class, are accounted for in the access class's next token rotation time computation.) If the "token hold timer" has a remaining positive value, the station can transmit frames at this access class until either the "token hold timer" times out or this access class's queue is empty. When either event occurs the station begins to service the next lower access class. When the lowest level is serviced the station performs any required logical ring maintenance and passes the token to its successor.

5.1.8 Token Rotation Timer Example. The following example describes a simplified system with only two active access classes, the highest and one other lower level. Assume there are four stations in the logical ring, with addresses 9, 7, 5, and 1. Assume stations 9 and 1 each send three high-priority "frames" per token revolution; while 7 and 5 send as many lower priority frames as possible. (The example assumes that propagation delays are negligible compared with the time to send data frames.)

The example begins after a period during which no data frames have been sent so that the token has been rotating as rapidly as possible. In Fig 5-2, each station is represented by a box which contains the station's address and target token rotation time value for the station's active frame queue. The values in the left-hand column under each station, labeled TRTC, are the token rotation "times" observed at that station for the previous rotation of the token. The values in the right-hand column, labeled XMIT, are the number of "frames" transmitted by the station each time it holds the token. Each row of this figure represents one rotation of the token. In this example station 9 is assumed to have three high-priority frames of 128 octets, stations 7 and 5 have only low-priority frames of 400 and 356 octets respectively, and station 1 has two high-priority frame of 305 octets. The token rotation "time" is given in octet_times and assumes 19 octet_times per token pass per station.

**Fig 5-2
Token Rotation Time "Priority" Example**

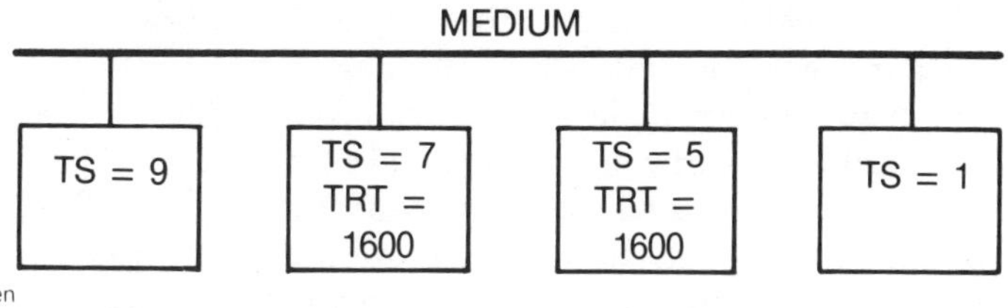

```
                              MEDIUM
    ─────────┬──────────────┬──────────────┬──────────────┬─────────
             │              │              │              │
         ┌───┴───┐      ┌───┴───┐      ┌───┴───┐      ┌───┴───┐
         │ TS = 9│      │ TS = 7│      │ TS = 5│      │ TS = 1│
         │       │      │ TRT = │      │ TRT = │      │       │
         │       │      │ 1600  │      │ 1600  │      │       │
         └───────┘      └───────┘      └───────┘      └───────┘
```

Token Rot.	TRTC	XMIT	TRTC	XMIT	TRTC	XMIT	TRTC	XMIT
1	76	3	460	3	1660	0	1660	2
2	2270	3	2270	0	1070	2	1782	2
3	1782	3	1782	0	1782	0	1070	2
4	1070	3	1070	2	1870	0	1870	2
5	1870	3	1870	0	1070	2	1782	2
6	1782	3	1782	0	1782	0	1070	2
7	1070	3	1070	2	1870	0	1870	2
8	1565	3	1565	1	1165	2	1877	1
9	1877	3	1877	0	1477	1	1121	1
10	1121	3	1121	2	1921	0	1565	1
11	1565	3	1565	1	1165	2	1877	1
12	1877	3	1877	0	1477	1	1121	1

Looking at the example we see that on the first token rotation, station 9 measures an effective rotation time of 76 (4*19) and sends three frames of high-priority data. Station 7 thus measures an effective rotation time of 460 (3*128+76), leaving 1140 units of "time" to send data before having to pass the token to station 5. Station 5 measures an effective token rotation time of 1660 (since 1660 octets of data have been sent since it last received the token). Station 5 cannot send low-priority data and shall immediately pass the token. (If station 7 had less data to send, it could have passed the token to station 5 sooner, giving station 5 an opportunity to send on this rotation.) Station 1 sends two frames of high-priority data, unconstrained by the lower priority rotation timer.

On the second rotation of the token station 7 cannot send, but the token arrives early enough for station 5 to send two frames of low-priority data.

On the third rotation of the token in the example, stations 9 and 1 continue to send three frames each of high-priority data. Neither stations 7 nor 5 can send low-priority data since the token is rotating too slowly on this circuit.

On the fourth and fifth rotations stations 9 and 1 continue to use most of the network bandwidth for high-priority frames. Stations 7 and 5 share the remaining bandwidth by each sending two frames on alternate token rotations.

Rotations 5 through 7 repeat the usage pattern shown in rotations 2 through 4, showing a stable cyclic bandwidth allocation pattern: over any three rotations, stations 9 and 1 use 66% of the bandwidth and stations 5 and 7 equally share the remaining 34%. If all stations always offer the same traffic, this sharing continues indefinitely.

On the eighth rotation of the token, station 1 begins to send only one frame of high-priority data, allowing the lower-priority stations more of the available network bandwidth. That a stable, cyclic usage pattern is again established can be seen by comparing token rotations 9 and 12. This usage pattern again repeats over three rotations. Stations 9 and 1, together, use 48% of the bandwidth and stations 5 and 7 equally share the remaining 52%.

This example demonstrates how the token rotation timer method allows lower access class traffic to fill in bandwidth which is not used by higher access class traffic. Note how the network bandwidth not used by stations with higher access class traffic is more or less equally shared among stations with lower access class traffic. Although in this example each station only sends traffic of one access class, this standard allows any station to send at any access class.

5.1.9 MAC acknowledged connectionless service. *The immediate-response mechanism, coupled with appropriate MAC-user functions, provides a MAC acknowledged connectionless service. When a higher layer entity requests a data transmission using the MAC acknowledged connectionless service, the MAC-user entity issues to the MAC entity a MA_DATA.request with a quality-of-service parameter specifying request_with_response.*

When the local MAC entity obtains the token, it sends the request_with _response frame and waits for another valid frame. If a timer expires without receiving a valid frame, the local MAC entity retransmits the original frame. This sequence is repeated until a valid frame is received or the allowed number of retries is exhausted.

When the remote (responding) MAC entity receives the frame specifying request _with_response, it passes the received frame to the remote MAC-user entity. That remote MAC-user entity generates an appropriate response and directs the remote MAC entity to send this response frame at once to the source of the request_with _response frame (that is, the originating station).

When the local (originating) MAC entity receives the response frame, or when the retry count is exhausted, it associates the frame (if available) with the request_with_response frame now being processed and notifies the originating MAC-user entity of the completion of its original request.

The retry mechanism of the immediate-response procedure prevents loss of frames at any arbitrary level of confidence determined by the max_retry_limit parameter (see 7.1.1). However, since the local station repeats the request_with _response frame when a response frame is not received, it is possible for the remote station to receive duplicates of the original request_with_response frame. The remote MAC-user entity should eliminate duplicate frames.

The local (originating) MAC entity engages in one immediate-response activity at a time. All retries and timeouts for that request are completed before the local MAC-entity processes another request or initiates the ring-maintenance/token-passing procedures.

5.1.10 Randomized Variables. Several of the variables used by the medium access protocol have two bit "random" values. Some of these randomized variables are used to improve error recovery probabilities under certain conditions. The randomization of max_inter_solicit_count forces stations to operate "out of step" when opening response windows.

5.2 Access Control Machine (ACM) States. The medium access logic in a station is described here as a computation machine which sequences through a number of distinct phases, called states. These states are introduced in the following subsections. The states and the transitions between them are illustrated in Fig 5-3. (The dashed lines group states into functional areas.) Section 7 contains the complete state transition table which provides a formal description of the token-passing bus access machine..

5.2.0 Offline. "Offline" is the state the access machine is in immediately following power-up or following the detection, by the MAC sublayer, of certain fault conditions. After powering up, a station tests itself and its connection to the medium without transmitting on the medium. This "internal" self-testing is station implementation dependent and does not affect other stations on the network. Thus, the self test procedure is beyond the scope of this standard.

After completing any power-up procedures, the station remains in the offline state until it has had all necessary internal parameters initialized and been instructed to go online.

5.2.1 Idle. "Idle" is the state where the station is listening to the medium and not transmitting.

If a MAC_control frame is received for which the station shall take action, the appropriate state is entered. For example, if a token frame, addressed to the station, is received, the station enters the "use token" state.

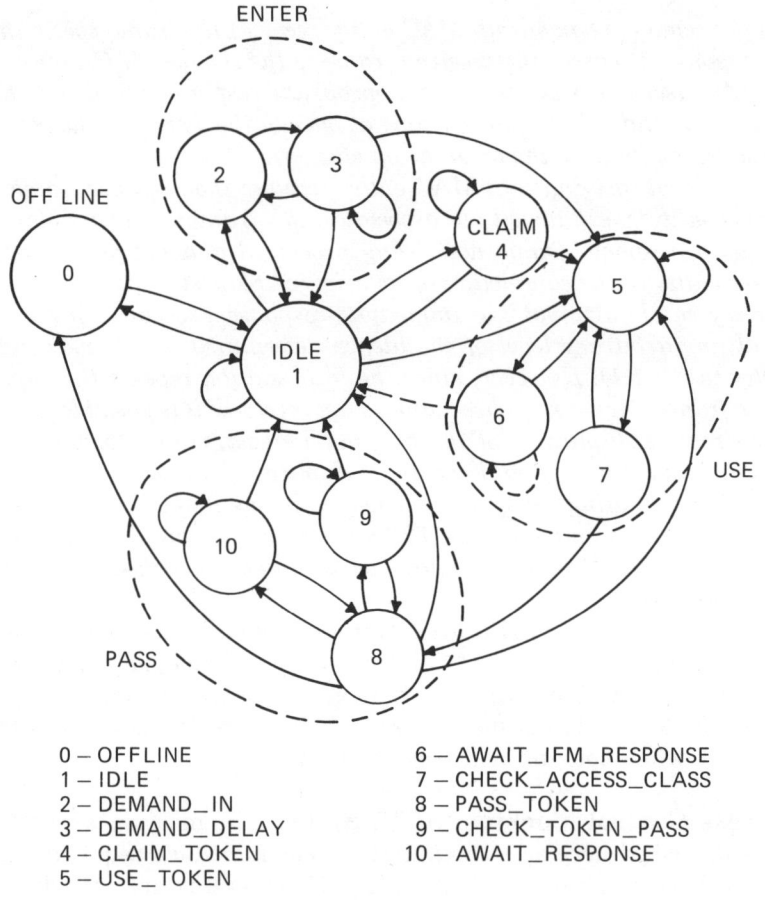

**Fig 5-3
MAC Finite State Machine Diagram**

0 – OFFLINE
1 – IDLE
2 – DEMAND_IN
3 – DEMAND_DELAY
4 – CLAIM_TOKEN
5 – USE_TOKEN
6 – AWAIT_IFM_RESPONSE
7 – CHECK_ACCESS_CLASS
8 – PASS_TOKEN
9 – CHECK_TOKEN_PASS
10 – AWAIT_RESPONSE

If the station goes for a long period of time (a defined multiple of the slot_time) without hearing any activity on the medium, it may infer that recovery of the logical ring is necessary. The station attempts to claim the token (enters the "claiming token" state) and (re)initialize the logical ring.

5.2.2 Demand In. The "demand-in" state is entered from the idle state if a solicit successor frame that spans the station's address is received by a station desiring logical ring entry. (The demand-in state is also entered from the demand-delay state during the contention resolution process discussed in Section 6.) In the demand-in state the contending station sends the token holder a set_successor frame and goes to the demand-delay state to await a response.

If a station intends to respond to a solicit_successor or a who_follows frame in the first response window, the station enters the demand-in state from the idle state with a zero delay and so immediately transmits a set_successor response and goes to the demand-delay state. If the station intends to respond in the second response window after a frame or is participating in the contention resolution process, the station delays in the demand-in state before transmitting a set _successor frame.

While delaying in the demand-in state, if the station hears any transmissions, it assumes that another station with a higher numbered address is requesting the token and so it shall return to the idle state.

5.2.3 Demand Delay. "Demand-delay" is the state the station enters after having sent a set_successor frame in the demand-in state. In the demand-delay state a station can expect to hear

(1) A token from the token holder indicating its set_successor frame was heard

(2) A resolve_contention frame from the token holder indicating that all stations which are still demanding into the logical ring should perform another step of the contention resolution process, or

(3) Set_successor frames from other stations, which the station ignores

If the station either hears nothing or hears a frame other than one of (1), (2), or (3), the station shall leave the demand-delay state. The station then abandons soliciting the token and returns to the idle state.

In (1) the token holder has heard the soliciting station and sent the token. The contention resolution process is over. The soliciting station upon receiving the token goes to the use token state and begins transmitting.

In (2) the token holder has heard responses from multiple stations soliciting the token and sent a resolve_contention frame. All stations currently in the demand-delay state respond to this frame. The responding stations first set a delay and return to the demand-in state where they listen for other demanders. If no other demanders have been heard by the time the delay period has expired, each station then sends another set_successor frame to the token holder.

The contention for the token by multiple stations is resolved by having each station delay a period of time in the demand-in state before transmitting another set_successor frame. The delay interval is chosen by taking the station's (unique) address and using two bits from that address to determine the delay interval. The first pass of the resolution process uses the most significant two address bits; the next pass the next two address bits; etc. Thus stations delay 0, 1, 2, or 3 slot times when entering the demand-in state before transmitting.

When multiple stations request to enter the logical ring, the desired result is for the token holding station to pass the token to the highest addressed station. To select the highest addressed contending station from multiple contenders, the one's complement of the station's address is used to determine the delay in the demand-in state. Thus, stations with numerically higher addresses delay shorter intervals and send their set_successor messages sooner than stations with lower addresses. Stations with numerically lower addresses hear the transmissions of the higher addressed stations and drop out of the contention process.

If two contending stations have the same value for the selected two address bits, they delay the same amount of time and transmit more or less simultaneously. If the token holder hears multiple responses and does not hear a valid set_successor from any station, it sends another resolve_contention frame, starting another step of the contention resolution process.

The contention resolution process can take at most 25 passes (48/2 + 1, for 48-bit addresses) of the following cycle:

(a) All remaining demanding stations send set_successor frames to the token holder.

(b) They all listen for a response from the token holder and ignore other set_successor frames.

(c) They all hear a resolve_contention frame from the token holder.

(d) They all delay a number of slot times based on the next two bits of their own addresses.

(e) If they hear another frame during the delay, they drop from contention.

The contention resolution process should resolve so that the contending station with the highest address is heard by the token holder and receives the token. However, if two stations are erroneously assigned the same station address, they will both sequence through the contention process using the same delays and may not resolve.

To permit eventual resolution in this error condition, a final resolution pass is taken, using a two-bit random number, after the station's address bits have all been used and the contention is still unresolved. If both stations choose the same random value or another error prevents resolution, then the token holder and the contending stations abandon the resolution process until the next response window is opened. (Thus two stations with the same address which consistently choose the same random number value may never be able to enter the logical ring.)

5.2.4 Claim Token. "Claim-token" is entered from the idle state after the inactivity timer expires (and the station desires to be included in the logical ring). In this state, the station attempts to initialize or reinitialize the logical ring by sending claim_token frames.

To resolve multiple simultaneous stations sending claim_token frames, each station delays for one slot_time after sending the claim_token frame, and then monitors the medium as previously described. If after this delay the bus is quiet, the station sends another claim_token frame.

If the station sends max_pass_count (where max_pass_count is half the number of bits in the station's address plus one, since the address bits are used in pairs) claim_token frames without hearing other transmissions, the station has successfully "claimed" the token, and goes to the use-token state.

5.2.5 Use Token. "Use-token" is entered after just receiving or claiming a token. This is the state in which a station can send data frames.

As the station enters this state, it starts the "token holding" timer, which limits how long the station may remain sending before passing the token. The value initially loaded in the holding timer, hi_pri_token_hold_time, is a system imposed parameter.

When a station's token holding timer has expired (and any transmission in progress is complete), or when the station has no more to transmit, it enters the check-access-class state.

When a station sends a data frame it sets the response window timer to 3 slot times and enters the await-IFM-response state.

5.2.6 Await IFM Response. "Await-IFM-response" is entered when a data frame has been sent. *The ACM may wait for the Interface Machine (IFM) to signal the reception of a response.*

If the frame sent in the use-token state was a request_with_no_response frame, no response is expected. The use-token state is again entered to check for another frame or holding timer timeout. *If the frame sent was a request_with_response frame, the station waits in the await-IFM-response state for one of the following*

(1) A response frame addressed to the requestor
(2) Any other valid frame
(3) A timeout

If a response frame addressed to the requestor is heard, the use-token state is again entered to check for another frame or holding-timer timeout. (The IFM passes the response frame to the specified MAC-user entity as it does all other data frames addressed to the station. The IFM also associates the response frame with the request_with_response frame just previously transmitted.)

If any other valid frame is heard, an error has occurred. The station returns to the idle state and processes the received frame.

If a timeout occurs before a valid frame is heard, the station repeats sending the request_with_response data frame. If the station repeats sending that frame the number of times specified by the max_retry_limit parameter, then the request is abandoned. The IFM notifies the MAC-user entity that no response to the frame was received. The use-token state is entered to check for another frame or token-holding-timer timeout.

5.2.7 Check Access Class. "Check-access-class" controls the transmission of frames for different access classes. If the priority option is not implemented all frames are considered to be high priority and the check-access-class state only serves to control entry to token passing.

If the priority option is implemented, a station may send frames for lower access classes before passing the token. Each access class other than the highest has a target token rotation time. At the time that the station has the token and begins to consider transmitting frames for that access class the residual time left in the target rotation timer is loaded into the token holding timer and the station transitions back to the use-token state. At this time the target rotation timer is also reloaded to its initial value.

Thus the station will alternate between use-token and check-access-class states for each access class. If time is available, data frames will be sent in the use-token state. When the lowest priority access class has been checked, the station will proceed to the pass token process, described next.

When a station has completed sending data frames, it shall enter the token passing state. Three conditions can occur

(1) The station knows its successor, so it simply passes the token and enters the check-token-pass state.

(2) The station knows its successor but shall first check if new stations desire to enter the logical ring. The station sends a solicit_successor frame and enters the await-response state.

(3) The station does not know its successor. (This condition occurs after initialization and under error conditions.) The station sends a solicit_successor frame opening response windows for all stations in the system and enters the await-response state.

5.2.8 Pass Token. "Pass token" is the state in which a station attempts to pass the token to its successor.

When its inter_solicit_count value is zero and time remains on the ring_maintenance_timer, the station allows new stations to enter the logical ring before passing the token. The token holding station does this by sending a solicit_successor_1 or solicit_successor_2 frame, as appropriate, and enters the await-response state. (See 5.1.4 for the details of this operation.)

If the address of the successor, NS, is known, the station performs a simple token pass following any new successor solicitation. (See 5.1.3 for details of this operation.) If the successor responds and the station hears a valid frame, the station has completed its token passing obligations.

If NS is not known, the station sends a solicit_successor_2 frame to itself. Since this frame has two response windows and identical source and destination addresses, it forces all stations on the network which desire to be in the logical ring (whether or not they were previously) to respond. Those stations whose addresses are lower than the sender of the token frame transmit in the first window; those with addresses higher transmit in the second window.

The station monitors the response windows for set_successor frames from potential successors, exactly as for the token pass. If no responses are heard, the station stops trying to maintain the logical ring and listens for transmissions from any other station. (See 5.1.3 for details of this operation.)

5.2.9 Check Token Pass. "Check-token-pass" is the state in which the station waits for a reaction from the station to which it just passed the token.

The station sending the token waits one slot time for the station receiving the token to transmit. The one slot time delay accounts for the time delay between receiving a frame and the recipient taking the response action.

If a valid frame is heard which started during the response window, the station assumes the token pass is successful. The frame is processed as if it were received in the idle state.

If nothing is heard in one slot time, the station sending the token assumes the token pass was unsuccessful and returns to the pass-token state to either repeat the pass or try another strategy.

If noise or an invalid frame is heard, the station continues to listen for additional transmissions, as described in detail in 5.1.3.

5.2.10 Await Response. "Await-response" is the state in which the station attempts to sequence candidate successors through a distributed contention resolution algorithm until one of those successors' set_successor frames is correctly received or until no successors appear. The state is entered from the pass-token-state whenever the station determines it is time to open a response window or if the station does not know its successor (as in initialization or when a token pass fails).

The station waits in the await-response state for a number of response window times. If nothing is heard for the entire duration of the window(s) opened, the station goes to the pass-token state, either to pass the token to its known successor or to try a different token-pass strategy.

If a set_successor frame is received, the station waits for the remainder of the response window time to pass. The station then enters the pass-token state and sends the token to the new successor.

If the received frame is other than a set_successor frame, the station drops the token (since some other station is acting as if it also has a token, thus creating a duplicate token situation) and re-enters the idle state.

If noise is heard during the response windows, the station cycles through a procedure of sending resolve_contention frames which each open four response windows, and waits for a distinguishable response that began in a response window. The loop repeats a maximum of max_pass_count times, each time instructing contending stations to select a different two bits of their address to determine which of the four opened windows to transmit in.

5.3 Interface Machine Description. The Interface Machine (IFM) acts as an intermediary between the other functional machines of the MAC sublayer and the MAC-user entities with which MAC communicates. Its internal operation is largely unspecified, because the MAC layer will function correctly, no matter how the IFM functional requirements are met.

The IFM has eight primary functions, three of which are optional

(1) Accept or generate the service primitives specified for the LLC - MAC and station management - MAC interfaces

(2) Queue pending service requests

(3) Recognize addresses of LLC and station management data frames destined for this station

(4) Map LLC and station management quality of service requests from LLC terms (service_class) into MAC terms (access_class)

(5) Optionally, maintain multiple queues of send requests separated by access_class (or by service class)

(6) Maintain FIFO ordering within each queue of pending service requests

(7) Optionally generate an ACM_RELEASE.indication to the ACM when a data frame is received whose quality parameter specifies response

(8) Optionally accept a response from the responding MAC-user entity following receipt of a frame specifying request_with_response, and send a response frame.

Since the service primitives are treated in detail elsewhere in this standard, they are not discussed further here.

The IFM should also handle address recognition for data frames not destined for the MAC layer itself. While some address recognition might be done in the receive machine, the need to check potentially large numbers of group addresses for relevance could place unreasonable demands on the RxM.

The notion of quality of service is similar to that of priority, though it is slightly less specific, and deliberately so. Higher protocol layers may rank their messages in some way which may be only approximately realizable by the lower layers. In the LAN case, the LLC layer may assign any one of eight service_class rankings to each frame it requests to be sent. The token bus MAC layer may not be able to provide different qualities of service, or MAC access_classes, so it shall be able to map all service_classes into one access_class. The MAC layer may, optionally, provide several distinct access_classes. When it does so, the IFM shall maintain multiple request queues, so that the requests may be handled according to both access_class (or service_class) and arrival order.

5.4 Receive Machine Description. The MAC receive machine (see Figs 1-3 and 5-4) accepts MAC-symbols (see 6.1.2) from the PHY layer and generates high-level data structures and signals for the MAC access-control machine and the MAC interface machine. The interface between the PHY layer and the MAC access machine is the PHY_DATA.indication primitive specified in Section 8. This description of the receive machine embodies the PHY_DATA.indication primitive as an encoded MAC-symbol and an associated PHY_clk. The other receive machine interfaces are internal to MAC and are composed of the following signals and data structures:

bus_quiet. This signal is asserted when the medium is inactive. It is set and cleared by the receive machine, and it is read by the access-control machine.

Rx_protocol_frame. A Boolean variable that is true when a valid MAC _control frame has been received. This variable is set by the receive machine, and it is read and cleared by the access machine.

Rx_data_frame. A Boolean variable which is true when a valid LLC_data or station_management frame has been received. This variable is set by the receive machine, read by both the access-control machine and the interface machine, but cleared only by the interface machine.

noise_burst. This signal indicates that there was activity on the medium that did not result in a valid frame (see 4.2.4 for the specification of invalid frames). This signal is set by the receive machine, and it is read and cleared by the access machine.

frame_buffer. When a valid frame has been received, this data structure contains the frame format, destination_address, source_address, data_unit and FCS fields of the received frame. The contents of this structure are written by the receive machine. When the Rx_protocol_frame signal is set, the contents of this structure are used by the access-control machine. When the Rx_data_frame signal is set, the contents of this structure are used by the interface machine.

There are four major functional blocks in the receive machine: the MAC-symbol interpreter, the FCS block, the deserializer and the receiver control block. (See Fig 5-4.) These blocks are described as synchronous machines clocked by PHY_clk. Where practical, these blocks are decomposed into finite state machines. See Figs 5-5, 5-6, and 5-7. In these figures, an unbracketed label on an arc is the condition for the arc; a label in brackets is an output of that arc.

TOKEN-PASSING BUS

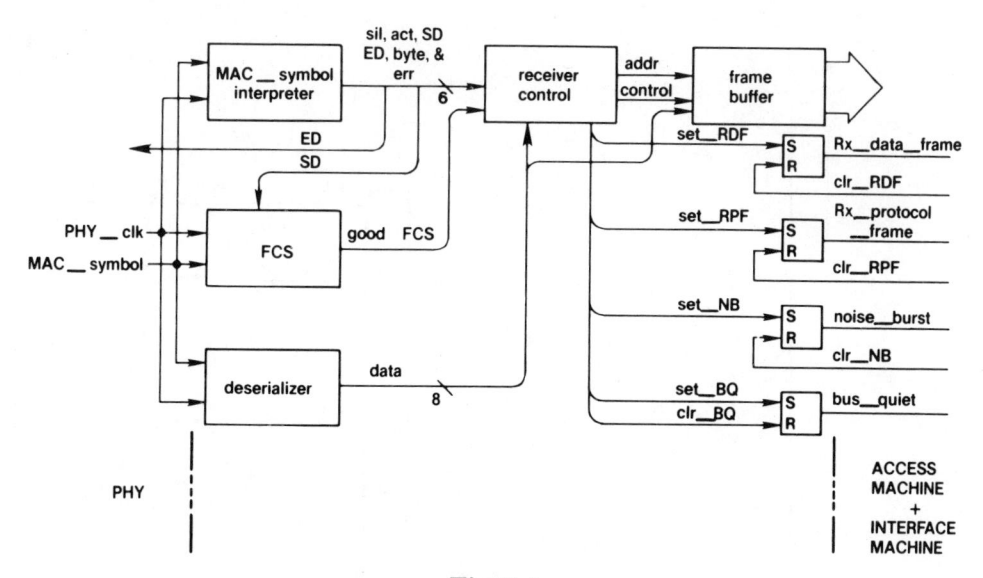

IEEE
Std 802.4-1985

**Fig 5-4
Receive Machine**

The MAC-symbol interpreter accepts MAC-symbols and generates the following signals:

sil, act. These signals represent transitions from activity to silence (sil) and from silence to activity (act) on the bus, respectively. The signals sil and act directly control set_BQ and clr_BQ (set and clear bus_quiet, respectively). The only reason they are not exactly equivalent is that the receiver control block shall maintain certain timing relationships among the bus_quiet, noise_burst, and valid_frame variables. The state machine shown only generates sil after eight MAC-symbols of silence (S), and requires three non-silence MAC-symbols to generate act. In part, this is merely to provide a degree of hysteresis in the receiver and the exact counts may be varied by the implementer; however, when a valid frame is received, the appropriate Rx_frame signal shall be set before bus_quiet is set. Failure to do so can cause the access-control machine to malfunction.

SD, ED. Any valid frame delimiter in the received MAC-symbol sequence is detected, regardless of context. The ED signal is returned to PHY for use by conditioning and synchronizing circuits.

byte, err. (State machine not shown.) The byte/err detector is unconditionally initialized by SD, establishing byte alignment. While only 0 and 1 MAC-symbols are subsequently received, byte strobes true every eight PHY_clk periods. The

Fig 5-5
sil/act Detector Finite State Machine

Fig 5-6
SD Detector Finite State Machine

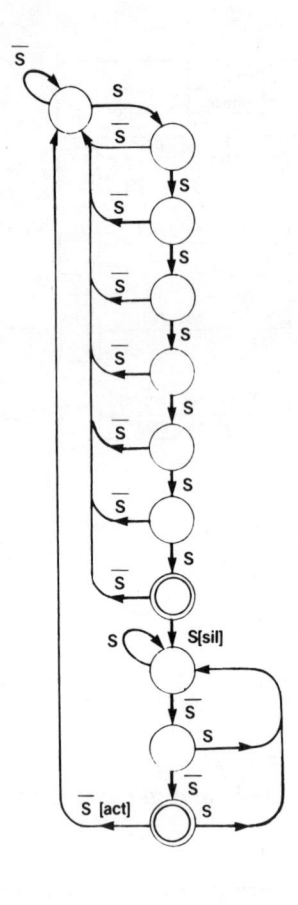

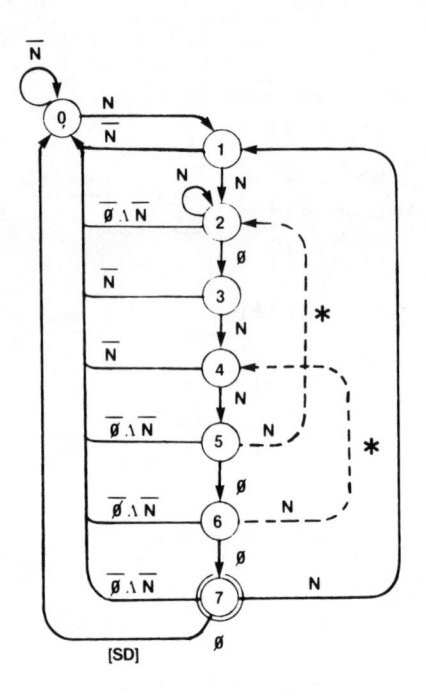

*The destination for these arcs may be state 1 or state 0 rather than the ones shown here.

reception of any MAC-symbol other than 0 or 1 starts an exit sequence. (See 6.1.2 for definitions of MAC-symbols.) Possible exit sequences are as follows:

(1) Reception of a P, B, or S MAC-symbol: report the error and terminate (wait for initialization).

(2) Reception of an N not on an octet boundary: report the error and terminate.

(3) Reception of an N on an octet boundary which does not prove to be a frame delimiter: report the error and terminate.

(4) Reception of an N on an octet boundary which introduces SD: initialize.

(5) Reception of an N on an octet boundary which introduces ED: terminate.

The FCS block implements the FCS calculation specified in 4.1.6. It is initialized by any SD, and shifts in data until a non-data symbol is received.

The output of the deserializer is defined only when SD, ED, or a data byte is reported.

TOKEN-PASSING BUS
IEEE
Std 802.4-1985

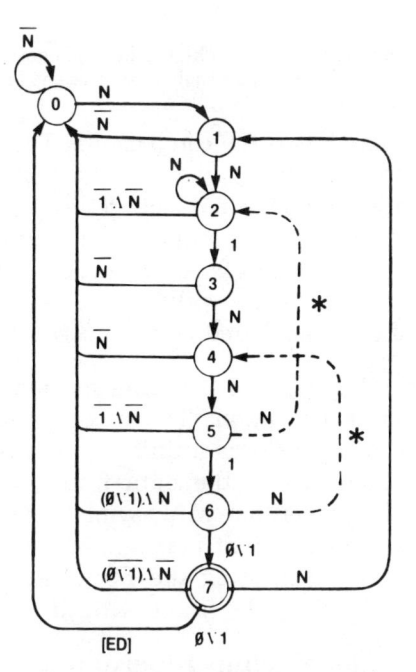

*The destination for these arcs may be state 1 or state 0 rather than the ones shown here.

**Fig 5-7
ED Detector Finite State Machine**

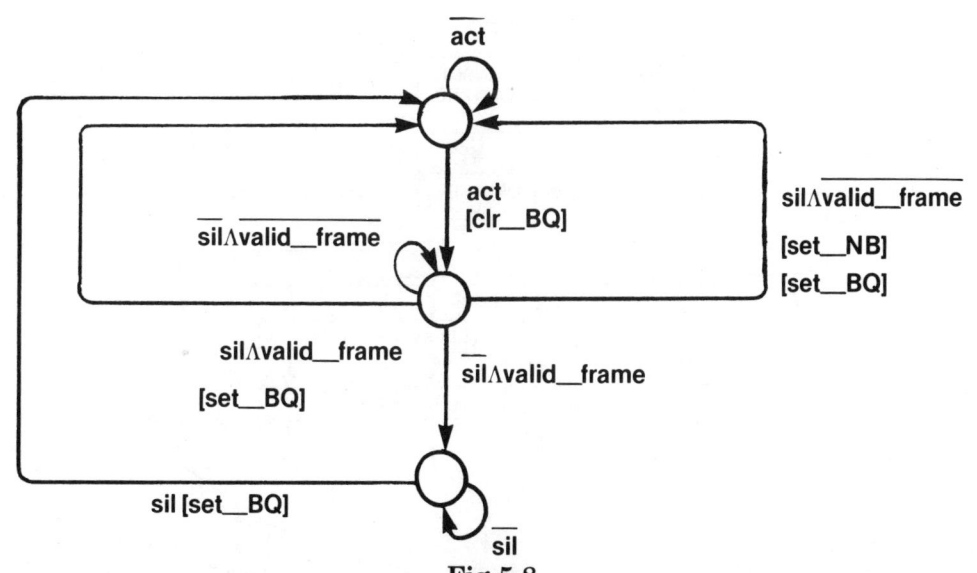

**Fig 5-8
noise—burst/bus—quiet (NB/BQ) Detector Finite State Machine**

NOTE: Reporting of the data bits in delimiters to higher layers is not required by this specification. Those data bits are not covered by the FCS and their correctness is not required for proper station operation.

The receiver control block has three components. The noise_burst/bus_quiet (NB/BQ) detector sets and clears bus_quiet, and it sets noise_burst on the rising edge of bus_quiet if a valid frame has not been received (see Fig 5-8). The frame control block transfers the deserializer output to the frame buffer, checks the FC field for LLC and station management frames, and determines whether the frame contained a legal number of octets. The valid frame detector further verifies that the FCS was correct and that the frame was composed of valid octets.

5.5 Transmit Machine Description. The transmit machine (TxM) has a fairly straightforward and simple operation. The access-control machine forwards frames for transmission to the TxM as a unit (at least for the purposes of this description). The TxM then passes the data frame, along with appropriate delimitation, to the physical layer, one MAC-symbol at a time, for transmission on the physical medium. The transmit machine is responsible for sending the proper amount of preamble, computing the FCS and including it within the transmitted frame, and delimiting the frame with SD and ED.

5.6 Regenerative Repeater Machine Description. Bus repeaters are used to connect electrically or frequency separate bus segments together into an extended logical bus network. A repeater has a separate receiver for each segment to which it is connected. Each receiver separates clock and MAC-symbols, and has a

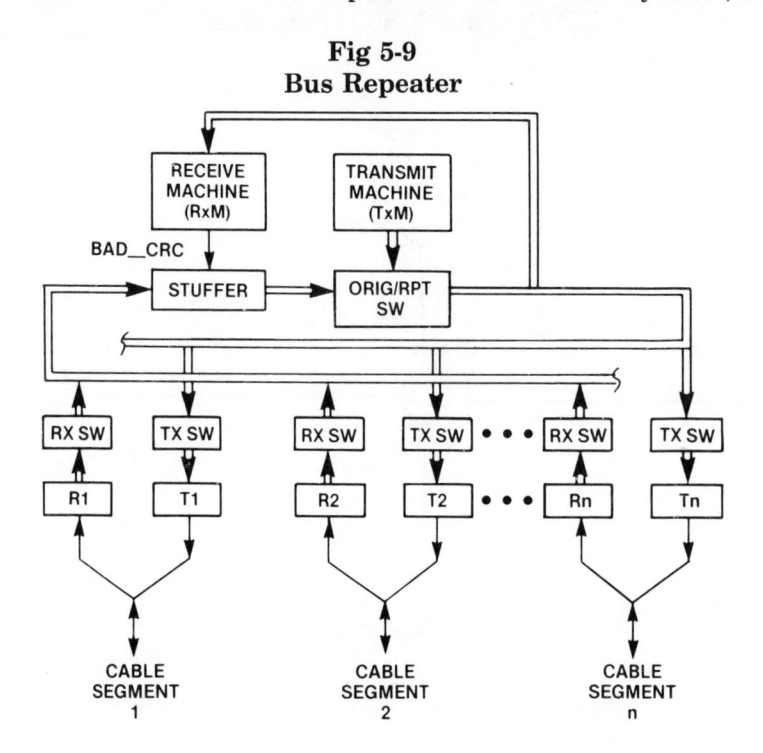

**Fig 5-9
Bus Repeater**

receive switch that controls which receiver is the MAC-symbol source for the stuffer. A receiver becomes the stuffer source by reporting non-silence when there is no other receiver acting as stuffer source. A stuffer source is not dropped until it reports silence.

Figure 5-9 shows a generalized repeater. Included in the figure are n distinct physical segments of a single bus. The simplest form of a repeater (a broadband head-end repeater) has only one transmitter/receiver pair.

The stuffer has three functions

(1) Re-insert preamble symbols that are lost in the receiver

(2) Transmit the abort sequence when bad_signal is reported to it. The abort sequence always begins on an octet boundary

(3) Set the E bit in the ED if the repeated frame has an FCS error

The output of the stuffer goes to one input of the originate/repeat switch; the other input to this switch comes from the transmit machine. When the transmit machine reports non-silence, the originate/repeat switch unconditionally selects that input. When the transmit machine reports silence, the switch selects the stuffer, after a short delay to guarantee that it does not repeat any symbols that originated in the local transmit machine.

While the originate/repeat switch is enabling the local transmit machine, all transmit switches are on, so the symbols are transmitted onto all segments. While the originate/repeat switch is selecting the stuffer, all transmit switches are on, except the one corresponding to the segment whose receiver is the current symbol source for the stuffer.

A repeater may or may not be a station within the network. If the repeater also functions as a station, the repeater's receiver and transmitter machines perform all the functions described in this standard. If the repeater does not function as a station, the receiver machine need only check the FCS of received frames, so as to compute the E bit value for the retransmitted ED. The transmitter machine of a non-station repeater continuously sends silence.

6. MAC Sublayer Definitions and Requirements

All of the aspects of the MAC sublayer operation and mechanism which are required for conformance to this standard and which are not specified in Sections 4 or 7 are specified in this section.

6.1 MAC Definitions. Critical MAC parameters which are constrained by this specification are defined as follows:

6.1.1 Immediate_response. The immediate transmission of a response to a received frame. This assumes that no other transmissions or actions were intervening.

6.1.2 MAC-symbols. The smallest unit of information exchanged between MAC sublayer entities. The six MAC-symbols are as follows:

NAME	ABBREVIATION
zero	0
one	1
non_data	N
pad_idle	P
silence	S
bad_signal	B

Where binary 0 and 1 data bits are discussed, they are sent and received as zero and one MAC-symbols respectively.

6.1.3 MAC_symbol_time. The time required to send a single MAC-symbol. This is the inverse of the LAN data rate.

Nominal Data Rate	Nominal MAC_symbol_time
1 Mb/s	1.0 μs
5 Mb/s	0.2 μs
10 Mb/s	0.1 μs

6.1.4 Octet_time. Corresponds to the time interval required to transmit eight MAC-symbols.

6.1.5 PHY-symbols (physical layer symbols). Correspond to the waveforms impressed on the physical medium. The PHY-symbol definitions are given in the following subsections:
  (1) 10.7.2 for Single-channel Phase Continuous FSK
  (2) 12.7.2 for Single-channel Phase Coherent FSK
  (3) 14.9.2 for Multilevel Duobinary AM/PSK (1 MAC-symbol/Bd)
  (4) 14.12 for Multilevel Duobinary AM/PSK enhanced

6.1.6 Transmission_path_delay. The worst case delay which transmissions experience going through the physical medium from a transmitter to a receiver. The following formula is a general definition of transmission_path_delay:

Transmission_path_delay = worst_case (physical_medium_delay
                            + Amplifier_delay
                            + Repeater_delay)

A detailed discussion of transmission_path_delay for each signaling technique is given in the following subsections:
  (1) 11.8 for Single_channel Phase Continuous FSK
  (2) 13.8 for Single_channel Phase Coherent FSK
  (3) 15.8 for Multilevel Duobinary AM/PSK

TOKEN-PASSING BUS
IEEE
Std 802.4-1985

6.1.7 Station_delay. The time from the receipt of the PHY-symbols corresponding to the last MAC-symbol of the received ED at the receiving station's physical medium interface to the impression of the first immediate_response PHY-symbols onto the physical medium by that station's transmitter.

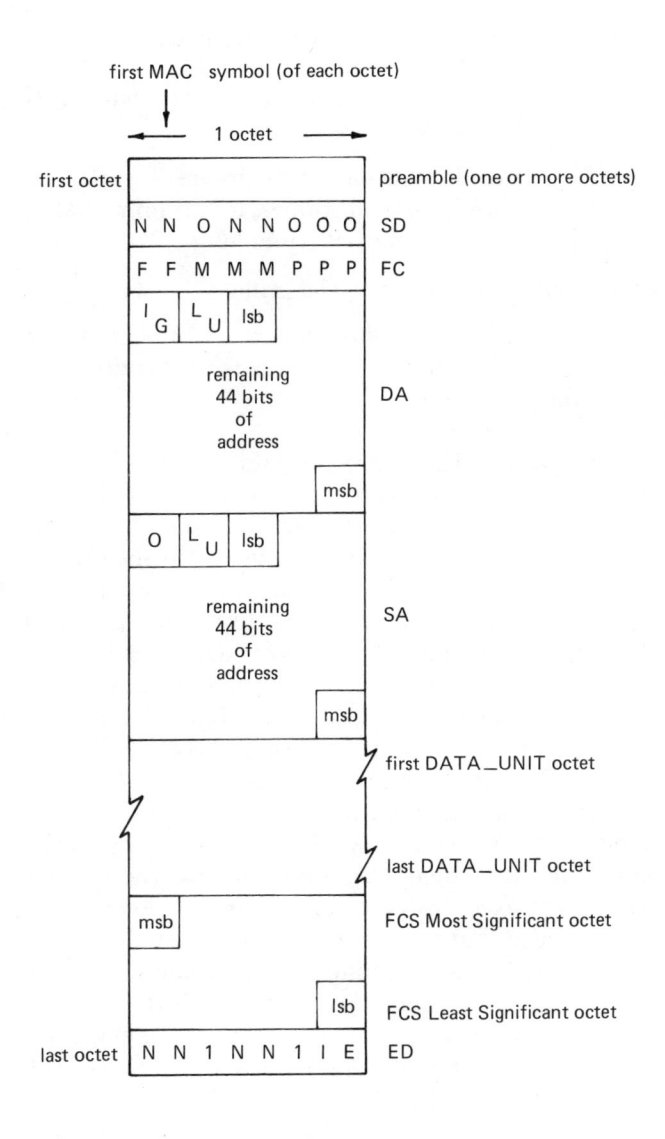

**Fig 6-1
MAC Protocol_data_unit Transmission Order**
(Shown for 48 bit Addresses)

77

6.1.8 Safety_margin. A time interval no less than one MAC_symbol_time.

$$\text{Safety\_margin} \geq \text{MAC\_symbol\_time}$$

6.1.9 Slot_time. The maximum time any station need wait for an immediate _response from another station. Slot_time is measured in octet_times, and is defined as

$$\begin{aligned}\text{slot\_time} = \text{INTEGER} (\{ &[2 * (\text{Transmission\_path\_delay} \\ &+ \text{Station\_delay}) \\ &+ \text{Safety\_margin}] / \text{MAC\_symbol\_time} \\ &+ 7\} \ / \ 8)\end{aligned}$$

6.1.10 Response_window. The basic time interval which the MAC protocol allows, following certain MAC_control frames, for an immediate_response from another station. This interval is one slot_time long

$$\text{response\_window duration} = \text{slot\_time}$$

If a station, waiting for a response, hears a transmission start during a response_window, that station shall not transmit again until at least the received transmission terminates.

6.2 Transmission Order. The frame formats used by the MAC sublayer and the detailed contents of the octets of those frames are specified in Section 4. The octets of a frame and the MAC-symbols of an octet shall be transmitted from the MAC sublayer to the physical layer, and vice versa, in the order specified in Fig 6-1; the first octet of the frame shall be transmitted first and the first MAC-symbol of each octet shall be transmitted first. The first octet and first MAC-symbol correspond to the top octet and the left-most MAC-symbol shown in Fig 6-1; Those notations within octets of Fig 6-1 which are not MAC-symbols are casual descriptions which are specified in Section 4. Figure 6-1 describes a complete general frame or MAC protocol_data_unit (m_pdu).

6.3 Delay Labeling. Vendors shall provide a worst_case value for equipment delay times. Vendors may optionally specify a minimum network slot time when their equipment anticipates some minimum delay in order to function correctly. When uncertain of the exact value of the delay, vendors shall state an upper bound. It is recommended that vendors of equipment conforming to this standard label the equipment with that equipment's contribuion to the station delay. A vendor of a complete station labels the station with the total station delay. A vendor of a component, intended to be assembled by an end user into a station, labels the component or otherwise documents the delays that contribute to station delay.

6.4 Miscellaneous Requirements

6.4.1 Station Initialization. On power-up, the station shall enter the offline state. While in the offline state the station shall not impress any signaling on the

LAN medium. The station shall progress from the offline state to the idle state only when it has been loaded with the basic station operating parameters needed for correct operation of the MAC protocols. These operating parameters include at least

    (1) TS   (station address)
    (2) address_length   (implicit in TS)
    (3) slot_time
    (4) hi_pri_token_hold_time
    (5) max_ac_4_rotation_time   (if priority is implemented)
    (6) max_ac_2_rotation_time   (if priority is implemented)
    (7) max_ac_0_rotation_time   (if priority is implemented)
    (8) max_ring_maintenance_rotation_time
    (9) ring_maintenance_timer_initial_value
    (10) max_inter_solicit_count
    (11) min_post_silence_preamble_length
    (12) in_ring_desired
    (13) max_retry_limit

6.4.2 Token Passing Order. The token shall be passed from station to station in station-address order, descending numerically except that the station with the lowest address shall pass the token to the station with the highest address, in order to close the logical ring. Figure 6-2 illustrates the address-order logical ring and shows the logical relationships which hold between addresses of adjacent stations in a logical ring with three or more members.

6.4.3 Station Receipt of Its Own Transmissions. In systems with significant transmission_path_delay, such as head-ended broadband systems, a transmitting station may receive its own transmissions after some small but significant delay. The MAC access mechanism of such a transmitting station shall not be misled by the receipt of its own transmissions. In Section 7 the state diagrams specify where a station should ignore its own transmissions.

6.4.4 Token Holding Time. The token holding station shall only begin transmitting a frame when there is time remaining on the token_hold_timer. A transmission may run past the expiration of the token_hold_timer by up to the time to transmit a maximum length data frame.

Use of the MAC acknowledged connectionless service (immediate response mechanism) may further exceed the token-holding time. The excess time may be caused by repeated retries with associated waiting periods.

6.4.5 Address Lengths. Addresses shall be either two octets (16 bits) or six octets (48 bits) long, including the Individual/Group bit and Local/Universal administration bit where appropriate. All stations operating on a single LAN shall be assigned and use addresses of the same length.

6.4.6 Randomized Variables. The station shall provide a two bit (that is, four valued) random variable for use in the MAC protocols. For the medium access protocol to benefit from the randomization, the technique used to create the random values shall be statistically independent between stations. Thus

IEEE
Std 802.4-1985   LOCAL AREA NETWORKS:

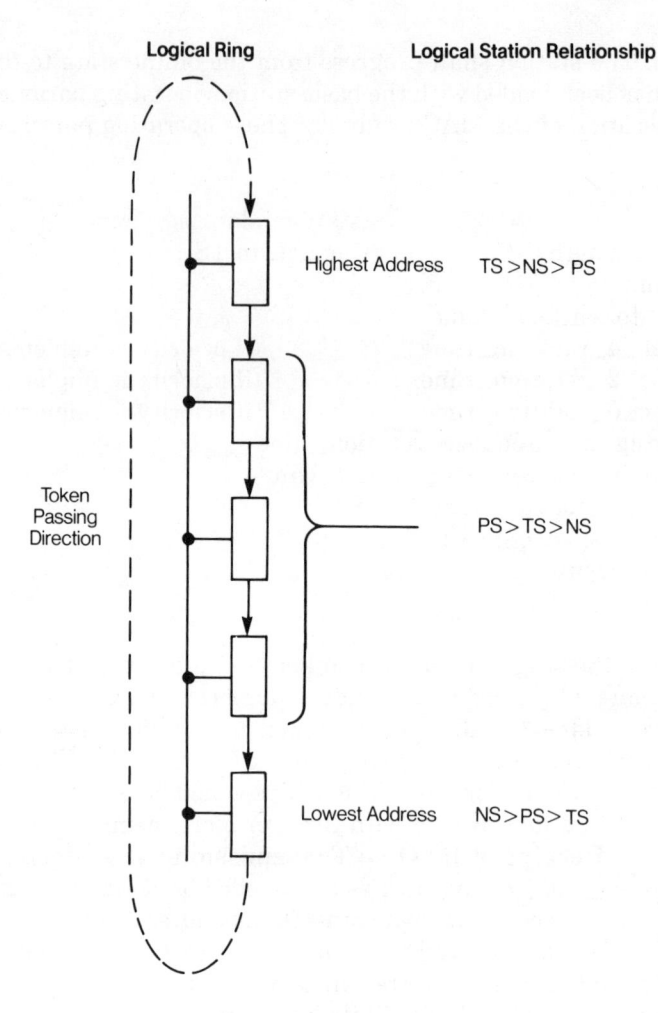

Fig 6-2
Logical Token-Passing Ring

random number generators tied in any way to the network data clock, for example, would not produce statistically independent variable values.

Section 7 states that the variables shall be rerandomized "periodically". Periodically shall be interpreted to mean either an interval not to exceed 50 ms, or every use of the random variable.

6.4.7 Contention Delay. If the station hears a solicit_successor or who _follows frame it determines which response window in which to contend based on the station's address and the SA/DA addresses in the frame. If the station wants to contend in the first window it loads the contention timer with zero, so the station proceeds immediately to the demand in state. If the station wants to contend in the second window, the contention timer is loaded with one, so the station listens during the first window.

Following receipt of a resolve_contention frame, if the station is contending, it loads the contention timer with the one's complement of two bits selected from its own address as indexed by the resolution pass count. The station thus listens zero, one, two, or three slot times before again contending.

6.4.8 Token Claiming. If the bus_idle_timer expires, a station may transmit a claim_token frame and set the claim_timer. When the claim_timer expires, if no transmissions are present at that instant, the station sends an additional claim token frame and repeats the delay and transmission check. This procedure is repeated until either transmissions from another station are heard or the value of the claim_pass_count equals max_claim_pass_count.

The length of the claim token frames are 0+, 2+, 4+, or 6+ slot_times as a function of two bits of the station's address. Indexing through the address performs an address sort in the claim process, leaving the station with the highest address claiming the token.

6.5 Use of Address Bits in Contention Algorithms. The contention processes used to claim a new token or demand logical ring entry both use the bits of the station address to accomplish a sorting-like resolution in which the station having the numerically largest or highest address value wins. The following paragraphs treat the address as an array of binary (0/1) values or address_bits; for notational purposes, "address_bit(i)" indicates the ith binary bit of the station's address, with address_bit(1) the most significant bit. These address _bits are used two at a time, starting with the most significant address_bits.

6.5.1 Claim_Token Frame Length. A station which is attempting to claim a new token first determines that no other station is transmitting, then transmits a claim_token frame containing a data_unit with a length equal to 0, 2, 4, or 6 slot_times. It then waits or delays one slot_time before again listening for other transmissions. The token claiming contention process shall consist of N cycles of listening, transmitting and delaying, where N is a function of the station's address length in bits:

$$N = (\text{address\_length} / 2) + 1$$

For a two octet address $N = 9$; for a six octet address $N = 25$.

The length, L, of the nth claim_token frame's data_unit, in octet_times (for the nth cycle of the token claiming process), shall be determined as follows:

    for $1 \leq n < N$
        bit_value := 2*address_bit((2*n)-1) + address_bit(2*n)
            L := 2*slot_time*bit_value

    for $n = N$
            L := 2*slot_time*random_4

where
    bit_value = 0, 1, 2, or 3 as a function of the two address bits used in cycle n, and
    random_4 is a random number = 0, 1, 2, or 3

6.5.2 Demand Delay Time Interval. A station which is demanding entry into the logical ring, first listens for other transmissions, delaying its next transmission for 0, 1, 2, or 3 slot_times, then, if it has heard no other transmssions, it transmits a fixed length set_successor frame. This delay preceding set_successor frame transmissions is called the demand_delay. The contention process for demanding logical ring entry shall consist of at most N cycles of transmission and listening delays, where N is a function of the address length in bits:

$$N = (\text{address\_length} / 2) + 1$$

The number of slot_times, D, to delay after the nth transmission (for the nth cycle of the contention resolution process) shall be determined as follows:

for $1 \leq n < N$
$\quad D := 3 - \text{bit\_value}$

for $n = N$
$\quad D := \text{random\_4}$

where bit_value and random_4 are as specified in 6.5.1.

6.6 Options Within MAC Sublayer

6.6.1 Priority Mechanism. The implementation of multiple per-frame classes of service, or priorities, is an option and is not required under this standard. A station which does not implement the optional priority mechanism shall transmit all MAC-user data frames with an access_class value of 6, corresponding to the highest priority.

Where the priority mechanism is implemented, it shall meet the requirements set forth in 6.6.1.1 through 6.6.1.3.

6.6.1.1 Access Classes. The priority mechanism shall provide four levels of service with respect to a frame's priority of access to the medium; these levels are called access_classes. The access_classes shall be identified as 0, 2, 4, and 6, and access_class 6 shall be the highest priority or most favored level of service.

6.6.1.2 Quality_of_Service to Access_Class Mapping. Where priority is implemented, the priority component of the MAC-user's quality_of_service parameter, contained in the MA_DATA.request, is eventually satisfied through use of the access_classes. The priority component of the quality_of_service request shall first be satisfied by assignment of the request to one of eight MAC service_classes. These MAC service_classes shall then be mapped into MAC access_classes as described in the following table:

service_class	access_class	priority
0, 1	0	lowest
2, 3	2	
4, 5	4	
6, 7	6	highest

6.6.1.3 Token Rotation Timers. A station which implements the priority mechanism shall provide three (actual or virtual) token_rotation_timers, one for each access_class. These timers shall all run concurrently, counting downward from an initial value to zero, at which point they shall stop counting and their status shall be "expired". These timers shall count in units of octet_times, and shall otherwise be managed as specified in Section 7.

6.6.2 Immediate Response Mechanism. *The ability for the MAC layer to send multiple request_with_response frames and to acknowledge such frames with a response frame is an option and is not required under this standard. A station which does not implement the immediate response mechanism shall not respond to request_with_response frames.*

6.7 Delegation of Right to Transmit. A station holding a token may request a second station to transmit a response without the second station holding the token. The first station, in effect, delegates the authority to transmit to another station. The secondary station shall conform to all of the requirements imposed by this standard on the token holder except for participating in the logical token passing ring and associated protocol mechanisms (unless the secondary is or needs to be in_ring). The secondary station need not be in the logical ring from an address sense. The secondary shall not transmit on the network unless

(1) Delegated as a transmitter by a token holder, or
(2) Transmitting is authorized by the procedures specified in Section 7.

7. Access Control Machine (ACM) Formal Description

The token bus medium access control mechanism is defined in this section. The section begins with a description of the variables and functions used in the definition of the algorithm. The second part of this section is a formal state machine description of the access control mechanism using the variables and functions discussed in the first part.

7.1 Variables and Functions. The variables and functions of the state machine description are grouped into categories as follows:
 (1) Variables defined by station management
 (2) Variables defined by the interface machine
 (3) Timers
 (4) Variables defined by the receive machine
 (5) Other ACM variables and functions

7.1.1 Station Management Variables. Station management provides the MAC machine with the station's address bit string (and thus implicitly with the length of all addresses). Also supplied by station management are other network parameters:

TS. This Station's address. A bit-string variable set to the value of the station's 16-bit or 48-bit address.

slot_time. An integer in the range of 1 to 2^{13} - 1 octet_times. See 5.1.1 and 6.1.9.

min_post_silence_preamble_length. An integer equal to the minimum number of octets of preamble to be transmitted at the beginning of a transmission after the station has been silent. The value of min_post_silence_preamble_length is determined by the type of physical layer used in the station.

max_pass_count. An integer equal to half the station's address length in bits, plus one. (Thus equal to 9 for a 16-bit address length and 25 for a 48-bit address length.)

The value of max_pass_count limits loops in the ACM. The value is used to limit the token contention process. After cycling through max_pass_count contention cycles the process shall be stopped if, due to an error, a single contender cannot be resolved.

The value of max_pass_count is also used to stop the token claiming process. After sending max_pass_count claim token frames, if no other station is heard, a station can claim the token.

max_inter_solicit_count. An integer number of token possessions within the range 2^4 to 2^8-1. This value, in addition to the ring_maintenance_timer, determines how often a station opens response windows. Normally, a station opens response windows prior to every Nth pass of the token, where N is the value of max_inter_solicit_count.

If all stations in the ring use the same max_inter_solicit_count, they could all consistently open response windows on the same token rotation. This action would lead to rapid token rotations where no response windows are opened, and occasional rotations where every station opens a response window before passing the token.

To avoid all stations in the ring having the same value of max_inter_solicit_count, the least significant two bits of the value shall be chosen randomly. The actual value used for the max_inter_solicit_count shall be changed by each station by rerandomizing the least significant two bits of the variable at least every 50 ms or on every use.

max_retry_limit. An integer constant in the range 0 to 7 that determines how many times a station resends a request_with_response frame for which it does not get a response.

target_rotation_time (access_class). An array of integers in the range 0 to 2^{21} - 1 octet_times, used with the priority option and with the ring_maintenance timer. (See 7.1.4 for a discussion of the variable's function.)

ring_maintenance_timer_initial_value. An integer in the range 0 to 2^{21} - 1 octet_times, used to determine the initial value of the ring_maintenance token_rotation_timer upon entry to the ring. A large value will cause the station to solicit successors immediately upon entry to the ring; a value of zero will cause the station to defer this solicitation for at least one rotation of the token.

hi_pri_token_hold_time. An integer in the range 0 to $2^{16} - 1$ octet_times. Used to control the maximum time a station can transmit frames at access class 6. If the priority option is not implemented, then hi_pri_token_hold_time determines how long a station can send frames of any access class.

in_ring_desired. A Boolean variable which determines the Access Control Machine's steady-state condition when it has no queued transmission requests. If the variable is true, the station should be in_ring (a participant in the token-passing logical ring). If false, the station should be out_of_ring (an observer of the token-passing logical ring).

7.1.2 Interface Machine Variables and Functions

get_pending_frame(access_class). A function provided by the interface machine of MAC. This function pops the first frame off the pending frame queue for the indicated access class, and returns it to the access control machine for transmission.

any_send_pending. A Boolean variable reflecting the logical OR of all the Boolean variables send_pending(access_class). any_send_pending is true if at least one of the pending frame queues is nonempty. If all queues are empty, the variable's value is false.

power_OK. A Boolean variable indicating that the ACM may begin operation. Provided by station management hardware.

7.1.3 Note on Logical Ring Membership Control.

The two Boolean variables in_ring_desired and any_send_pending determine the operation of the ACM with respect to contending for the token and being in the logical ring as follows:

Variables and States		ACM Actions
in_ring_desired	any_send_pending	
false	false	Do not contend for token. Drop out if currently in token-passing logical ring.

Variables and States		ACM Actions
in_ring_desired	any_send_pending	
false	true	Contend for token. Send data, which may empty the pending frame queues and make any_send_pending false. Exit logical ring if any_send_pending becomes false.
true	false	Contend for token if not sole active station. Remain in token-passing logical ring even without data to send.
true	true	Contend for token. Remain in token-passing logical ring and send data.

7.1.4 Timers. A number of timers are used in the description of the state machine. A timer is expressed as a set of procedures and a Boolean variable. The procedures are named xx_timer.start(value), where xx is the timer name and value is an integer that sets the timer delay. xx_timer.value returns the current value of the counter. The Boolean variables are named xx_timer.expired and have a value of false while the timer is running and true when the timer has expired.

For example, the bus_idle timer is set to a value of one (slot time) by executing bus_idle_timer.start(1). The variable bus_idle_timer.expired is then false for one slot time.

7.1.4.1 Slot_time Interval Timers. The first five timers (bus_idle_timer, contention_timer, claim_timer, response_timer and token_pass_timer) work in integral multiples of the network slot_time. (The first five timers are not used concurrently; thus they could be implemented in a single hardware timer.)

bus_idle_timer. Controls how long a station listens in the idle state for any data on the medium before entering the claiming token state and re-initializing the network. Most stations wait seven slot times. The one station in the network having lowest_address true waits six slot times. The function max_bus_idle returns the value 6 or 7 depending on the state of lowest_address.

claim_timer. Controls how long a station listens between sending claim_token frames. The claim_timer is always loaded with the value 1.

response_window_timer. Controls how long a station which has opened a response window listens before transmitting its next frame.

When sending a solicit_successor, who_follows or resolve_contention frame this timer controls the length of time a station solicits responses. After sending a solicit_successor frame, the sending station loads the response_window timer with the number of windows opened. The timer thus determines how long the station remains in the await response state listening for stations to respond. If the timer expires and nothing is heard, the station goes to the pass_token state and passes the token to its successor.

When sending a request_with_response data frame the response_window timer controls how long a station waits for a response frame before repeating the request_with_response frame.

contention_timer. Controls how long a station listens in the demand_in state after hearing a resolve_contention, solicit_successor or who_follows frame when the station wants to contend for the token. If the station hears a transmission while listening, it has lost the contention and shall return to the idle state.

token_pass_timer. Controls how long a station listens after passing the token to its successor.

If any frame is heard before the token_pass timer expires, the station assumes that its successor has accepted the token. If the timer expires and a frame is not heard, the station assumes its successor did not accept the token and sequences to the next stage of the pass token procedure.

7.1.4.2 Octet_time Interval Timers.

The remaining timers have a granularity of one octet transmission time, rather than one network slot_time. They are used to implement the access class structure and limit the time during which a station may start to transmit frames for each access class.

token_rotation_timer(access_class). This is a set of four timers, one for each of the lower three access classes and one for ring maintenance. The first three of these timers only exist for stations implementing the priority option. The fourth timer, ring_maintenance, always exists.

When the station begins processing the token at a given access class the associated timer is reloaded with the value of the target_rotation_time for that level. When the station again receives the token it may send data of that access class until the residual time in the associated token_rotation_timer has expired.

Upon initial entry to the ring, the first three priority timers are set to a value of zero (expired), and the ring_maintenance timer is set to the value ring_maintenance_timer_initial_value.

token_hold_timer. The residual time from the current token_rotation_timer is loaded into the token_hold_timer just before the token_rotation_timer is reloaded. The station may send data frames of the corresponding access class as long as the token_hold_timer has not expired.

When the station is sending highest access class messages the value of hi_pri_token_hold_time is loaded into the token_hold_timer. Thus highest access class messages are limited to only a fixed number of bytes regardless of current network loading.

7.1.5 Receive Machine Variables and Functions. The outputs of the receive machine are several state variables and a data frame, as described in the following paragraphs.

bus_quiet. A Boolean variable which is true whenever the physical layer is reporting that silence is being received. False when something other than silence is being received. bus_quiet is set and reset by the receiver machine and is only read by the ACM.

Rx_frame. A record written by the receiver machine. The record is updated to reflect the contents of the most recently received valid frame. The major fields in the record are
    FC. The one octet frame control field
    DA. The two or six octet destination address field
    SA. The two or six octet source address field
    data_unit. The multi-octet data unit field
    FCS. The four octet frame check sequence field.

Rx_protocol_frame. This signal indicates that a valid frame has been received, and that the frame type is one of the MAC protocol frame types. This signal is set by the receive machine, and it is read and cleared by the access machine.

Rx_data_frame. This signal indicates that a valid frame has been received, and that the frame type is a LLC_frame or station_management frame. This signal is set by the receive machine and read by both the access control machine and the interface machine; it is cleared only by the interface machine.

noise_burst. A Boolean variable set by the receive machine when bus quiet goes true (the bus goes from non-silence to silence) and neither Rx_protocol_frame nor Rx_data_frame were set during the transmission (that is, no valid frame was heard). It is reset by the access control machine when the noise burst condition has been processed.

7.1.6 Other Variables and Functions. The following variables and functions are local to the MAC access control machine (ACM).

TH - Token Holder's address. The address of the current token holder. A temporary buffer loaded from the SA field of a solicit_successor, who_follows or resolve_contention frame. If a set_successor frame is sent by the station as part of the contention process, the DA address is taken from TH.

NS - Next Station's address. The address of a station's successor in the logical ring. NS is set when a station that does not know its successor hears a solicit_successor frame and contends for the token. The station sets NS to the value of the Destination Address field of the frame. (If the station successfully contends in a response window, it will receive the token and eventually pass it to the station whose address was loaded into NS.) For example, suppose a station with address 25 is not in the logical ring, and wants to enter. If this station hears a solicit_successor frame sent by station 30 with a DA address of 20, it will set NS to 20, the DA address in the frame. If the station contends in the window and is heard by station 30, it will be passed a token. When the station has completed sending data frames it passes the token to its successor station 20.

The NS variable is also loaded whenever the station receives a set_successor frame addressed to it.

Whenever the value of NS is changed, a MA_EVENT.indication is given to station management, if enabled.

NOTE: Once a station thinks it knows the value of NS it no longer reloads NS when a contention window is opened spanning the station's address. The reason is that under error recovery conditions, stations will send solicit_successor_2 frames addressed to themselves that open response windows for all stations. If all stations reset their NS variables at this point, any logical ring that existed would collapse.

NS_known. A Boolean variable that indicates whether the station thinks it knows the address of its successor. NS_known is set true whenever the station receives a set_successor frame addressed to it. Normally the set_successor frame follows a successful contention, as in the previous example.

NS_known is set false whenever the station leaves the logical ring.

PS - Previous Station's address. The variable is set to the value of the source address of the last token addressed to the station.

If a who_follows frame is heard, the contents of the data field of the frame are compared with the contents of PS. If they are equal, the station responds to the who_follows request with a set_successor frame.

An example will clarify the use of PS. If a logical ring contains stations with addresses 30, 25, and 20, the station with address 20 will have 25 in its PS register, since this is the address of the station that sends it the token. If station 25 fails, when station 30 tries to send the token to station 25 it will get no response. After two tries at passing the token, station 30 sends a "who follows 25?" frame. Station 20 responds by sending a "set your successor to 20" frame. In this manner the failed station, 25, is quickly patched out of the ring.

max_access_class. An integer constant used to initialize the sequencing of the processing of the pending frame queues. The value of max_access_class is 6, the highest priority access class.

access_class. An integer which is used to sequence through the access classes while transmitting data frames.

The first, or highest priority, access_class equals the value of max_access_class (that is, 6). The variable access_class is then decremented (by 2) through all classes until less than zero, and then the station performs its ring maintenance functions and passes the token.

in_ring. A Boolean variable set true when the station receives a token frame addressed to it or when the station successfully completes the claiming token process. Set false if the station sets itself out of the ring.

sole_active_station. A Boolean variable used to mute stations that have defective receivers. If a station's receiver becomes inoperative in an undetected manner, the station otherwise will disrupt the operation of the system by continually claiming the token and then soliciting a successor station.

If the sole_active_station variable is true, a station is prevented from entering the claiming token process unless it has data to send. Thus a station with an inoperative receiver and no data to send will remain passively out of the ring.

If a station is a member of the ring and its receiver fails, it will be unable to hear its successor claiming the token. The station will cycle through the token passing recovery algorithm, quickly reaching the point where it has sent a solicit_successor_2 frame addressed to itself and received no response. At this point, the station sets sole_active_station true and becomes passive.

Sole_active_station is set false whenever the station hears a valid frame from another station.

lowest_address. A Boolean variable set true if the station's successor address is greater than the station's address.

At any one time there should be only one station in the logical ring with lowest_address set true. This is the station with the lowest address of all those currently in the logical ring. When this station opens response windows during a token pass, it shall open two windows. The first window is used by stations that have an even lower address that wish to enter the ring. The second window is used by stations that have a higher address than the recipient of the token, the station currently with the highest address in the ring.

Lowest_address is computed and set by a station whenever NS is changed.

Lowest_address is used for a second purpose unrelated to token passing. If the token-holding station fails, another station shall recover the token. The bus_idle_timer is a "watchdog" timer. If no frames are heard by a station for an interval greater than this timer, the claim token process is started.

In an effort to minimize interference during the claiming process, one station is selected to use a shorter bus_idle_timer value than the other stations. This station recovers all lost token failures, except ones it causes. The station with lowest_address true is always unique, so it is assigned this role.

just_had_token. A Boolean variable set true when the station passes the token and set false if the station hears a valid frame from another station.

Just_had_token is used to detect duplicate addressing failures on the network.

TOKEN-PASSING BUS

If a station hears a valid frame with a source address equal to its own address and just_had_token is false, the station cannot have sent the frame. If such a frame is heard, the MAC sublayer notifies station management of the detection of another station on the network using the same MAC address; the MAC sublayer then enters the offline state.

heard. A three_state variable used in the await response state. The states are:
 nothing. The station has heard nothing (except its own transmissions) since beginning the resolve process.
 collision. A noise burst has been heard.
 successor. A valid set_successor frame has been received. At the end of the resolution period, the station will send the token to the station whose address was in the protocol data unit field of (one of) the valid set_successor frame(s).

claim_pass_count. An integer with a range from 0 to max_pass_count. Used as an index to TS to select two bits from the station's address. The value of the selected bits (times twice the slot time) determines the length of the information field of the claim_token frame to be sent. After each claim_token frame the value of the variable claim_pass_count is incremented by one.

contend_pass_count. An integer with a range from 0 to max_pass_count. Used as an index to TS to select two bits from the station's address. The one's-complement of the selected bits (times the slot time) determine the length of time a station delays in the demand in state after receiving a resolve_contention frame. If no other frames are heard before the contention_timer expires, the station sends a set_successor frame to the token holder, increments the value of contend_pass_count, goes to the demand delay state, and waits for the token or for another resolve_contention frame.

contention_delay(cycle). An integer function which returns the value 0, 1, 2, or 3. This value is based upon the one's complement of a pair of address bits which are indicated by the cycle in the address sort. The value is used to control the number of slot_times the station delays before transmitting when demanding entry to the logical ring.

resolution_pass_count. An integer with a range from 0 to max_pass_count. Used to count the number of resolve contention passes the token-holding station makes. If the counter reaches the value of max_pass_count, the resolution process is abandoned and the token passed to the station's successor.

inter_solicit_count. An integer in the range 0 to 2^8-1. Determines when a station shall open a response window. Before passing the token, the value of inter_solicit_count is checked. If the value is zero, a new successor is solicited by opening a response window. If the value is not zero, the counter is decremented and the token is passed. Whenever anything is heard during the response windows following the solicit_successor frame, the counter value is set to zero so that it will again be zero when the station next receives and passes the token. Thus receipt of a set_successor frame during a response window causes the station to reopen the response window before that next token pass.

remaining_retries. *An integer in the range 0 to max_retry_limit. Used to count the number of retransmissions upon timeout of a frame specifying request_with _response.*

suppress_FCS. A Boolean variable used within the ACM to indicate that the current frame should be transmitted without having the transmitter state machine append a FCS.

transmitter_fault_count. An integer in the range of 0 to 7. Used to infer that the station's transmitter has probably failed and thus that the station's transmissions cannot be heard correctly by other stations on the network.

The value of transmitter_fault_count is incremented each time the station sequences to the end of the token contention process or fails to pass the token to any successor. Neither of these failures occurs during normal operation. The value of transmitter_fault_count is reset to zero if the station either wins the demand_in token contention process or successfully passes the token, since such an event indicates that another station correctly heard a transmission from the station.

If the value of transmitter_fault_count is incremented to max_transmitter _fault_count, the station reports a faulty_transmitter to station management and enters the offline state. The value of max_transmitter_fault_count is set to a maximum of 7, allowing for an occasional protocol sequencing impasse due to noise. If the station cannot enter the ring or pass the token (if already in the logical ring) seven times in a row, the inference made is that something has failed in the station, probably in the transmitter, and so the station removes itself from the logical ring.

first_time. A Boolean variable that controls processing of noise bursts in the await response state. Set true upon entry to the state. Set false when the first noise burst is heard. If a noise burst is heard when first_time is false, the station returns to the idle state.

pass_state. A multistate variable used to control the operation of the pass _token substates. The action taken in the state depends on the value of the variable pass_state as follows: (The actions are listed in the order taken by a station soliciting successors and failing.)

pass_state value	action
solicit_successor	Send solicit_successor frame. Enter await response state.
pass_token	Send token to successor. Enter check token pass state.
repeat_pass_token	Same action as pass_token substate.
who_follows	Send who follows frame. Enter await response state.
repeat_who_follows	Same action as who follows substate.
solicit_any	Send solicit_successor_2 frame with DA = TS, opening 2 response windows that span all other stations. Enter await response state.
total_failure	Set sole_active_station true and either silently pass the token back to itself (if the station has more data to send) or enter the idle state. This station will not transmit again unless it has data to send or it hears a valid frame from another station.

7.2 Access Control Machine Formal Description. The access control machine (ACM) is described formally in this subsection. The description model used is a hybrid of finite state machine and procedural programming language notations and concepts. The ACM may be in any one of 11 major states at any given time. Its actions and its transition into another state are determined by its evaluation of the MAC state variables discussed in the previous subsection.

The conditions evaluated and the actions taken for each state machine transition are expressed using syntax based upon Ref [2]. The ACM variables and other information units used by the ACM are described using Ada-like [2] data declarations. Where an information unit cannot be expressed using Ada [2] syntax, a descriptive statement, enclosed in angle brackets (<>) is used.

The remainder if this section presents a list of words appearing in the ACM description; programming language style declarations of most of the variables, functions, and procedures used in the state machine description; a summary of the ACM state transitions (arcs) appearing in 7.2.4; and, finally, the ACM state transition tables.

The state transition tables present the current state, transition name, and the next state on one line at the beginning of each transition description. Below this line are

(1) The conditions which shall be true for the particular transition to be taken, and

(2) The actions to be taken before going to the prescribed next state.

7.2.1 List of Unique ACM Words. This is a list of unique words arranged in alphabetical sequence that are used in the MAC ACM state transition tables of 7.2.4. This list includes only words from the EXIT CONDITION and ACTION TAKEN parts of these tables; Current State, Transition Name, Next State, and comments (strings beginning with – –) were excluded.

```
access_class
any_send_pending
bus_idle_timer
bus_idle_timer.expired
bus_idle_timer.start
bus_quiet
cdu
claim_data_unit
claim_pass_count
claim_timer
claim_timer.expired
claim_timer.start
claim_token
collision
contend_pass_count
contention_delay
contention_timer contention_timer.expired
contention_timer.start
DA
data_unit
destination
duplicate_address
faulty_transmitter
FC
FCS_suppression
first_time
frame_control
get_pending_frame
heard
hi_pri_token_hold_time
in_ring
in_ring_desired
inter_solicit_count
just_had_token
```

```
lowest_address
max_access_class
max_bus_idle
max_inter_solicit_count
max_pass_count
```
max_retry_limit
```
max_transmitter_fault_count
MA_FAULT_REPORT.indication
MA_INITIALIZE_PROTOCOL.request
noise_burst
nothing
NS
NS_known
octet_time
pass_state
pass_token
power_ok
```
remaining_retries
```
ring_maint_timer_init_value
token_pass_timer.expired
token_pass_timer.start
tok_pass_substate'succ
total_failure
transmitter_fault_count
TS
who_follows
```

7.2.2 ACM Data Declarations

NOTE: Constants are represented as numeric values, rather than the transmission-order bit strings of Section 4.

```
-- constants and parameters

-- These are all treated as constants in this declaration,
--   with the understanding that many of them are actually
--   station parameters set by station management.

  symbol_time: constant duration := 1 / <network data rate>;
   octet_time: constant duration := 8 * symbol_time;
    slot_time: constant duration := <network specific>;
                 -- in octet_times
address_length: constant (16, 48);  -- network parameter
   timer_size: constant integer := (2**21) * octet_time;
                 -- example only
max_pass_count: constant integer := (address_length/2) + 1;
max_inter_solicit_count: constant integer range 16 .. 255
                            := <network specific>;

max_frame_length: constant integer := (2**13 - 1); -- 8191
max_data_unit_length: constant integer :=
         (max_frame_length - ( 5 + 2*address_length/8 ) );
         -- This gives 8174 for 48 bit addresses,
         --        and 8182 for 16 bit addresses.

max_access_class: constant integer := 6;
ring_maintenance: constant integer := -2;
                 -- min value of access class
max_transmitter_fault_count: constant integer := 7;

max_retry_limit: constant integer := 3;   -- typical value

-- the following time limit values are examples only

hi_pri_token_hold_time: constant time :=  1000 * octet_time;
max_ac_4_rotation_time: constant time := 40000 * octet_time;
mac_ac_2_rotation_time: constant time := 20000 * octet_time;
max_ac_0_rotation_time: constant time := 10000 * octet_time;
max_ring_maintenance_time: constant time :=
                                       25000 * octet_time;
-- end of timer example constants
```

```
-- type definitions
type address is integer range 0 .. (2**address_length - 1);

type addr_index is integer range 1 .. address_length ;
type pass_count is integer range 0 .. max_pass_count;

type LLC_priority is integer range 0 .. 7;

type MAC_priority is (0, 2, 4, 6);

type MAC_actions is ( request_with_no_response,
                      request_with_response,
                      response );
type MAC_symbol is (zero, one, non_data,
                    pad_idle, bad_signal, silence);
    -- also referred to as (0, 1, N, P, B, S)
subtype data_symbol is MAC_symbol range zero .. one;
    -- also referred to as D

type data_octet is array (0 .. 7) of data_symbol;

type data_unit_type is
    record
        length: integer range 0 .. max_data_unit_length := 0;
         data: array (0 .. max_data_unit_length)
                of data_octet;
end  record;
type frame_identifier is ( MAC_control,              -- 2#00#
                           station_management_data,  -- 2#01#
                           LLC_data,                 -- 2#10#
                           special_purpose_data );   -- 2#11#
type frame_ctrl_typ is (fid: frame_identifier)
    record
        case fid is
           when MAC_control => mftyp: integer range 0 .. 63;
           when LLC_data,
                station_management_data,
                special_purpose_data=>
                    record
                        MAC_action: MAC_actions :=
                                request_with_no_response;
                        priority: LLC_priority := 7;
                    end record;
        end case;
--  end record;
```

```
      for frame_ctrl_typ use      -- define subfield structure
         record at mod 8
               fid         at 0 range 0..1;
               mftyp       at 0 range 2..7;
               MAC_action  at 0 range 2..4;
               priority    at 0 range 5..7;
         end record;
quality_of_service renames frame_ctrl_type;

type FCS_type is array (0 .. 3) of data_octet;

type general_frame is
    record
              FC: frame_ctrl_typ;
              DA: address;
              SA: address;
         data_unit: data_unit_type;
              FCS: FCS_type;
    end record;

-- State 8 (PASS_TOKEN) has seven substates, each representing
--    a different aspect of the token passing process. These
--    substates are kept track of by the state variable
--    pass_state, which is of type tok_pass_substate
      type tok_pass_substate is
              ( solicit_successor,
                pass_token,
                repeat_pass_token,
                send_who_follows,
                repeat_who_follows,
                solicit_any,
                total_failure );
```

```
-- constant definitions

       null_data_unit: data_unit_type;   -- has a length of zero

          claim_token: frame_ctrl_typ := ( MAC_control,
                                           mftyp => 2#000000# );
   solicit_successor_1: frame_ctrl_typ := ( MAC_control,
                                           mftyp => 2#100000# );
   solicit_successor_2: frame_ctrl_typ := ( MAC_control,
                                           mftyp => 2#010000# );
          who_follows: frame_ctrl_typ := ( MAC_control,
                                           mftyp => 2#110000# );
    resolve_contention: frame_ctrl_typ := ( MAC_control,
                                           mftyp => 2#001000# );
                token: frame_ctrl_typ := ( MAC_control,
                                           mftyp => 2#000100# );
        set_successor: frame_ctrl_typ := ( MAC_control,
                                           mftyp => 2#001100# );
```

```
-- procedures and packages

-- generic timer package
generic
      type time is integer range 0 .. timer_size;
      type tick is integer range symbol_time .. slot_time;
      -- time_int defines the timer granularity
              --    or counting interval
package timer( time_int: tick := octet_time )
      procedure start( init: in time );
      function value return time;
      function expired return Boolean;
end timer;

           -- timers count from a "start" value down to zero.
           -- timers are "expired" when their value is zero.
           -- each count corresponds to one "tick", which
           --    corresponds either to one slot_time
           --    or to eight symbol_times on the medium.

function max_bus_idle return slot-time;
           -- returns a 6 or 7 slot_time time interval
           -- if lowest_address then return 6*slot_time
           --                   else return 7*slot_time .
```

```
function claim_data_unit( cycle: in pass_count )
                        return data_unit_type;
        -- returns a data unit with arbitrary contents
        --     and with its length (and thus its transmission
        --     time) equal to 0, 2, 4 or 6 slot_times.

        -- this length depends upon the two bits of the
        --     address indicated by the cycle of the address
        --     sort.

function response_delay( below_TH: in Boolean )
        --                      return slot-time;
        -- returns a 0 or 1 times slot_time time interval;
        -- if below_TH then return 0
        --              else return slot_time .

function contention_delay( cycle: in pass_count )
                        return slot-time;
    -- returns a 0, 1, 2 or 3 times slot_time time interval
    --    based on the one's complement of two bits of the
    --    address indicated by the cycle of the address sort.
function send_pending( queue: in MAC_quality_of_service )
        --              return Boolean;
        -- returns TRUE if there is a pending frame
        --    in the indicated pending frame queue.

function any_send_pending return Boolean;
        -- returns TRUE if there is a pending frame in
        --    any of the pending frame queues.

procedure get_pending_frame( queue: in MAC_quality_of_service;
                             FC: out frame_ctrl_typ;
                             DA: out address;
                             SA: out address;
                      data_unit: out data_unit_type;
                 FCS_suppression: out Boolean );
        -- returns the first frame from the indicated
        --    pending frame queue.
```

TOKEN-PASSING BUS

IEEE Std 802.4-1985

```
procedure send( FC: in frame_ctrl_typ;
                DA: in address := <TS OR global OR any well
                                            formed address>;
                SA: in address := <TS>;
         data_unit: in data_unit_type := null_data_unit;
   FCS_suppression: in Boolean := false );
     -- sends the indicated frame by passing it symbol by
     --   symbol to the Physical Layer for transmission.
     -- if FCS_suppression is requested, an FCS is not
     --   appended and the last four octets of the data_unit
     --   serve as the FCS.
```

```
-- Boolean state variables

            bus_quiet: Boolean;
          noise_burst: Boolean;
           first_time: Boolean;
              in_ring: Boolean;
      in_ring_desired: Boolean;
       just_had_token: Boolean;
       lowest_address: Boolean;
             NS_known: Boolean;
             power_ok: Boolean;
     Rx_protocol_frame: Boolean;
         Rx_data_frame: Boolean;
    sole_active_station: Boolean;
         suppress_FCS: Boolean;
```

```
-- address variables
           TS: address;         -- This Station
           NS: address;         -- Next Station
           PS: address;         -- Previous Station
           TH: address;         -- Token Holder
  destination: address;         -- destination address
       source: address;         -- source address
```

```
-- counters

       claim_pass_count: pass_count;
     contend_pass_count: pass_count;
  resolution_pass_count: pass_count;
     inter_solicit_count: integer range
                          0 .. max_inter_solicit_count;
transmitter_fault_count: integer range
                          0 .. max_transmitter_fault_count;
```

```
-- protocol or frame data units

cdu: data_unit_type;
sdu: data_unit_type;
```

```
-- miscellaneous variables

          heard: (nothing, collision, successor);

     pass_state: tok_pass_substate;

   access_class: integer range -2 .. max_access_class;

       Rx_frame: general_frame;

remaining_retries: integer range 0 .. max_retry_limit;
```

Summary List of States and Transition Arcs

| Current State | Transition Name | Next State |
|---|---|---|ои

7.2.3 ACM State Transition Summary

Current State	Transition Name	Next State
0. OFFLINE	initialize	1. IDLE
1. IDLE	new_successor	1. IDLE
1. IDLE	no_successor_1	1. IDLE
1. IDLE	receive_token	5. USE_TOKEN
1. IDLE	entry_demand_in	2. DEMAND_IN
1. IDLE	repair_demand_in	2. DEMAND_IN
1. IDLE	own_frame_1	1. IDLE
1. IDLE	duplicate_address_1	0. OFFLINE
1. IDLE	ring_patch	2. DEMAND_IN
1. IDLE	non_idle_bus	1. IDLE
1. IDLE	no_token	4. CLAIM_TOKEN
1. IDLE	idle_station	1. IDLE
1. IDLE	other_heard	1. IDLE
2. DEMAND_IN	continue_contention	3. DEMAND_DELAY
2. DEMAND_IN	lost_contention_2	1. IDLE
3. DEMAND_DELAY	contention_delay	2. DEMAND_IN
3. DEMAND_DELAY	won_contention	5. USE_TOKEN
3. DEMAND_DELAY	lost_contention_3	1. IDLE
3. DEMAND_DELAY	end_contention	1. IDLE
3. DEMAND_DELAY	end_all_contention	0. OFFLINE
3. DEMAND_DELAY	unexpected_frame_3	1. IDLE
3. DEMAND_DELAY	ignore_contenders	3. DEMAND_DELAY
3. DEMAND_DELAY	ignore_noise	3. DEMAND_DELAY
3. DEMAND_DELAY	long_bus_idle	1. IDLE
4. CLAIM_TOKEN	lose_address_sort	1. IDLE
4. CLAIM_TOKEN	continue_address_sort	4. CLAIM_TOKEN
4. CLAIM_TOKEN	win_address_sort	5. USE_TOKEN
5. USE_TOKEN	send_frame	6. AWAIT_IFM_RESPONSE
5. USE_TOKEN	no_send	7. CHECK_ACCESS_CLASS
6. AWAIT_IFM_RESPONSE	no_timeout	5. USE_TOKEN
6. AWAIT_IFM_RESPONSE	retry	6. AWAIT_IFM_RESPONSE
6. AWAIT_IFM_RESPONSE	no_response_6	5. USE_TOKEN
6. AWAIT_IFM_RESPONSE	unexpected_frame_6	1. IDLE
6. AWAIT_IFM_RESPONSE	own_frame_6	6. AWAIT_IFM_RESPONSE
6. AWAIT_IFM_RESPONSE	ignore_noise_6	6. AWAIT_IFM_RESPONSE
7. CHECK_ACCESS_CLASS	next_access_class	5. USE_TOKEN
7. CHECK_ACCESS_CLASS	leave_ring	8. PASS_TOKEN
7. CHECK_ACCESS_CLASS	do_solicit_successor	8. PASS_TOKEN
7. CHECK_ACCESS_CLASS	do_pass_token	8. PASS_TOKEN
7. CHECK_ACCESS_CLASS	do_solicit_any	8. PASS_TOKEN

Summary List of States and Transition Arcs *(Continued)*

Current State	Transition Name	Next State
7.2.3 ACM State Transition Summary (Continued)		
0. OFFLINE	initialize	1. IDLE
8. PASS_TOKEN	open_1_response_window	10. AWAIT_RESPONSE
8. PASS_TOKEN	open_2_response_windows	10. AWAIT_RESPONSE
8. PASS_TOKEN	pass_token	9. CHECK_TOKEN_PASS
8. PASS_TOKEN	who_follows_query	10. AWAIT_RESPONSE
8. PASS_TOKEN	solicit_any	10. AWAIT_RESPONSE
8. PASS_TOKEN	silent_pass_to_self	5. USE_TOKEN
8. PASS_TOKEN	sole_station	1. IDLE
8. PASS_TOKEN	no_successor_8	1. IDLE
8. PASS_TOKEN	no_future	0. OFFLINE
9. CHECK_TOKEN_PASS	token_pass_failed	8. PASS_TOKEN
9. CHECK_TOKEN_PASS	own_frame_9	9. CHECK_TOKEN_PASS
9. CHECK_TOKEN_PASS	pass_ok	1. IDLE
9. CHECK_TOKEN_PASS	not_sure	9. CHECK_TOKEN_PASS
9. CHECK_TOKEN_PASS	probably_ok	1. IDLE
10. AWAIT_RESPONSE	no_response	8. PASS_TOKEN
10. AWAIT_RESPONSE	resolution_succeeded	8. PASS_TOKEN
10. AWAIT_RESPONSE	own_address_10	10. AWAIT_RESPONSE
10. AWAIT_RESPONSE	hear_successor	10. AWAIT_RESPONSE
10. AWAIT_RESPONSE	collision	10. AWAIT_RESPONSE
10. AWAIT_RESPONSE	unexpected_frame_10	1. IDLE
10. AWAIT_RESPONSE	send_resolve	10. AWAIT_RESPONSE
10. AWAIT_RESPONSE	resolution_failed	8. PASS_TOKEN

TOKEN-PASSING BUS

IEEE
Std 802.4-1985

Current State
  Exit Condition
    Action Taken
	Transition Name	Next State

7.2.4 ACM State Transition Tables
7.2.4.0 Offline State

```
0. OFFLINE                   initialize                    1. IDLE

     power_OK    AND MA_INITIALIZE_PROTOCOL.request

        -- MAC configuration information supplied by station
        --    management
        -- It is station management's responsibility to initialize
        --    the MAC sublayer on station power-up.
        -- This includes values for:
        --        slot_time       (as octet-time multiple)
        --        TS              (This Station's address)
        --        address_length       (implicit in TS)
        --        target_rotation_time (one each for
        --                         access_classes 4, 2 and 0)
        --        hi_pri_token_hold_time
        --        max_inter_solicit_count
        --        ring_maintenance_timer_initial_value
        --    and other variables which may need to be initialized.
        -- Initialize the timers used in the Access Control Machine
        package bus_idle_timer        is
                                      new timer(time_int
                                          => slot_time);
        package contention_timer      is
                                      new timer(time_int
                                          => slot_time);
        package claim_timer           is
                                      new timer(time_int
                                          => slot_time);
        package response_window_timer is
                                      new timer(time_int
                                          => slot_time);
        package token_pass_timer      is
                                      new timer(time_int
                                          => slot_time);
        package token_hold_timer      is
                                      new timer(time_int
                                          => octet_time);
        package token_rotation_timer
                is array( ring_maintenance .. 4 ) of new timer
                   (time_int => octet_time);  -- only -2,0,2,4 used
```

Current State
   Exit Condition
      Action Taken
	Transition Name	Next State

0. OFFLINE	initialize	1. IDLE

```
        in_ring := false;        -- set initial values
        NS_known := false;       -- of variables
        lowest_address := false;
        sole_active_station := false;
        just_had_token := false;
        transmitter_fault_count := 0;
        MA_EVENT.indication( no_successor );
        bus_idle_timer.start( max_bus_idle );
```

7.2.4.1 Idle State

```
1. IDLE                   receive_token              5. USE_TOKEN

    Rx_protocol_frame
    AND Rx_frame.FC = token
    AND Rx_frame.SA /= TS
    AND Rx_frame.DA = TS
    AND in_ring

        -- token receipt
        sole_active_station := false;
        PS := Rx_frame.SA;              -- set predecessor
        -- set access_class to highest level
        access_class := max_access_class;
        token_hold_timer.start( hi_pri_token_hold_time );
        Rx_protocol_frame := false;


1. IDLE                   new_successor              1. IDLE

    Rx_protocol_frame
    AND Rx_frame.FC = set_successor
    AND Rx_frame.SA /= TS
    AND Rx_frame.DA = TS
    AND Rx_frame.data_unit /= TS

        -- new successor heard
        NS := Rx_frame.data_unit;
        lowest_address := ( NS > TS );
        NS_known := true;
        sole_active_station := false;
        inter_solicit_count := 0;
        just_had_token := false;
        MA_EVENT.indication( new_successor );
        bus_idle_timer.start( max_bus_idle );
        Rx_protocol_frame := false;


1. IDLE                   no_successor_1             1. IDLE

    Rx_protocol_frame
    AND Rx_frame.FC = set_successor
    AND Rx_frame.SA /= TS
    AND Rx_frame.DA = TS
    AND Rx_frame.data_unit = TS

        -- successor is myself - one station ring
        NS := Rx_frame.data_unit;
        NS_known := false;              -- no one station rings
        sole_active_station := false;
        inter_solicit_count := 0;
        just_had_token := false;
        MA_EVENT.indication( no_successor );
        bus_idle_timer.start( max_bus_idle );
        Rx_protocol_frame := false;
```

Current State Exit Condition Action Taken	Transition Name	Next State

1. IDLE   entry_demand_in   2. DEMAND_IN

```
   Rx_protocol_frame
   AND Rx_frame.SA /= TS
   AND Rx_frame.DA /= TS
   AND NOT in_ring          -- not part of functioning ring
   AND ( in_ring_desired OR any_send_pending )
   AND (  ( Rx_frame.FC = solicit_successor_1
            AND Rx_frame.SA > TS
            AND Rx_frame.DA < TS )
       OR ( Rx_frame.FC = solicit_successor_2
            AND ( Rx_frame.SA > TS
                 OR Rx_frame.DA < TS ) ) )

      -- solicit_successor heard which allows this station
      --    to respond as a potential successor
      -- contention is anticipated
      contend_pass_count := 0;
      inter_solicit_count := 0;
      just_had_token := false;
      TH := Rx_frame.SA;      -- save address of current token holder
      NS := Rx_frame.DA;
      lowest_address := ( TS < NS );
      sole_active_station := false;
      -- initialize token_rotation timers to "expired"
      token_rotation_timer( 4 ).start( 0 );
      token_rotation_timer( 2 ).start( 0 );
      token_rotation_timer( 0 ).start( 0 );
      token_rotation_timer( ring_maintenance ).start(
                           ring_maintenance_timer_initial_value );
      contention_timer.start( response_delay( TS < TH ) );
      Rx_protocol_frame := false;
```

TOKEN-PASSING BUS

IEEE
Std 802.4-1985

Current State
   Exit Condition
      Action Taken
	Transition Name	Next State

---

  1. IDLE   repair_demand_in   2. DEMAND_IN

```
    Rx_protocol_frame
    AND Rx_frame.SA /= TS
    AND Rx_frame.DA /= TS
    AND in_ring
    AND ( in_ring_desired OR any_send_pending )
    AND (   ( Rx_frame.FC = solicit_successor_1
              AND Rx_frame.SA > TS
              AND Rx_frame.DA < TS )
         OR ( Rx_frame.FC = solicit_successor_2
              AND ( Rx_frame.SA > TS
                 OR Rx_frame.DA < TS ) ) )

        -- This station was in ring, but is now
        --    being skipped for some reason.
        -- solicit_successor heard which allows this station
        --    to respond as a potential successor
        -- contention is anticipated
        contend_pass_count := 0;
        inter_solicit_count := 0;
        just_had_token := false;
        TH := Rx_frame.SA;
        sole_active_station := false;
        contention_timer.start( response_delay( TS < TH ) );
        Rx_protocol_frame := false;
```

---

  1. IDLE   own_frame_1   1. IDLE

```
    ( Rx_protocol_frame OR Rx_data_frame )
    AND Rx_frame.SA = TS
    AND just_had_token

        -- ignore own frame
        bus_idle_timer.start( max_bus_idle );
        Rx_protocol_frame := false;
```

---

  1. IDLE   duplicate_address_1   0. OFFLINE

```
    ( Rx_protocol_frame OR Rx_data_frame )
    AND Rx_frame.SA = TS
    AND NOT just_had_token

        -- detect a duplicate station address.
        -- report to Network Management
        MA_FAULT_REPORT.indication( duplicate_address );
```

Current State
  Exit Condition
    Action Taken
	Transition Name	Next State

1. IDLE   ring_patch   2. DEMAND_IN

```
Rx_protocol_frame
AND Rx_frame.FC = who_follows
AND Rx_frame.SA /= TS
AND Rx_frame.data_unit = PS
AND in_ring

    -- Recognize who_follows message from predecessor's
    --    predecessor. Respond with a set_successor message to
    --    patch a failed station (TS's predecessor) out of the
    --    ring. Contention is possible
    contend_pass_count := 0;
    inter_solicit_count := 0;
    just_had_token := false;
    TH := Rx_frame.SA;
    sole_active_station := false;
    contention_timer.start( 0 );
    Rx_protocol_frame := false;
```

1. IDLE   non_idle_bus   1. IDLE

```
noise_burst

    -- bus not idle
    -- reset bus_idle timer
    bus_idle_timer.start( max_bus_idle );
    noise_burst := false;
```

1. IDLE   no_token   4. CLAIM_TOKEN

```
bus_idle_timer.expired
AND bus_quiet
AND NOT ( Rx_protocol_frame OR Rx_data_frame OR noise_burst )
AND ( any_send_pending
      OR ( in_ring_desired AND NOT sole_active_station ) )
                    -- in case TS's receiver has failed

    -- no token, so claim one
    claim_pass_count := 1;
    cdu := claim_data_unit( claim_pass_count );
    send( FC => claim_token,
          data_unit => cdu );
    claim_timer.start ( 1 );
```

TOKEN-PASSING BUS

IEEE
Std 802.4-1985

Current State
   Exit Condition
      Action Taken
	Transition Name	Next State

1. IDLE	idle_station	1. IDLE

```
bus_idle_timer.expired
AND bus_quiet
AND NOT ( Rx_protocol_frame OR Rx_data_frame OR noise_burst )
AND NOT any_send_pending
AND ( NOT in_ring_desired OR sole_active_station )

    -- ring has collapsed
    --    and TS does not need to be in the ring.
    -- reset bus_idle timer just to keep it running
    lowest_address := false;
    in_ring := false;
    NS_known := false;
    MA_EVENT.indication( no_successor );
    bus_idle_timer.start( max_bus_idle );
```

111

Current State
   Exit Condition
      Action Taken
	Transition Name	Next State

```
   1. IDLE                   other_heard                   1. IDLE

     -- NOTE: The following codifies the converse of the union
     --   of all of the above frame_received conditions
     --   i.e. this is supposed to have the same effect as an
     --   "otherwise" or a "none_of_the_above" clause.

     ( RX_data_frame
        AND NOT Rx_frame.SA = TS )

     OR ( Rx_protocol_frame
        AND NOT              -- any of the following

          ( Rx_frame.SA = TS

            OR ( Rx_frame.FC = set_successor
               AND Rx_frame.DA = TS )

            OR ( Rx_frame.FC = token
               AND Rx_frame.DA = TS
               AND in_ring )

            OR ( Rx_frame.FC = solicit_successor_1
               AND ( in_ring_desired OR any_send_pending )
               AND Rx_frame.DA < TS
               AND Rx_frame.SA > TS )

            OR ( Rx_frame.FC = solicit_successor_2
               AND ( in_ring_desired OR any_send_pending )
               AND Rx_frame.DA < TS )

            OR ( Rx_frame.FC = solicit_successor_2
               AND ( in_ring_desired OR any_send_pending )
               AND Rx_frame.DA /= TS
               AND Rx_frame.SA > TS )

            OR ( Rx_frame.FC = who_follows
               AND Rx_frame.data_unit = PS
               AND in_ring )                    ) )

        just_had_token := false;
        sole_active_station := false;
        bus_idle_timer.start( max_bus_idle );
        Rx_protocol_frame := false;
```

TOKEN-PASSING BUS
IEEE
Std 802.4-1985

Current State
   Exit Condition
      Action Taken
	Transition Name	Next State

7.2.4.2 Demand In State

```
2. DEMAND_IN          continue_contention      3. DEMAND_DELAY

   contention_timer.expired
   AND bus_quiet
   AND NOT ( Rx_protocol_frame OR Rx_data_frame OR noise_burst )

       send( FC => set_successor,
             DA => TH,              -- most recent reliable SA
             data_unit => TS );
       bus_idle_timer.start( max_bus_idle );
```

```
2. DEMAND_IN            lost_contention_2         1. IDLE

   ( Rx_protocol_frame OR Rx_data_frame OR noise_burst )

       -- drop contention and reprocess event in state 1
       -- NO ACTION
```

Current State	Transition Name	Next State
Exit Condition		
Action Taken		

7.2.4.3 Demand Delay State

3. DEMAND_DELAY   contention_delay   2. DEMAND_IN

```
Rx_protocol_frame
AND Rx_frame.FC = resolve_contention
    -- delay till next contention transmission
    -- delay time depends on bits of address,
    --    indexed into by contend_pass_count
    contend_pass_count := contend_pass_count + 1;
    contention_timer.start( contention_delay
                                ( contend_pass_count ) );
    Rx_protocol_frame := false;
```

---

3. DEMAND_DELAY   won_contention   5. USE_TOKEN

```
Rx_protocol_frame
AND Rx_frame.FC = token
AND Rx_frame.DA = TS
    -- token being passed here, so this station is in the ring
    in_ring := true;
    NS_known := true;
    sole_active_station := false;

    PS := Rx_frame.SA;
    transmitter_fault_count := 0;
    -- set access_class to highest level
    access_class := max_access_class;
    MA_EVENT.indication( new_successor );
    token_hold_timer.start( hi_pri_token_hold_time );
    Rx_protocol_frame := false;
```

---

3. DEMAND_DELAY   lost_contention_3   1. IDLE

```
Rx_protocol_frame
AND Rx_frame.DA /= TS
AND Rx_frame.FC = token
AND contend_pass_count < max_pass_count
    -- token was passed to another station. contention is
    -- over. go back to IDLE state and reprocess the event.
    -- NO ACTION
```

---

3. DEMAND_DELAY   end_contention   1. IDLE

```
Rx_protocol_frame
AND Rx_frame.DA /= TS
AND Rx_frame.FC = token
AND contend_pass_count = max_pass_count
AND transmitter_fault_count < max_transmitter_fault_count
    -- ran to end of contention process, so count
    --    consecutive occurrences to catch faulty transmitter
    transmitter_fault_count := transmitter_fault_count + 1;
    bus_idle_timer.start( max_bus_idle );
```

TOKEN-PASSING BUS   IEEE
                                                    Std 802.4-1985

Current State
   Exit Condition
      Action Taken
	Transition Name	Next State

3. DEMAND_DELAY	end_all_contention	0. OFFLINE

    Rx_protocol_frame
    AND Rx_frame.DA /= TS
    AND Rx_frame.FC = token
    AND contend_pass_count = max_pass_count
    AND transmitter_fault_count >= max_transmitter_fault_count

        -- probable "faulty transmitter" condition
        -- assume worst case
        MA_FAULT_REPORT.indication(faulty_transmitter);

---

3. DEMAND_DELAY	unexpected_frame_3	1. IDLE

    Rx_data_frame
    OR (Rx_protocol_frame
       AND Rx_frame.FC /= token
       AND Rx_frame.FC /= resolve_contention
       AND Rx_frame.FC /= set_successor)

        -- synchronization error, so contention must be over
        --   so go back to IDLE state and reprocess the event
        -- NO ACTION

---

3. DEMAND_DELAY	ignore_contenders	3. DEMAND_DELAY

    Rx_protocol_frame
    AND Rx_frame.FC = set_successor

        -- ignore any set_successor messages, from TS or others,
        Rx_protocol_frame := false;

---

3. DEMAND_DELAY	ignore_noise	3. DEMAND_DELAY

    noise_burst

        -- ignore any unrecognizable signal streams
        noise_burst := false;

---

3. DEMAND_DELAY	long_bus_idle	1. IDLE

    bus_idle_timer.expired
    AND bus_quiet
    AND NOT (Rx_protocol_frame OR Rx_data_frame OR noise_burst)

        -- bus_idle timeout, so go back to IDLE state
        --   immediately, and process it there
        -- NO ACTION

Current State   Transition Name   Next State
Exit Condition
Action Taken

7.2.4.4 Claim Token State

4. CLAIM_TOKEN   lose_address_sort   1. IDLE

```
claim_timer.expired
AND NOT bus_quiet

    -- other stations heard so drop from contention
    bus_idle_timer.start( max_bus_idle );
```

---

4. CLAIM_TOKEN   continue_address_sort   4. CLAIM_TOKEN

```
claim_timer.expired
AND bus_quiet
AND claim_pass_count < max_pass_count

    -- do an iteration of multipass address_sort algorithm
    claim_pass_count := claim_pass_count + 1;
    -- create a data_unit 0, 2, 4 or 6 slot_times long
    cdu := claim_data_unit( claim_pass_count );
    send( FC => claim_token,
          data_unit => cdu );
    claim_timer.start( 1 );    -- one slottime delay
```

---

4. CLAIM_TOKEN   win_address_sort   5. USE_TOKEN

```
claim_timer.expired
AND bus_quiet
AND claim_pass_count = max_pass_count

    -- token now claimed
    in_ring := true;
    -- initialize token_rotation timers to "expired"
    token_rotation_timer( 4 ).start( 0 );
    token_rotation_timer( 2 ).start( 0 );
    token_rotation_timer( 0 ).start( 0 );
    token_rotation_timer( ring_maintenance ).start(
                    ring_maintenance_timer_initial_value );
    inter_solicit_count := 0;
    -- set access_class to highest level
    access_class := max_access_class;
    token_hold_timer.start( hi_pri_token_hold_time );
```

TOKEN-PASSING BUS

IEEE
Std 802.4-1985

Current State
   Exit Condition
      Action Taken
	Transition Name	Next State

7.2.4.5 Use Token State

5. USE_TOKEN	send_frame	6. AWAIT_IFM_RESPONSE

    send_pending(access_class)
    AND NOT token_hold_timer.expired

```
            -- send one MAC-user frame of current access_class level
            get_pending_frame( queue => access_class,
                               FC => frame_control,
                               SA => source,
                            -- SA shall equal TS except in relay nodes
                               DA => destination,
                               data_unit => sdu,
                               FCS_suppression => suppress_FCS );
      max_retry_limit => remaining_retries;
      send( FC => frame_control,
            DA => destination,
            SA => source,
            data_unit => sdu,
            FCS_suppression => suppress_FCS );
      response_window_timer.start( 3 );
```

5. USE_TOKEN	no_send	7. CHECK_ACCESS_CLASS

    NOT send_pending(access_class)
    OR token_hold_timer.expired

```
            -- time to relinquish the token
            -- set access_class to next lower level
            access_class := access_class - 2;
```

Current State Exit Condition Action Taken	Transition Name	Next State

7.2.4.6 Await IFM Response State

6. AWAIT_IFM_RESPONSE	no_timeout	5. USE_TOKEN

```
frame_control.MAC_action = no_response_requested
OR signal_received( ACM_RELEASE.indication )
            -- generated by the Interface Machine
            -- upon receiving the response.

    -- check for another serviceable request
    -- NO ACTION
```

6. AWAIT_IFM_RESPONSE	retry	6. AWAIT_IFM_RESPONSE

```
response_window_timer.expired
AND bus_quiet
AND remaining_retries > 0

    remaining_retries := remaining_retries - 1;
    send( FC => frame_control,
          DA => destination,
          SA => source,
          data_unit => sdu,
          FCS_suppression => suppress_FCS );
    response_window_timer.start( 3 );
```

6. AWAIT_IFM_RESPONSE	no_response_6	5. USE_TOKEN

```
response_window_timer.expired
AND bus_quiet
AND remaining_retries = 0

    -- notify interface machine of non-response
    IFM_REPORT.indication( response_overdue );
    -- check for another serviceable request
```

6. AWAIT_IFM_RESPONSE	unexpected_frame_6	1. IDLE

```
Rx_frame.SA /= TS
AND ( Rx_protocol_frame
    OR ( Rx_data_frame
        AND Rx_frame.DA /= TS ) )

    -- some other station thinks it has the token, so defer
    --    by notifying interface machine of the situation
    --    and dropping out
    IFM_REPORT.indication( distributed_ACM_error );
```

TOKEN-PASSING BUS

Current State 　　Exit Condition 　　　　Action Taken	Transition Name	Next State
6. *AWAIT_IFM_RESPONSE* 　　*Rx_frame.SA = TS* 　　*AND (Rx_protocol_frame OR Rx_data_frame)* 　　　　*-- ignore own frame* 　　　　*Rx_protocol_frame := false;*	*own_frame_6*	6. *AWAIT_IFM_RESPONSE*
6. *AWAIT_IFM_RESPONSE* 　　*noise_burst* 　　　　*noise_burst := false;*	*ignore_noise_6*	6. *AWAIT_IFM_RESPONSE*

IEEE
Std 802.4-1985   LOCAL AREA NETWORKS:

| Current State   Transition Name   Next State |
| Exit Condition |
| Action Taken |

7.2.4.7 Check Access Class State

7. CHECK_ACCESS_CLASS   next_access_class   5. USE_TOKEN

    access_class > ring_maintenance

```
      -- load token_hold_timer with residual from the
      --   token_rotation_timer for this access_class level
      token_hold_timer.start(
                  token_rotation_timer( access_class ).value;
      -- restart token rotation timer
      token_rotation_timer( access_class ).start(
                  target_rotation_time( access_class ) );
```

7. CHECK_ACCESS_CLASS   leave_ring   8. PASS_TOKEN

```
access_class = ring_maintenance
AND NS_known
AND NOT in_ring_desired
AND NOT any_send_pending
AND inter_solicit_count > 0

      -- all access levels checked and all queues emptied
      -- remove self from ring
      --    and pass token to next station
      send( FC => set_successor,
            DA => PS,
            data_unit => NS );
      in_ring := false;
      NS_known := false; -- NS will be unknown after token pass
      pass_state := pass_token;
      MA_EVENT.indication( no_successor );
```

7. CHECK_ACCESS_CLASS   do_solicit_successor   8. PASS_TOKEN

```
access_class = ring_maintenance
AND NS_known
AND inter_solicit_count = 0
AND NOT token_rotation_timer( ring_maintenance ).expired

      -- all access_class levels checked and accessed,
      --    when possible
      -- offer entry to new stations now
      pass_state := solicit_successor;
      -- restart ring maintenance token rotation timer
      token_rotation_timer( ring_maintenance ).start(
                  target_rotation_time) ring_maintenance ) );
```

120

TOKEN-PASSING BUS   IEEE
                                                      Std 802.4-1985

Current State	Transition Name	Next State
Exit Condition		
Action Taken		

7. CHECK_ACCESS_CLASS   do_pass_token   8. PASS_TOKEN

    access_class = ring_maintenance
    AND NS_known
    AND (in_ring_desired OR any_send_pending)
    AND (inter_solicit_count > 0
        OR token_rotation_timer(ring_maintenance).expired)

       -- all access_class levels checked and accessed,
       --   when possible
       -- pass the token to next_station
    pass_state := pass_token;
    inter_solicit_count := max(inter_solicit_count - 1 , 0);
    -- restart ring maintenance token rotation timer
    token_rotation_timer(ring_maintenance).start
           (target_rotation_time(ring_maintenance));

7. CHECK_ACCESS_CLASS   do_solicit_any   8. PASS_TOKEN

    access_class = ring_maintenance
    AND NOT NS_known

       -- all access_class levels checked and accessed,
       --   when possible
       -- need to find some successor
    pass_state := solicit_any;
    -- restart ring maintenance token rotation timer
    token_rotation_timer(ring_maintenance).start(
            target_rotation_time(ring_maintenance));

Current State
   Exit Condition
      Action Taken
	Transition Name	Next State

7.2.4.8 Pass Token State

```
-- Note on State 8. PASS_TOKEN substates and sequencing:
--      State 8 has seven substates, each representing a different
--      aspect of the token passing process. These substates are kept
--      track of by the state variable "pass_state", which is of type
--      "tok_pass_substate". The type definition is repeated below.
--      The function "tok_pass_substate'succ( )" is the Ada [4]
--      built-in successor function - it allows sequencing to the next
--      substate without knowing the current substate name.
--
--      type tok_pass_substate is (solicit_successor,
--                                 pass_token,
--                                 repeat_pass_token,
--                                 send_who_follows,
--                                 repeat_who_follows,
--                                 solicit_any,
--                                 total_failure );
```

8. PASS_TOKEN   open_one_response_window   10. AWAIT_RESPONSE

```
    pass_state = solicit_successor
    AND NOT lowest_address

        -- open 1 response window
        --    for stations with addresses between TS and NS
        resolution_pass_count := 0;
        heard := nothing;
        Rx_protocol_frame := false;
        noise_burst := false;
        send( FC => solicit_successor_1,
              DA => NS );
        response_window_timer.start( 1 );
```

8. PASS_TOKEN   open_two_response_windows   10. AWAIT_RESPONSE

```
    pass_state = solicit_successor
    AND lowest_address

        -- open two response windows
        --    for stations with addresses smaller or larger
        --    than any now in ring
        resolution_pass_count := 0;
        heard := nothing;
        Rx_protocol_frame := false;
        noise_burst := false;
        send( FC => solicit_successor_2,
              DA => NS );
        response_window_timer.start( 2 );
```

TOKEN-PASSING BUS

IEEE
Std 802.4-1985

Current State
  Exit Condition
    Action Taken
	Transition Name	Next State

8. PASS_TOKEN   pass_token   9. CHECK_TOKEN_PASS

```
pass_state = pass_token
OR pass_state = repeat_pass_token

    -- pass token
    send( FC => token,
          DA => NS );
    just_had_token := true;
    first_time := true;        -- used in CHECK_TOKEN_PASS
    Rx_protocol_frame := false;
    noise_burst := false;
    token_pass_timer.start( 1 );
```

8. PASS_TOKEN   who_follows_query   10. AWAIT_RESPONSE

```
pass_state = send_who_follows
OR pass_state = repeat_who_follows

    resolution_pass_count := 0;
    heard := nothing;
    Rx_protocol_frame := false;
    noise_burst := false;
    send( FC => who_follows,
          data_unit => NS );
    response_window_timer.start( 3 );   -- long delay
```

8. PASS_TOKEN   solicit_any   10. AWAIT_RESPONSE

```
pass_state = solicit_any

    -- pass token to self with two response windows
    --     soliciting all potential successors,
    resolution_pass_count := 0;
    heard := nothing;
    Rx_protocol_frame := false;
    noise_burst := false;
    send( FC => solicit_successor_2,
          DA => TS );
    response_window_timer.start( 2 );
```

8. PASS_TOKEN   silent_pass_to_self   5. USE_TOKEN

```
pass_state = total_failure
AND any_send_pending

    -- no one else is out there, so pass token to self
    --     until transmit queues are empty
    -- set access class to highest level
    access_class := max_access_class;
    token_hold_timer.start( hi_pri_token_hold_time );
```

Current State
  Exit Condition
    Action Taken
	Transition Name	Next State

8. PASS_TOKEN	sole_station	1. IDLE

    pass_state = total_failure
    AND NOT any_send_pending
    AND sole_active_station

        -- reached this state last time
        -- this is probably the only active station,
        --   so just idle
        in_ring := false;
        NS_known := false;
        lowest_address := false;
        bus_idle_timer.start(max_bus_idle);

| 8. PASS_TOKEN | no_successor_8 | 1. IDLE |

    pass_state = total_failure
    AND NOT any_send_pending
    AND NOT sole_active_station
    AND transmitter_fault_count < max_transmitter_fault_count

        -- no successor found. Possible "deaf receiver" or
        --   "faulty transmitter" condition
        -- assume fault present; don't pass token to self
        in_ring := false;
        NS_known := false;
        lowest_address := false;
        sole_active_station := true;
        transmitter_fault_count := transmitter_fault_count + 1;
        MA_EVENT.indication(no_successor);
        bus_idle_timer.start(max_bus_idle);

| 8. PASS_TOKEN | no_future | 0. OFFLINE |

    pass_state = total_failure
    AND NOT any_send_pending
    AND NOT sole_active_station
    AND transmitter_fault_count >= max_transmitter_fault_count

        -- no successor found
        -- probable "faulty transmitter" condition
        -- assume worst case
        MA_FAULT_REPORT.indication(faulty_transmitter);

TOKEN-PASSING BUS
IEEE
Std 802.4-1985

Current State
  Exit Condition
    Action Taken
	Transition Name	Next State

7.2.4.9 Check Token Pass State

9. CHECK_TOKEN_PASS   token_pass_failed   8. PASS_TOKEN

```
token_pass_timer.expired
AND bus_quiet
AND NOT ( Rx_protocol_frame OR Rx_data_frame OR noise_burst )

    -- successor failed to accept and use token
    --   so proceed to next PASS_TOKEN substate
    pass_state := tok_pass_substate'succ( pass_state );
```

9. CHECK_TOKEN_PASS   own_frame_9   9. CHECK_TOKEN_PASS

```
( Rx_protocol_frame OR Rx_data_frame )
AND Rx_frame.SA = TS

    -- ignore own transmissions
    -- also ignore prior noise
    first_time := true;
    Rx_protocol_frame := false;
```

9. CHECK_TOKEN_PASS   pass_ok   1. IDLE

```
( Rx_protocol_frame OR Rx_data_frame )
AND Rx_frame.SA /= TS

    -- some station is using the token
    -- reprocess the frame in state 1 (IDLE)
    -- NO ACTION
```

9. CHECK_TOKEN_PASS   not_sure   9. CHECK_TOKEN_PASS

```
noise_burst
AND first_time

    -- something heard - either:
    --   1) a frame sent by token recipient,
    -- or 2) the token TS sent was garbled
    -- Watch for another frame
    first_time := false;   -- allow only one pass on this arc
    noise_burst := false;
    token_pass_timer.start( 4 );
```

Current State
    Exit Condition
        Action Taken
	Transition Name	Next State

9. CHECK_TOKEN_PASS	probably_ok	1. IDLE

```
    token_pass_timer.expired
    AND bus_quiet
    AND NOT ( Rx_protocol_frame OR Rx_data_frame )
    AND noise_burst
    AND NOT first_time

        -- heard a second noise burst - cannot be my token
        --   so successor probably transmitting
        -- reprocess event in state 1
        -- NO ACTION
```

TOKEN-PASSING BUS
IEEE
Std 802.4-1985

Current State
  Exit Condition
    Action Taken
	Transition Name	Next State

7.2.4.10 Await Response State

10. AWAIT_RESPONSE   no_response   8. PASS_TOKEN

```
response_window_timer.expired
AND bus_quiet
AND NOT ( Rx_protocol_frame OR Rx_data_frame OR noise_burst )
AND resolution_pass_count = 0
AND heard = nothing

    -- response windows expired, unused
    --    ( bus was quiet for entire time )
    inter_solicit_count := max_inter_solicit_count;
    pass_state := tok_pass_substate'succ( pass_state );
```

10. AWAIT_RESPONSE   resolution_succeeded   8. PASS_TOKEN

```
response_window_timer.expired
AND bus_quiet
AND heard = successor

    -- new successor found so resolution process is complete
    -- pass token to new successor
    --    and open response window again next pass
    pass_state := pass_token;
    MA_EVENT.indication( new_successor );
    noise_burst := false;
```

10. AWAIT_RESPONSE   own_address_10   10. AWAIT_RESPONSE

```
( Rx_protocol_frame OR Rx_data_frame )
AND Rx_frame.SA = TS

    -- ignore own transmissions
    --    and those of demanders with same address
    -- also ignore prior noise bursts
    heard := nothing;
    Rx_protocol_frame := false;
```

Current State
  Exit Condition
    Action Taken
	Transition Name	Next State

10. AWAIT_RESPONSE   hear_successor   10. AWAIT_RESPONSE

```
    Rx_protocol_frame
    AND Rx_frame.FC = set_successor
    AND Rx_frame.SA /= TS
    AND Rx_frame.DA = TS

        -- some successor heard "in the clear"
        NS := Rx_frame.data_unit;
        lowest_address := ( NS > TS );
        NS_known := ( NS /= TS );
        sole_active_station := false;
        heard := successor;
        inter_solicit_count := 0;
        Rx_protocol_frame := false;
        transmitter_fault_count := 0;
        -- Note: The way this specification is written the last
        --       valid set_successor message heard will be used to
        --       determine the successor's address.
        --       A conformant station is not required to use the
        --       last set_successor message; any such message,
        --       correctly received, may be used.
```

10. AWAIT_RESPONSE   collision   10. AWAIT_RESPONSE

```
    noise_burst
    AND heard /= successor

        -- infer a collision from presence of signal
        --    without a valid frame
        -- wait out balance of response windows
        heard := collision;
        noise_burst := false;
```

10. AWAIT_RESPONSE   unexpected_frame_10   1. IDLE

```
    Rx_frame.SA /= TS
    AND ( Rx_data_frame
          OR ( Rx_protocol_frame
               AND ( Rx_frame.FC /= set_successor
                     OR ( Rx_frame.FC = set_successor
                          AND Rx_frame.DA /= TS ) ) ) )

        -- some other station thinks it has the token, so defer
        --   by dropping out
        -- re-process the frame in state 1 (IDLE)
        -- NO ACTION
```

TOKEN-PASSING BUS

IEEE
Std 802.4-1985

Current State
   Exit Condition
      Action Taken
	Transition Name	Next State

10. AWAIT_RESPONSE   send_resolve   10. AWAIT_RESPONSE

    response_window_timer.expired
    AND bus_quiet
    AND NOT (Rx_protocol_frame OR Rx_data_frame OR noise_burst)
    AND heard = collision
    AND resolution_pass_count < max_pass_count

        -- another 4 response_window resolution pass is called for
        heard := nothing;
        resolution_pass_count := resolution_pass_count +1;
        send(FC => resolve_contention);
        response_window_timer.start(4);

10. AWAIT_RESPONSE   resolution_failed   8. PASS_TOKEN

    response_window_timer.expired
    AND bus_quiet
    AND NOT (Rx_protocol_frame OR Rx_data_frame OR noise_burst)
    AND ((heard = nothing AND resolution_pass_count > 0)
        OR (heard /= successor
            AND resolution_pass_count = max_pass_count))

        -- no resolution reached, and no more demands heard or
        --   possible, so pass token to known successor
        inter_solicit_count := 0;
                        -- solicit successors on next pass
        pass_state := tok_pass_substate'succ(pass_state);

8. MAC - Physical Layer Interface Service Specification

The services provided to the MAC sublayer by the physical layer of this standard are specified in this section. This section specifies these services in an abstract way. It does not specify or constrain the implementation entities and interfaces within a computer system. The relationship of this section to other sections of this standard and to LAN specifications is illustrated in Fig 8-1.

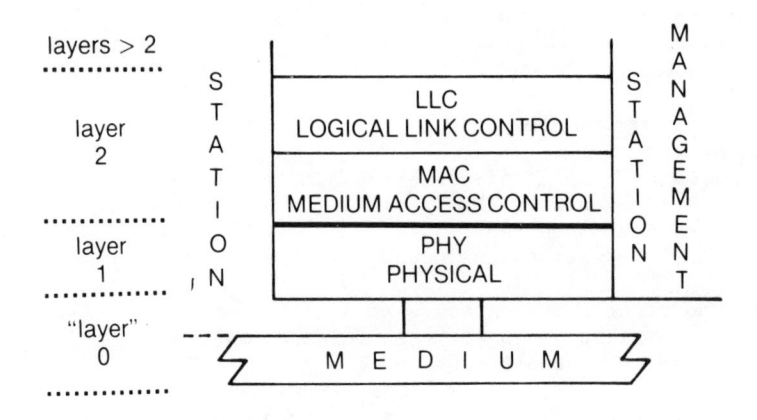

**Fig 8-1
Relation to LAN Model**

8.1 Overview of the LAN Physical Layer Service

8.1.1 General Description of Services Provided by the Layer. The services provided by the physical layer are informally described here. These services provide for the transmission and reception of MAC-symbols, each with a duration of one MAC-symbol period. Jointly, they provide the means by which cooperating MAC entities can coordinate their transmissions and exchange information by way of a shared communications medium.

8.1.2 Model Used for the Service Specification. The model and descriptive method are detailed in Appendix A.

8.1.3 Overview of Interactions. The primitives associated with symbol transmission and reception are

PHY_DATA.request
PHY_DATA.indication

PHY_MODE.request
PHY_NOTIFY.request

8.1.3.1 PHY_DATA request and indication. The PHY_DATA.request primitive is passed to the physical layer to request that a symbol be impressed on the local area network's communications medium. Only one such request is accepted per MAC-symbol-period. The PHY_DATA.indication primitive is passed from the physical layer to indicate the reception of a MAC-symbol from the medium.

8.1.3.2 PHY_MODE request. The PHY_MODE.request primitive is passed to the physical layer to establish the transmission mode for subsequent PHY_DATA. request primitives, either transmission to all connected media segments or, when the station is functioning as a bus repeater, transmission to all connected media segments other than the one which is the current source of symbols for the PHY_DATA.indication primitive. This primitive also affects the source of the station's MAC-symbol timing.

8.1.3.3 PHY_NOTIFY request. The PHY_NOTIFY.request primitive is passed to the physical layer to notify the physical layer that an end-of-frame delimiter has just been detected, and that the following received symbols should be either silence or the results of a properly-transmitted pad_idle sequence.

8.1.4 Basic Services and Options. All PHY_DATA services are required in all implementations, and both of the PHY_DATA primitives are mandatory. The PHY_MODE primitive is mandatory only in stations which can function both as originating and as repeating stations in the network. The PHY_NOTIFY primitive is mandatory only in stations which can function as repeating stations in the network.

8.2 Detailed Specifications of Interactions with the Physical Layer Entity. This subsection describes in detail the primitives and parameters associated with the physical layer services. Note that the parameters are specified in an abstract sense. The parameters specify the information that shall be available to the receiving layer entity. A specific implementation is not constrained in the method of making this information available.

8.2.1 PHY_DATA.request

8.2.1.1 Function. This primitive is the service request primitive for the symbol transfer service.

8.2.1.2 Semantics. This primitive shall provide parameters as follows:

PHY_DATA.request
 (symbol)

symbol shall specify one of

IEEE
Std 802.4-1985   LOCAL AREA NETWORKS:

(1) <u>zero</u> —corresponds to a binary 0
(2) <u>one</u> —corresponds to a binary 1
    <u>data</u> is the collective name for <u>zero</u> and <u>one</u>.
(3) <u>non_data</u>   — used in delimiters, always sent in pairs, and always in octets with the form:

non_data non_data data non_data non_data data data data

(4) <u>pad_idle</u>   — send one symbol of preamble/inter-frame-idle (preamble is a physical entity specific sequence of <u>data</u> symbols)

(5) <u>silence</u>—send silence (or pseudo-silence) for a duration of one MAC-symbol-period

8.2.1.3 When Generated. This primitive is passed from the MAC sublayer to the physical layer to request that the specified symbol be transmitted on the local area network medium. This primitive shall be passed to the physical layer once for each PHY_DATA.indication that the MAC sublayer receives from the physical layer. There shall be an implementation-dependent constant phase relationship, determined by MAC, between a PHY_DATA.indication and the next subsequent PHY_DATA.request.

8.2.1.4 Effect on Receipt. Receipt of this primitive causes the physical layer to attempt to encode and transmit the symbol using signaling appropriate to the local area network medium. The physical layer signals its acceptance of the primitive by responding with a locally-defined confirmation primitive.

8.2.1.5 Constraints

pad_idle symbols, which are referred to collectively as <u>preamble</u>, are transmitted at the start of each MAC frame, both to provide a training signal for receivers and to provide a nonzero minimum separation between consecutive frames. The following constraints apply

(1) An originating station shall transmit a minimum number of octet multiples of <u>pad_idle</u> so that their duration is at least 2 μs, and after completing transmission of the last required octet, it may (but need not) transmit more octets of <u>pad_idle</u> symbols before the first frame-delimiter.

(2) A repeating station on a single-channel bus (for example, an FSK repeater) shall retransmit at least the same minimum number of octets of <u>pad_idle</u>, and may transmit more <u>pad_idle</u> symbols, before repeating the first frame-delimiter and the remainder of the transmission.

(3) The head-end remodulator on a dual-channel (for example, broadband) system, which transmits continuous signaling in the forward channel as a training and synchronization signal for all of the other stations in the local area network, shall retransmit at least one-half octet of <u>pad_idle</u> before repeating the first frame-delimiter and the remainder of a transmission. It need not retransmit the entire <u>pad_idle</u> signal as originated, since the primary purpose of the initial <u>pad_idle</u> sequence, that of a synchronizing sequence for stations in a switched-carrier environment, does not apply to the above-described forward channel.

<u>non_data</u> symbols shall be used only within frame delimiters, where they always shall be requested in pairs. The symbol sequences of those frame delimiters shall be:

non_data non_data data non_data non_data data data data

where each data symbol is either the symbol zero or the symbol one.

When data symbols are transmitted between frame delimiters, the number of data symbols transmitted, not including those data symbols within the eight-symbol frame delimiter sequences, shall always be a multiple of eight. (That is, only complete octets of data symbols shall be transmitted between frame delimiters.) When pad_idle symbols are transmitted between frame delimiters, the number of pad_idle symbols transmitted shall always be a multiple of eight. Octets of pad_idle symbols and octets of data symbols shall always be separated by frame delimiter octets, or a sequence of silence symbols, or both. (That is, pad_idle octets and data octets cannot be intermixed.)

The jitter in the implementation-dependent constant phase relationship between consecutive PHY_DATA.indicate and PHY_DATA.request primitives shall not be greater than 2%.

8.2.1.6 Additional Comments. The confirmation of this request is a timed confirmation, which can only be made once per transmit MAC-symbol-period. Consequently, this request shall only be repeated once per transmit MAC-symbol-period.

8.2.2 PHY_DATA.indication

8.2.2.1 Function. This primitive is the service indication primitive for the symbol transfer service.

8.2.2.2 Semantics. This primitive shall provide parameters as follows:

PHY_DATA.indication
 (symbol)

symbol shall specify one of:
(1) zero—corresponds to a binary 0
(2) one—corresponds to a binary 1
(3) non_data—used in delimiters, always sent in pairs
(4) pad_idle—corresponds to one MAC-symbol-period during which preamble / inter-frame-idle was received and not reported as either zero or one
(5) silence —corresponds to one MAC-symbol-period of received silence (or pseudo-silence)
(6) bad_signal —corresponds to one MAC-symbol-period during which inapropriate signaling was received

8.2.2.3 When Generated. This primitive is passed from the physical layer to the MAC sublayer to indicate that the specified symbol was received from the local area network medium.

8.2.2.4 Effect on Receipt. The effect of receipt of this primitive by the MAC sublayer entity is unspecified.

8.2.2.5 Additional Comments. This indication is a timed indication, which can only be made once per received MAC-symbol period. Consequently, this indication shall only be repeated once per received MAC-symbol period.

Each transmission begins with pad_idle symbols, and it is expected that some, but not all, of these initial symbols may be "lost in transit" between the transmitting station and the receiving stations, and consequently reported as silence.

Where the physical layer encoding for successive pad_idles is a modulation-specific sequence of the encodings for zero and one, receivers are permitted to decode such a transmitted sequence of pad_idles as a sequence of zeros and ones and report them as such to the MAC entity. In other words, a receiver need not have the ability to detect and report pad_idle as such; rather it may report the corresponding signaling as data.

In the absence of errors or colliding transmissions, and with the above two exceptions for symbols transmitted as pad_idle, the sequence of symbols reported is identical to the sequence of symbols transmitted by the associated PHY_DATA.requests.

8.2.3 PHY_MODE.request

8.2.3.1 Function. This primitive is the service request primitive for the symbol transfer mode-setting service.

8.2.3.2 Semantics. This primitive shall provide parameters as follows:

PHY_MODE.request
   (mode)

mode shall specify one of:

(1) originating —MAC entity shall originate symbols to be transmitted on all segments of the connected LAN medium

(2) repeating —MAC entity shall function as a repeater, interpreting and repeating the symbols which the PHY entity is receiving from one segment to all the other segments of the connected LAN medium.

8.2.3.3 When Generated. This primitive is passed from the MAC sublayer to the physical layer to establish the specified operational mode of the PHY entity.

8.2.3.4 Effect on Receipt. Receipt of this primitive causes the physical layer to select the appropriate mode of operation for succeeding PHY_DATA.request primitives. The originating mode causes the PHY entity to transmit symbols at a locally-determined rate onto all segments of the medium connected to the station. The repeating mode causes the PHY entity to monitor all attached segments, selecting a segment on which symbols other than silence are being signaled (where possible) as the source of the received symbols reported by the PHY_DATA.indication primitive and as the source of both the receive and transmit symbol timing. The repeating mode also inhibits transmission onto the selected medium segment from which data and timing are being received.

8.2.3.5 Additional Comments. This mode selection shall be performed dynamically within a bus repeater which can also operate as an originating station; it may be performed statically (for example, at design time) in all other cases. Additional information on the use of this primitive can be found in the various physical layer entity specifications (see 10.6, 12.6, 14.8).

8.2.4 PHY_NOTIFY.request

8.2.4.1 Function. This primitive is the service request primitive for the potential-end-of-reception notification service.

8.2.4.2 Semantics. This primitive shall be parameterless, as follows:

PHY_NOTIFY.request

8.2.4.3 When Generated. This primitive is passed from the MAC sublayer to the physical layer to notify the physical layer that an end-frame-delimiter has just been detected, and that the following received symbols should be either silence or the results of a properly-transmitted pad_idle sequence.

8.2.4.4 Effect on Receipt. The effect of receipt of this primitive by the physical layer entity is implementation-determined. (It may cause the physical layer entity to make special provisions for detecting silence (for example, by checking for the known pad_idle sequence) or for switching its AGC and clock-recovery circuitry to a high-speed acquisition mode.)

9. Generic Station Management - Physical Layer Interface Service Specification

The generic set of services provided to the station management functions by physical layers of this standard is specified in this section. There is another subsection in the specification of each physical layer entity which specifies how this generic set of services applies to that particular type of physical layer entity. The relationship of this section to other sections of this standard and to LAN specifications is illustrated in Fig 9-1.

**Fig 9-1
Relation to LAN Model**

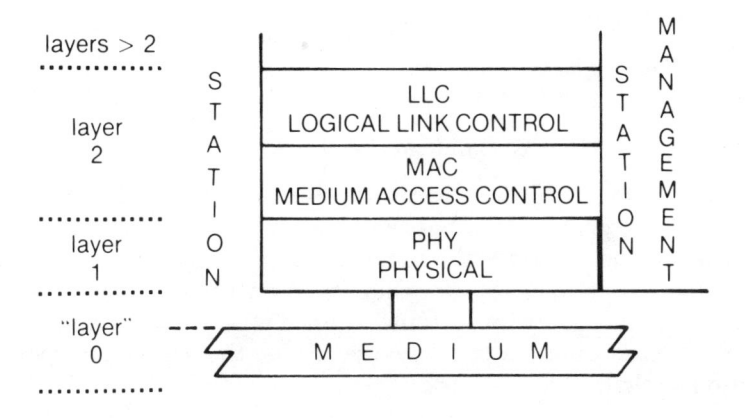

9.1 Overview of the LAN Physical Layer Management Service

9.1.1 General Description of Services Provided at Interface. The services provided to the station management functions by physical layers are described informally in this section. These services are all local administrative services between the physical layer and its manager. This set of services provides the means and method of

(1) Resetting the physical layer entity and determining the local area network topology and the physical layer entity's role in that local area network, and thus the specific form of token-passing protocol required of the MAC entity which uses the services of this physical layer entity, for example, token_bus, token_bus_repeater.

(2) Determining the available and current operating modes of the physical layer entity, selecting the appropriate operating modes, and, optionally, notifying of changes in current operating modes not caused by a PHY_MODE.select request. Modal choices for buses can include

  (a) Transmit and receive channel assignments
  (b) Transmitted power level adjustment (per drop cable)
  (c) Transmitter output enable/disable (per drop cable)
  (d) Received signal source (either a drop cable or a specified Loop_3 loopback point)
  (e) Signaling mode selection and reporting
  (f) Received signal level reporting.

9.1.2 Model Used for the Service Specification. The model and descriptive method are detailed in Appendix A.

9.1.3 Overview of Interactions. The primitives associated with local administrative services are:

PHY_RESET.request
PHY_RESET.confirmation

PHY_MODAL_CAPABILITY_QUERY.request
PHY_MODAL_CAPABILITY_QUERY.confirmation

PHY_MODE_QUERY.request
PHY_MODE_QUERY.confirmation

PHY_MODE_SELECT.request
PHY_MODE_SELECT.confirmation

PHY_MODE_CHANGE.indication

9.1.3.1 PHY_RESET request and confirmation. The PHY_RESET.request primitive is passed to the physical layer to reset the entire physical layer and to verify the topology of the associated local area network (that is, token−bus) and the physical layer entity's role in that network (for example, originate_only or originate_and_repeat). It elicits an immediate PHY_RESET.confirmation primitive specifying the network's topology type and the station's role in that network.

9.1.3.2 PHY_MODAL_CAPABILITY_QUERY request and confirmation. The PHY_MODAL_CAPABILITY_QUERY.request primitive is passed to the physical layer to determine the physical layer entity's actual capabilities with respect to a specified class of modal operation. It elicits an immediate PHY_MODAL_CAPABILITY_QUERY.confirmation primitive specifying the physical layer entity's actual capabilities in the class queried.

9.1.3.3 PHY_MODE_QUERY request and confirmation. The PHY_MODE_QUERY.request primitive is passed to the physical layer to determine the physical layer entity's current mode of operation with respect to a specified class of modal operation. It elicits an immediate PHY_MODE_QUERY.confirmation primitive specifying the physical layer entity's current mode of the class queried.

9.1.3.4 PHY_MODE_SELECT request and confirmation. The PHY_MODE_SELECT.request primitive is passed to the physical layer to select the physical layer entity's mode of operation with respect to a specified class of modal operation. It elicits an immediate PHY_MODE_SELECT.confirmation primitive specifying the success or failure of the selection request.

9.1.3.5 PHY_MODE_CHANGE indication. The PHY_MODE_CHANGE.indication primitive is passed to the station management entity to notify it of the occurrence of a non-commanded change in one of the physical layer entity's modes of operation (for example, transmitter disabling by way of activation of the physical layer entity's jabber inhibit function).

9.1.4 Basic Services and Options. Local administrative services are required in all implementations. Within these services certain primitives are mandatory in all implementations. Other primitives are optional but desirable. In general, the mandatory primitives are basic to the service offered. The desirable primitives are expected to be provided by specific implementations, but are not absolutely necessary to provide the service. The mandatory and optional primitives are summarized in the listing below. An M in the listing indicates a mandatory primitive. An O in the listing indicates a desirable but optional primitive.

M PHY_RESET.request
M PHY_RESET.confirmation

O PHY_MODAL_CAPABILITY_QUERY.request
O PHY_MODAL_CAPABILITY_QUERY.confirmation

O PHY_MODE_QUERY.request
O PHY_MODE_QUERY.confirmation

M PHY_MODE_SELECT.request
M PHY_MODE_SELECT.confirmation

O PHY_MODE_CHANGE.indication

9.2 Detailed Specifications of Interactions with the Station Management Entity. The primitives and parameters associated with the physical layer administrative services are described here in detail. Note that the parameters are specified in an abstract sense. The parameters specify the information that shall be available to the receiving entity. A specific implementation is not constrained in the method of making this information available. For example, the representation of received signal source choices is not specified.

9.2.1 PHY_RESET.request

9.2.1.1 Function. This primitive is the service request primitive for the physical layer reset service. It also functions as a topology type and station role query service request primitive.

9.2.1.2 Semantics. This primitive shall be parameterless, as follows:

PHY_RESET.request

9.2.1.3 When Generated. This primitive is passed from the station management entity to the physical layer entity to request that the physical layer entity reset itself and report the topology type of the associated local area network and the physical layer entity's role in that network.

9.2.1.4 Effect on Receipt. Receipt of this primitive causes the physical layer entity to reset itself exactly as at power-on and to generate a PHY_RESET.confirmation primitive to indicate the topology type of the associated local area network and the physical layer entity's role in that network.

9.2.2 PHY_RESET.confirmation

9.2.2.1 Function. This primitive is the service confirmation primitive for the physical layer reset service.

9.2.2.2 Semantics. This primitive shall provide parameters as follows:
PHY_RESET.confirmation
 (LAN_topology_type,
   PHY_role)

LAN_topology_type specifies whether the associated LAN is a token_bus (on a broadcast medium) or some other form of LAN.

PHY_role specifies whether the physical layer entity should function as an originate_only station or as an originate_and_repeat (bus repeater) station.

9.2.2.3 When Generated. This primitive is passed from the physical layer entity to the station management entity in confirmation to the previous associated physical reset request.

9.2.2.4 Effect on Receipt. The station management entity uses the LAN topology type and PHY role information to determine which protocol the associated MAC entity should employ.

9.2.3 PHY_MODAL_CAPABILITY_QUERY.request [OPTIONAL]

9.2.3.1 Function. This primitive is the service request primitive for the physical layer capability query service.

9.2.3.2 Semantics. This primitive shall provide parameters as follows:

PHY_MODAL_CAPABILITY_QUERY.request
 (mode_class)

TOKEN-PASSING BUS   IEEE
                                            Std 802.4-1985

mode_class shall specify one of
(1) min_post_silence_preamble_length
(2) channel_assignments
(3) transmitted_power_level_adjustments
(4) transmitter_output_inhibits
(5) received_signal_sources
(6) signaling_modes
(7) received_signal_level_reporting

The specific values which are relevant for any particular physical layer entity shall be specified in the appropriate application subsection. All other values of the mode_class parameter shall elicit an undefined_mode_class confirmation.

9.2.3.3 When Generated. This primitive is passed from the station management entity to the physical layer entity to request that the physical layer entity report its capabilities with regard to the designated class of capabilities.

9.2.3.4 Effect on Receipt. Receipt of this primitive causes the physical layer entity to generate a PHY_MODAL_CAPABILITY_QUERY.confirmation primitive to report its capabilities with respect to the queried modal capability class.

9.2.4 PHY_MODAL_CAPABILITY_QUERY.confirmation [OPTIONAL]

9.2.4.1 Function. This primitive is the service confirmation primitive for the physical layer capability query service.

9.2.4.2 Semantics. This primitive shall provide parameters as follows:

PHY_MODAL_CAPABILITY_QUERY.confirmation
  (mode_class,
    capability_report)

mode_class shall take one of the values specified in 9.2.3. All other values of the mode_class parameter shall elicit an undefined_mode_class confirmation.

capability_report provides the requested report of the physical layer entity's capabilities in the queried area, or the undefined_mode_class confirmation if for an unknown mode_class.

9.2.4.3 When Generated. This primitive is passed from the physical layer entity to the station management entity in confirmation of the previous associated capability query request.

9.2.4.4 Effect on Receipt. The effect of receipt of this primitive by the station management entity is unspecified.

9.2.5 PHY_MODE_QUERY.request [OPTIONAL]

9.2.5.1 Function. This primitive is the service request primitive for the physical layer current mode query service.

9.2.5.2 Semantics. This primitive shall provide parameters as follows:

PHY_MODE_Query.request
  (mode_class)

mode_class shall take one of the values specified in 9.2.3. All other values of the mode_class parameter shall elicit an undefined_mode_class confirmation.

9.2.5.3 When Generated. This primitive is passed from the station management entity to the physical layer entity to request that the physical layer entity report its current mode with regard to the designated class of modes.

9.2.5.4 Effect on Receipt. Receipt of this primitive causes the physical layer entity to generate a PHY_MODE_QUERY.confirmation primitive to report its current mode with respect to the queried mode class.

9.2.6 PHY_MODE_QUERY.confirmation [OPTIONAL]

9.2.6.1 Function. This primitive is the service confirmation primitive for the physical layer current_mode query service.

9.2.6.2 Semantics. This primitive shall provide parameters as follows:

PHY_MODE_QUERY.confirmation
(mode_class,
  current_mode)

mode_class shall take one of the values specified in 9.2.3. All other values of the mode_class parameter shall elicit an undefined_mode_class confirmation.

current_mode provides the requested report of the physical layer entity's current mode in the queried area, or the undefined_mode_class confirmation if for an unknown mode_class.

9.2.6.3 When Generated. This primitive is passed from the physical layer entity to the station management entity in confirmation to the previous associated mode query request.

9.2.6.4 Effect on Receipt. The effect of receipt of this primitive by the station management entity is unspecified.

9.2.7 PHY_MODE_SELECT.request

9.2.7.1 Function. This primitive is the service request primitive for the physical layer current_mode select service.

9.2.7.2 Semantics. This primitive shall provide parameters as follows:

PHY_MODE_SELECT.request
(mode_class,
  new_mode)

mode_class shall take one of the values specified in 9.2.3. All other values of the mode_class parameter shall elicit a failure confirmation status.

new_mode specifies the desired mode of the designated mode_class.

9.2.7.3 When Generated. This primitive is passed from the station management entity to the physical layer entity to request that the physical layer entity change its current operating mode of the designated mode_class to the mode specified by new_mode.

9.2.7.4 Effect on Receipt. Receipt of this primitive causes the physical layer entity to attempt to change its operating mode of the designated mode_class to the specified mode, and to generate an PHY_MODE_SELECT.confirmation primitive to indicate the status of the requested change.

9.2.8 PHY_MODE_SELECT.confirmation

9.2.8.1 Function. This primitive is the service confirmation primitive for the physical layer current_mode select service.

9.2.8.2 Semantics. This primitive shall provide parameters as follows:

PHY_MODE_SELECT.confirmation
 (mode_class,
   status)

mode_class shall take one of the values specified in 9.2.3. All other values of the mode_class parameter shall elicit a <u>failure</u> confirmation status.

status indicates the <u>success</u> or <u>failure</u> of the operating mode selection request.

9.2.8.3 When Generated. This primitive is passed from the physical layer entity to the station management entity in confirmation to the previous associated mode select request to indicate the success or failure of that request.

9.2.8.4 Effect on Receipt. The effect of receipt of this primitive by the station management entity is unspecified.

9.2.9 PHY_MODE_CHANGE.indication [OPTIONAL]

9.2.9.1 Function. This primitive is the service indication primitive for the physical layer non-commanded mode change notification service.

9.2.9.2 Semantics. This primitive shall be parameterless, as follows:

PHY_MODE_CHANGE.indication

9.2.9.3 When Generated. This primitive is passed from the physical layer entity to the station management entity to indicate that one or more of the physical layer entity's current modes, as reportable by the PHY_MODE_QUERY.confirmation primitive of 9.2.6, has changed since the previous PHY_MODE_SELECT.confirmation or PHY_MODE_CHANGE.indication primitive.

9.2.9.4 Effect on Receipt. The effect of receipt of this primitive by the station management entity is unspecified.

9.2.9.5 Additional Comments. This primitive is used to provide timely notification of non-commanded mode changes, such as automatic transmitter output inhibit due to activation of the physical layer's jabber inhibit function.

10. Single-Channel Phase-Continuous-FSK Bus Physical Layer Specification

The functional, electrical, and mechanical characteristics of one specific form of physical layer (single-channel phase-continuous-FSK bus) of this standard are specified in this section. This specification includes the physical layer embodiments found in stations which could attach to the single-channel phase-continuous-FSK bus local area network. The relationship of this section to other sections of this standard and to LAN specifications is illustrated in Fig 10-1. The relationship of this section to the single-channel phase-continuous-FSK physical layer entity and medium is illustrated in Fig 10-2.

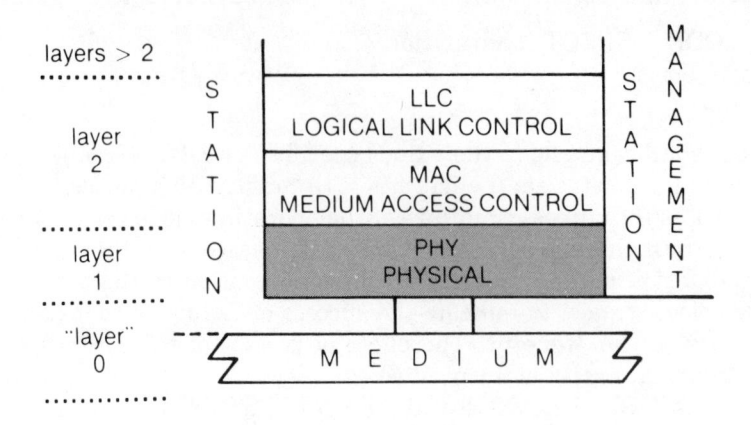

Fig 10-1
Relation to LAN Model

This standard specifies these physical layer entities only in so far as necessary to ensure
 (1) The interoperability of implementations conforming to this specification, and
 (2) The protection of the local area network and those using it.

10.1 Nomenclature. Some terms used in this section whose meanings within the section are more specific than indicated in the glossary of Ref [1] are as follows:

drop cable. The very short 35 Ω to 50 Ω stub cable which connects the station to a tee connector on the trunk cable.

FSK, Frequency Shift Keying. A modulation technique whereby information is impressed upon a carrier by shifting the frequency of the transmitted signal to one of a small set of frequencies.

Manchester encoding. A means by which separate data and clock signals can be combined into a single, self-synchronizable data stream, suitable for transmission on a serial channel.

phase-continuous FSK. A particular form of FSK where the translations between signaling frequencies is accomplished by a continuous change of frequency (as opposed to the discontinuous replacement of one frequency by another, such as might be accomplished by a switch). Thus it is also a form of frequency modulation.

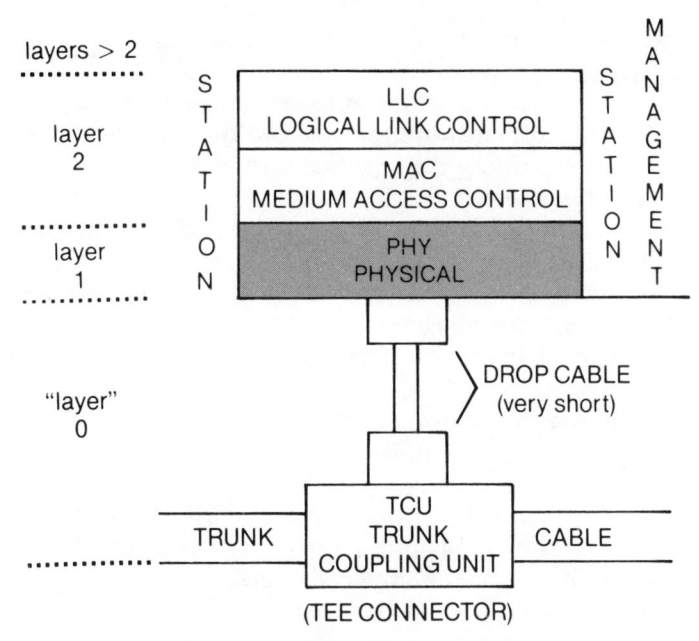

**Fig 10-2
Physical Hardware Partitioning,
Token-Passing Bus Local Area Network**

regenerative repeater. A device used to extend the length, topology, or interconnectivity of a local area network beyond that imposed by the minimum transmit and receive level specifications of the station and the connectivity restrictions of the medium. Regenerative repeaters perform the basic actions of restoring signal amplitude, waveform, and timing. They also prefix enough pad_idle symbols to a transmission to compensate for any symbols lost in transmission from the prior station or repeater.

single-channel FSK coaxial system. A system whereby information is encoded, frequency modulated onto a carrier, and impressed on the coaxial transmission medium. At any point on the medium, only one information signal at a time can be present within the channel without disruption.

station. Equipment connected to the local area network. For the purposes of this standard, regenerative repeaters are considered stations, whether or not they have functionality beyond that of a repeater.

trunk cable. The main 75 Ω coaxial cable of a single-channel phase-continuous FSK coaxial cable system.

10.2 Object. The object of this specification is to
 (1) Provide the physical means necessary for communication between local network stations employing the local area network token bus access method

described in this standard and a single-channel phase-continuous-FSK bus medium.

(2) Define a physical interface that can be implemented independently among different manufacturers of hardware and achieve the intended level of compatibility when interconnected to a common single-channel phase-continuous-FSK bus local area network medium.

(3) Provide a communication channel capable of high bandwidth and low bit error rate performance. The resultant mean bit error rate at the MAC service interface (see Section 8) shall be less than 10^{-8}, with a mean undetected bit error rate of less than 10^{-9} at that interface.

(4) Provide for ease of installation and service in a wide range of environments.

(5) Provide for high network availability.

(6) Facilitate low-cost implementations.

10.3 Compatibility Considerations. This standard applies to physical layer entities which are designed to operate on a 75 Ω coaxial trunk cable with the approximate configuration of an unbranched trunk, as specified in Section 11. All single-channel phase-continuous-FSK bus coaxial cable systems shall be compatible at the (drop cable) medium interface. Specific implementations based on this standard may be conceived in different ways provided compatibility at the medium is maintained.

10.4 Overview of the Single-Channel Phase-continuous-FSK Bus Medium. The communications medium specified in Section 11 consists of a long unbranched trunk cable which connects to stations by way of tee connectors and very short stubbed drop cables. Extension of the topology to a branched trunk usually is accomplished by way of active regenerative repeaters which are connected to span the branches.

10.5 Overview of the Phase-Continuous-FSK Bus Physical Layer

10.5.1 General Description of Functions. The functions performed by the single-channel phase-continuous-FSK bus physical layer entity are described informally here. Jointly these functions provide a means whereby symbols presented at the MAC interface of one physical layer entity can be conveyed to all of the physical layer entities on the bus for presentation to their respective MAC interfaces.

10.5.1.1 Symbol Transmission and Reception Functions. Successive symbols presented to the physical layer entity at its MAC service interface are applied to an encoder which produces as output a three PHY-symbol code: {H}, {L}, {off}. The output is then applied to a two-tone FSK modulator which represents each {H} as the higher frequency tone, each {L} as the lower frequency tone, and each {off} as no tone. This modulated signal is then ac coupled to the single-channel bus medium and conveyed by the medium to one or more receivers.

Each receiver is also ac coupled to the single-channel bus medium. It bandpass filters the received signal to reduce received noise, demodulates the filtered signal and then infers the transmitted PHY-symbol from the presence of carrier and the frequency of the received signal. It then decodes that inferred PHY-symbol by an approximate inverse of the encoding process and presents the resultant decoded MAC-symbols at its MAC service interface.

For all MAC-symbols except pad_idle, this decoding process is an exact inverse of the encoding process in the absence of errors. The pad_idle symbols, which are referred to collectively as preamble, are transmitted at the start of each MAC frame, to provide a training signal for receivers and to provide a nonzero minimum separation between consecutive frames. Since each transmission begins with pad_idle symbols, it is expected that some of these initial symbols may be "lost in transit" between the transmitter and receivers. Additionally, in phase-continuous FSK systems the MAC-symbol encodings for successive pad_idles is identical with the encoding for an alternating series of ones and zeros, and receivers are permitted to decode the transmitted representation of successive pad_idles as an alternating series of ones and zeros and report it as such to the MAC entity.

10.5.1.2 Regenerative Repeater Functions. Regenerative repeaters may be used to extend the network size beyond the maximum signal loss budget of an unassisted station, or the topology to that of a branched trunk. They do so by connecting two or more media segments and repeating anything "heard" on one segment to the other segments. For the purposes of this standard, regenerative repeaters are considered stations, whether or not they have functionality beyond that of a repeater.

10.5.1.3 Jabber-Inhibit Function. To protect the local area network from most faults in a station, each station contains a jabber-inhibit function. This function serves as a "watchdog" on the transmitter; if the station does not turn off its transmitter after a prolonged time (roughly one-half second), then the transmitter output shall be automatically disabled for at least the remainder of the transmission.

10.5.1.4 Local Administrative Functions. These are optional functions which select various modes of operation. They are activated either manually, or by way of the physical layer entity's station management interface, or both. They can include

(1) Enabling or disabling each transmitter output. (A redundant medium configuration has two or more transmitter outputs.)

(2) Selecting the received signal source: any single medium (if redundant media are present), or any available loopback point.

NOTE: If a loopback point is selected, then all transmitter outputs shall be inhibited.

10.5.2 Model Used for the Functional Specification. The detailed functional specifications are modeled after CCITT V Series modem specifications Refs [16] and [17], particularly the V.36 specification, with additional detail added where necessary.

10.5.3 Basic Functions and Options. Symbol transmission and reception functions and jabber-inhibit functions are required in all implementations. All other functions are optional.

10.6 Detailed Application of Section 9, Generic Station Management to Physical Layer Interface Service Specification. The range of permissible values for the parameters specified in Section 9 are as follows:

LAN_topology_type parameter of PHY_RESET.confirmation primitive. The value of this parameter shall be token_bus.

PHY_role parameter of PHY_RESET.confirmation primitive. The value of this parameter shall be originate_and_repeat for bus repeater stations, and originate_only for all other stations.

Mode_class parameter of PHY_MODAL_CAPABILITY_QUERY and PHY_MODE_QUERY primitives. The mode_class parameter shall specify min_post_silence_preamble_length, transmitter_output_inhibits, or received_signal_sources. The value read for min_post_silence_preamble_length shall be equal to one octet. All other values of the mode_class parameter shall elicit an undefined_mode_class confirmation.

Mode_class parameter of PHY_MODE_SELECT primitives. The mode_class parameter shall specify transmitter_output_inhibits or received_signal_sources. All other values of the mode_class parameter shall elicit a failure confirmation.

10.7 Single-Channel Phase-Continuous-FSK Bus Physical Layer Functional, Electrical, and Mechanical Specifications. Unless otherwise stated, all voltage and power levels specified are in rms and dB (1 mV, 37.5 Ω) rms, respectively, based on transmissions of arbitrary data patterns.

10.7.1 Data Signaling Rates. The standard data signaling rate for phase-continuous FSK systems is 1 Mb/s. The permitted tolerance for this signaling rate is ±0.01% for an originating station, and is ±0.015% for a repeater station while repeating. When a composite physical layer entity is embodied in a regenerative repeater, it shall originate signaling on all trunks at the exact same data rate.

10.7.2 Symbol Encoding. The physical layer entity transmits MAC-symbols presented to it at its MAC interface by the medium access control sublayer entity. The possible MAC-symbols are (see 8.2.1.2): zero, one, non_data, pad_idle, and silence. Each of these MAC-symbols is encoded into a pair of PHY-symbols from a different three-symbol {H}, {L}, {off} code and then transmitted. The encoding action to be taken for each of the input MAC-symbols is:

(1) Silence—Each silence symbol shall be encoded as the sequence {off off}.

(2) Pad_idle—pad_idle symbols are always originated in octets. Each pair of consecutive pad_idle symbols shall be encoded as the sequence {L H} {H L}.

(3) Zero—Each zero symbol shall be encoded as the sequence {H L}.

(4) One—Each one symbol shall be encoded as the sequence {L H}.

(5) Non_data —Non_data symbols are transmitted by the MAC sublayer entity in pairs. Each such pair of consecutive non_data symbols shall be encoded as the sequence {L L} {H H}. Thus the (start frame delimiter) subsequence

    non_data   non_data   zero   non_data   non_data   zero

shall be encoded as the sequence

{L L} {H H} {H L} {L L} {H H} {H L},

and the (end frame delimiter) subsequence

non_data   non_data   one   non_data   non_data   one

shall be encoded as the sequence

{L L} {H H} {L H} {L L} {H H} {L H}.

10.7.3 Modulated Line Signal (at the line output of the station). The PHY-symbols resulting from the encoding of 10.7.2 shall be applied to an FSK modulator with the result that each {H} shall be represented by the higher of the modulator's two signaling frequencies, each {L} shall be represented by the lower of the modulator's two signaling frequencies, and each {off} shall be represented by the absence of both carrier and modulation. The resultant modulated carrier shall be coupled to the single-channel bus medium as specified in 10.7.5.

10.7.3.1 The line signal shall correspond to an FSK signal with its carrier frequency at 5.00 MHz, varying smoothly between the two signaling frequencies of 3.75 MHz ± 80 kHz and 6.25 MHz ± 80 kHz.

10.7.3.2 Each of the PHY-symbols resulting from the encoding of 10.7.2 shall be transmitted for a period equal to one-half of the inter-arrival time of the MAC-symbols which the MAC entity presents at the MAC interface. The maximum jitter in this periodicity shall be less than 1% of that MAC-symbol inter-arrival time.

10.7.3.3 When transitioning between the two signaling frequencies, the FSK modulator shall change its frequency in a continuous and monotonic manner within 100 ns, with amplitude distortion of at most 10%.

10.7.3.4 The output level of the transmitted signal at the modulated carrier frequency into a 37.5 Ω resistive load shall be between +54 dB and +60 dB (1 mV, 37.5 Ω).

NOTE: The signal level on the cable due to a single transmitter is propagated along the very short (stub) drop cable to a tee connector and thence along the trunk cable in two directions. Thus the two half sections of the 75 Ω trunk cable appear as a 37.5 Ω load to the transmitting entity.

10.7.3.5 When in the transmitter-off state (that is, while "transmitting" the PHY-code {off}), the station shall present a dc shunt impedance of 50 kΩ or more at its medium interface. When in the transmitter-on state (that is, while transmitting the PHY-codes {H} and {L}), the station shall function as a voltage source with an impedance of 38 Ω or less at its medium interface. In either state, the station shall present a maximum shunt capacitance of 25 pF at that medium interface.

10.7.3.6 The residual or leakage transmitter-off output signal (that is, while "transmitting" the PHY-code {off}) shall be no more than -26 dB (1 mV, 37.5 Ω).

10.7.4 Jabber Inhibit. Each physical layer entity shall have a self-interrupt capability to inhibit modulation from reaching the local area network medium. Hardware within the physical layer (with no external message other than the prolonged detection of an output-on condition within the transmitter) shall provide a nominal window of one-half second ±25% during which time a normal data link transmission may occur. If a transmission is in excess of this duration, the jabber inhibit function shall operate to inhibit any further output from reaching the medium. Reset of this jabber inhibit function shall occur upon receipt of a station management PHY_RESET.request (see 9.2.1). Additional resetting means are permitted.

10.7.5 Coupling to the Medium. The physical layer functions are intended to operate satisfactorily with a medium consisting of a 75 Ω bidirectional coaxial trunk cable, tee connectors, and short stubbed 37 Ω to 51 Ω drop cables. The mechanical coupling of the station to the medium shall be to the 37 Ω to 51 Ω drop cable by way of a 50 Ω male BNC-series connector, as specified in Section 11.

Both the transmitter and the receiver shall be ac coupled to the center conductor of one of the medium's drop cables, and the breakdown voltage of that ac coupling means shall be at least 500 V ac rms. In addition to this coupling, the shield of the coaxial cable medium shall be connected to chassis ground, and the impedance of that connection shall be less than 0.1 Ω.

10.7.6 Receiver Sensitivity and Selectivity. The physical layer entity shall be capable of providing an undetected bit error rate of 10^{-9} or lower, and a detected bit error rate of 10^{-8} or lower, when receiving signals with a level of +24 dB to +60 dB (1 mV, 37.5 Ω), in a system with an in-band noise floor of +4 dB (1 mV, 37.5 Ω) or less, as measured at the point of connection to the station.

10.7.7 Symbol Timing. Each physical layer entity shall recover the PHY-symbol timing information contained within the transitions between signaling frequencies of the received signal, and shall use this recovered timing information to determine the precise rate at which MAC-symbols should be delivered to the MAC interface. The jitter in this reported MAC-symbol timing relative to the PHY-symbol timing within the received signaling shall be less than 8%. When receiving silence from the medium, it shall be reported at the MAC interface at a rate determined by 10.7.1.

10.7.8 Symbol Decoding. After demodulation and determination of each received signaled PHY-symbol, that PHY-symbol shall be decoded by the process inverse to that described in 10.7.2, and the decoded MAC-symbols shall be reported at the MAC interface. (As noted in 10.5.1.1, receivers are permitted to decode the transmitted representation of pad_idle as zero or one.) Whenever a signaled PHY-symbol sequence is received for which the encoding process has no inverse, those PHY-symbols shall be decoded as an appropriate number of bad_signal MAC-symbols and reported as such at the MAC interface. In such cases, the receiving entity should resynchronize the decoding process as rapidly as possible.

10.7.9 Transmitter Enable/Disable and Received Signal Source Selection [OPTIONAL]. The ability to enable and disable the transmission of modulation onto the single-channel bus medium as directed by the station management entity is recommended but optional.

The ability to select the source of received signaling, either a loopback point within the physical layer entity or (one of) the (possibly redundant) media, as directed by the station management entity, is recommended but optional. When such an option is invoked and the selected source is other than (one of) the media, transmission to all connected bus media shall be disabled automatically while such selection is in force.

10.7.10 Redundant Media Considerations. Embodiments of this standard which can function with redundant media are not precluded, provided that the embodiment as delivered functions correctly in a nonredundant single-cable environment. Where redundant media are employed, the provisions of 10.7.4 and 10.7.9 shall apply separately and independently to each single medium interface, and much of 10.7.9 shall be mandatory. Specifically, separate jabber inhibit monitoring shall exist for each medium (although common inhibition is permissible), receiver signal source selection shall be provided capable of selecting any one of the redundant media, and it shall be possible to enable or disable each single transmitter independently of all other redundant transmitters when the source of received signaling is one of the redundant media.

10.7.11 Reliability. The physical layer entity shall be designed so that its probability of causing a communication failure among other stations connected to the medium is less than 10^{-6} per hour of continuous (or discontinuous) operation. For regenerative repeaters this requirement is relaxed to a probability of 10^{-5} per hour of operation. Connectors and other passive components comprising the means of connecting the station to the coaxial cable medium shall be designed to minimize the probability of total network failure.

10.7.12 Regenerative Repeater Considerations. The physical layer entity of a regenerative repeater can be considered to be a composite entity, with separate electrical and mechanical low-level transmit and receive functions for each connected trunk segment (that is, each port), all under a common encoding, decoding, timing-recovery and control function.

The basic mode of operation, originating or repeating, shall be determined by the superior MAC entity and conveyed by the PHY_MODE.request primitive (see 8.2.3). When originating, the repeater physical layer entity shall originate the symbol timing provided to the MAC entity and transmit the encoded MAC-symbols onto all connected trunk segments. It shall use either internal loopback or any one of the attached trunks as the source of PHY-symbols which are decoded and reported by way of the PHY_DATA.indicate primitive.

When switching to repeating, the repeater physical layer entity shall delay for an implementation-dependent amount of time (typically a few symbol-durations) to prevent repeating the end of the just-prior transmission, and shall then scan the connected ports for one on which signaling is being received. During the delay period, and while this scan for signal is unsuccessful, the repeater physical layer entity shall indicate silence symbols to its MAC entity using its locally-originated symbol timing. Upon detecting signaling at one or more ports, the repeater entity shall select one of those active ports as the source of its received signaling. It shall then temporarily disable that selected port's low-level transmitter function, decode the received signaling, retime that signaling before or after decoding so that the implementation-determined constant phase relationship between PHY_DATA. indicate and PHY_DATA.request is maintained (see 8.2.4), and indicate the decoded MAC-symbols to its associated MAC entity. It should then vary the frequency of the MAC-symbol timing, within the bounds of this subsection (10.7), as necessary to maintain the proper relationship with the frequency of the received PHY-symbol timing.

When repeating, after decoding the MAC-symbol silence received from the active port, the repeater physical layer entity shall await the MAC-entity's transmission of silence by way of a PHY_DATA.request, shall then re-enable the temporarily disabled low-level transmitter function, and shall then again follow the procedure outlined in the prior paragraph just as if the MAC entity had just switched to repeating.

In summary, when the MAC entity is originating

(1) The physical layer entity alone shall determine the MAC-symbol timing

(2) Transmission occurs on all attached trunks (unless disabled by the provisions of 10.7.9)

(3) Internal loopback or any one of the attached trunks can be used as the source of PHY-symbols which are decoded and reported by way of the PHY_DATA.indicate primitive.

When the MAC entity is repeating

(a) The physical layer entity first delays long enough to ensure that the prior transmission is not repeated, then scans all attached trunks for signaling and selects one of those trunks with signaling as the source of received signaling

(b) Transmission to the selected trunk is temporarily inhibited

(c) The received signaling from the selected trunk is decoded and indicated to the MAC entity

(d) The frequency of MAC-symbol timing is varied as necessary (at most ±0.015%) to track the frequency of the peer transmitter's MAC-symbol timing

(e) Upon detecting a loss of signaling (that is, receiving silence) from the selected trunk, the physical layer entity first waits until the MAC entity requests transmission of silence, and then repeats the whole procedure.

10.8 Environmental Specifications

{NOTE: Subsection 10.8 is not a part of the ISO standard. The subject of international standards in this area is under study by the International Electrotechnical Commission and other organizations.}

10.8.1 Safety Requirements. Recommendations and guidelines related to safety are given in this subsection. The list is incomplete; neither does it address all possible safety concerns. The designer is urged to consult the relevant local, national, and international safety codes and regulations to ensure compliance with the appropriate codes and standards. EIA CB 8-1981[9] provides additional guidance on many relevant regulatory requirements.

Local area network cable systems as described in Section 11 are subject to at least four direct electrical safety hazards during their use, and designers of connecting equipment should be aware of these hazards. The hazards are

(1) Direct contact between local network components and power or lighting circuits

(2) Static charge buildup on local network cables and components

(3) High-energy transients coupled onto the local network cabling system

(4) Potential differences between safety grounds to which various network components are connected

These electrical safety hazards, to which all similar cabling systems are subject, should be alleviated properly for a local network to perform properly. In addition to provisions for properly handling these faults in an operational system, special measures should be taken to ensure that the intended safety features are not negated when attaching or detaching equipment from the local area network medium of an existing network.

Sound installation practice, as defined by ANSI/NFPA 70-1984[3], Article 820 and applicable local codes and regulations shall be followed in every instance in which such practice is applicable.

10.8.2 Electromagnetic and Electric Environment. Sources of interference from the environment include electromagnetic fields, electrostatic discharge, transient voltages between earth connections, etc. Several sources of interference contribute to voltage buildup between the coaxial cable and the earth connection, if any, of the station.

The physical layer entity embodiment shall meet its specifications when operating in an ambient plane-wave field of

(1) 2 V/m from 10 kHz through 30 MHz

(2) 5 V/m from 30 MHz through 1 GHz

10.8.3 Temperature and Humidity. Any embodiment of this standard is expected to operate over a reasonable range of environmental conditions related to temperature, humidity, and physical handling such as shock and vibration. Specific requirements and values for these parameters are considered to be beyond the scope of this standard. Manufacturers are requested to indicate in the literature associated with system components and equipment (and on the components if possible) the operating environment specifications to facilitate selection, installation, and maintenance of these components.

10.8.4 Regulatory Requirements. The following regulatory requirements may apply to local area network equipment and media:

ANSI/NFPA 70-1984[3] Articles 250, 800, and 820, ANSI/UL 94-1979[4] Rated under V-0, ANSI/UL 114-1982[5], ANSI/UL 478-1979[6], CSA Standard C22.2 No 154-M 1983[8], FCC Docket 20780-1980[10], Part 15, Subpart J, and IEC 716-1983[11].

10.9 Labeling. It is recommended that each embodiment (and supporting documentation) of a physical layer entity conformant to this standard be labeled in a manner visible to the user with at least these parameters

(1) Specific sections of the LAN standards to which the equipment conforms

(2) Data rate capability in Mb/s (that is, 1 Mb/s)

(3) Worst-case round-trip delay (for nonrepeaters) or one-way delay (for repeaters) which this equipment induces on a two-way transmission exchange between stations, as specified in 6.1.9.

IEEE
Std 802.4-1985   LOCAL AREA NETWORKS:

(4) Operating modes and selection capabilities as defined in 10.7.9 and 10.7.10.
Additionally, when the station has multiple BNC-series connectors (for example, for redundant media) the role of each such connector shall be designated clearly by markings on the station in the vicinity of that connector.

11. Single-Channel Phase-Continuous-FSK Bus Medium "Layer" Specification

The functional, electrical and mechanical characteristics of one specific form of medium layer (single-channel phase-continuous-FSK bus) of this standard are specified in this section. This specification includes the medium "layer" embodiments of a single-channel phase-continuous-FSK bus local area network.

The relationship of this section to other sections of this standard and to LAN specifications is illustrated in Fig 11-1. The relationship of this section to the single-channel phase-continuous-FSK bus physical layer and medium "layer" entities is illustrated in Fig 11-2.

**Fig 11-1
Relation to LAN Model**

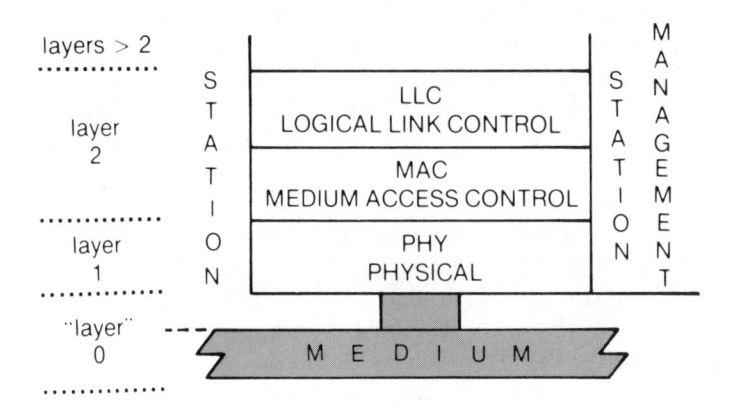

TOKEN-PASSING BUS

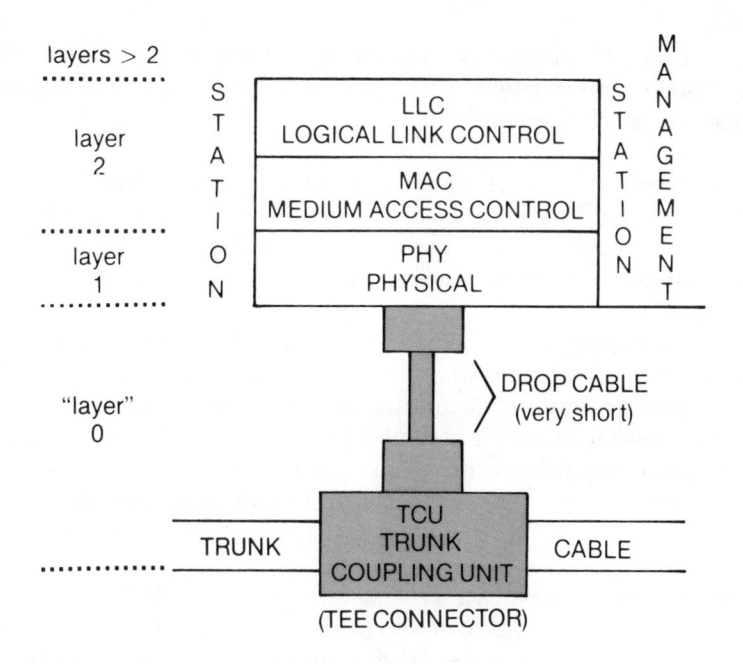

IEEE
Std 802.4-1985

**Fig 11-2
Physical Hardware Partitioning,
Token-Passing Bus Local Area Network**

This standard specifies the medium "layer" only in so far as necessary to ensure
(1) The interoperability of physical layer entities conforming to Section 10 when connected to a medium layer conformant to this section
(2) The protection of the local area network and those using it.

11.1 Nomenclature. Terms used in this section whose meanings within the section are more specific than indicated in the glossary of Ref [1] are as follows:

BNC-connector. A 50 Ω BNC-series coaxial cable connector (of the kind commonly found on rf equipment).

single-channel FSK coaxial system. A system whereby information is encoded, frequency modulated onto a carrier, and impressed on the coaxial transmission medium. At any point on the medium, only one information signal at a time can be present within the channel without disruption.

drop cable. The very short 35 Ω to 50 Ω stub coaxial cable which connects the station to a tee connector on the trunk cable.

FSK, Frequency Shift Keying. A modulation technique whereby information is impressed upon a carrier by shifting the frequency of the transmitted signal to one of a small set of frequencies.

phase-continuous FSK. A particular form of FSK where the translations between signaling frequencies is accomplished by a continuous change of frequency (as opposed to the discontinuous replacement of one frequency by another, such as might be accomplished by a switch).

regenerative repeater. A device used to extend the length, topology, or interconnectivity of a single-channel bus local area network beyond the limits imposed by the minimum transmit and receive level specifications of the station. Regenerative repeaters perform the basic actions of restoring signal amplitude, waveform, and timing. They also prefix enough pad_idle symbols to a transmission to compensate for any symbols lost in transmission from the prior station or repeater.

(impedance-matching) splitter. A small module which electrically and mechanically couples one trunk cable to other trunk cables, providing a branching topology for the single-channel FSK trunk. An impedance-matching splitter combines signal energy received at its ports, splitting any signal energy received from a trunk symmetrically among the other trunks. It contains only passive electrical components (R, L, C).

station. Equipment connected to the local area network. For the purposes of this standard, regenerative repeaters are considered stations, whether or not they have functionality beyond that of a repeater.

tee connector. A small module, usually a T-shaped connector, which electrically and mechanically couples the trunk cable to a very short drop cable. It splits the signal energy received from each trunk cable very asymmetrically, with the bulk of that energy passed to the other trunk cable and only a small percentage passed to the drop cable. It splits a part of the signal energy received from the drop cable equally among the trunk cables, and reflects the rest of that signal energy back to the transmitting station; it does not impedance-match the drop cable to the bidirectional trunk cable. It contains only passive electrical components (R, L, C).

trunk cable. The main cable of a single-channel phase-continuous-FSK bus coaxial cable system.

11.2 Object. The object of this specification is to
(1) Provide the physical medium necessary for communication between local network stations employing the LAN token-bus access method defined in this standard and a single-channel phase-continuous-FSK bus physical layer

(2) Provide for ease of installation and service in a wide range of environments
(3) Provide for high network availability
(4) Facilitate low-cost implementations

11.3 Compatibility Considerations. This standard applies to medium "layer" entities which are designed to operate as nondirectional single-channel coaxial cable bus systems. Such systems generally use a long flexible trunk cable connected by way of tee connectors to very short (stubbed) drop cables to stations. This specification applies to a single trunk system in which two-way communication is accomplished through the use of nondirectional tee connectors and splitters and, in large systems, multidirectional regenerative repeaters.

All implementations of medium "layer" entities conformant to this standard shall be compatible at their station interfaces. Specific implementations based on this standard may be conceived in different ways provided compatibility at the actual station interfaces is maintained.

11.4 Overview of the Phase-Continuous-FSK Bus Medium "Layer"

11.4.1 General Description of Functions. The functions performed by the single-channel phase-continuous-FSK bus medium "layer" entity are described informally here. Jointly these functions provide a means whereby signaling presented at the station interfaces of very short 35 Ω to 50 Ω drop cables can be combined and conveyed to all of the stations on all of the medium's drop cables. Thus stations connected to these drop cables can communicate.

11.4.1.1 Operational Overview of the Single-Channel Phase-Continuous-FSK Bus Medium. Stations are connected to the long trunk coaxial cable(s) of single-channel phase-continuous-FSK bus systems by very short drop cables and tee connectors (which do not impedance-match the drop cable to the trunk). These tee connectors are passive devices, usually simple connectors, which are nondirectional (that is, omnidirectional) with regard to signal propagation. The nondirectional characteristics of the tee connectors permit the station's signal to propagate in both directions along the trunk cable. The very short length of the drop cables minimizes the effect of the reflections on the drop cable due to the impedance mismatch between the 35 Ω to 50 Ω drop cable and the 37.5 Ω apparent impedance of the bidirectional trunk cable.

The topology of the single-channel phase-continuous-FSK bus system is that of a very long unbranched tree trunk, with the stations connected as leaves to the very short stubs (drop cables) extending from the trunk. Branching is accomplished in the trunk itself by way of regenerative repeaters (described below) and splitters, which provide nondirectional coupling of the signaling carried on the trunk cables. The splitters employ only passive electrical components (R, L, C only).

Regenerative repeaters provide both branching and the ability to extend a system topology beyond that permitted by the minimum transmit and receive level specifications of an unassisted station. The regenerative repeaters of the single-channel phase-continuous-FSK bus system are connected to trunk cables by tee connectors and drop cables and function as specialized stations which normally repeat signaling received on any branch to all other branches of the trunk cable system.

11.4.1.2 Regenerative Repeater Functions. In an actual single-channel phase-continuous-FSK bus system, regenerative repeaters may be used to connect trunk segments into a highly branched topology, or to extend the length of, or number of tee connectors and drops on, a trunk beyond that which the unassisted station's minimum transmit and receive level specifications would allow.

In performing its repeating functions, the regenerative repeater (see 10.7.12) serves as a relay station, with a composite physical-layer entity (one sub-entity per connected trunk) and one medium-access entity monitoring and repeating the received composite signaling. When not transmitting for itself, the repeater's medium-access entity interprets the symbols received from the composite physical-layer entity. When a symbol other than silence is received, the composite physical-layer entity determines which trunk carried the symbol, and it then selects that trunk as the source of reported signaling. Concurrently, the medium access entity begins to retransmit all symbols reported (onto the other trunks). When a collision or noise is detected (for example, bad_signal reported), the repeater's medium-access entity sends an abort sequence (see 4.1.8) in lieu of repeating the received MAC-symbols.

11.4.2 Model Used for the Functional Specification. The detailed functional specifications are modeled after CCITT H. series media specifications, REfs [18] and [19], and particularly the H.14 specification, with additional detail added where necessary.

11.4.3 Basic Characteristics and Options. All signal-conveyance characteristics and station-interface characteristics are mandatory. All other characteristics are optional.

11.5 Bibliography

RHEINFELDER, W., *CATV Circuit Engineering,* TAB Books, Blue Ridge Summit, PA, 1975.

11.6 Single-Channel Phase-Continuous-FSK Bus Medium "Layer" Functional, Electrical and Mechanical Specifications. The single-channel phase-continuous-FSK bus medium "layer" entity is an entity whose sole function (relative to this standard) is signal transport between the stations of a single-channel phase-continuous-FSK bus local area network. Consequently only those characteristics of the medium "layer" entity which impinge on station to station signal transport, or on human and equipment safety, are specified in this standard.

An implementation of the medium "layer" entity shall be deemed conformant to this standard if it provides the specified signal transport services and characteristics for the stations of a single-channel phase-continuous-FSK bus local area network, and if it meets the relevant safety and environmental codes.

All measurements specified in the following paragraphs are to be made at the point of station or regenerative repeater connection to the medium. Unless otherwise stated, all voltage and power levels specified are in rms and dB (1 mV, 37.5 Ω) rms, respectively, based on transmissions of arbitrary data patterns.

11.6.1 Coupling to the Station. The connection of the single-channel phase-continuous-FSK bus medium to the station shall be by way of a flexible 34 Ω to 51 Ω drop cable terminated in a female BNC-series 50 Ω connector; this combination shall mate with a male BNC-series 50 Ω connector mounted on the station.

In addition to this coupling, the shield(s) of the coaxial drop cable medium shall be connected to the outer barrel of the terminating female connector and the impedance of that connection shall be less than 0.1 Ω. Also, the impedance of a connection between the outer barrel of that female connector and the shell of a mated male connector shall be less than 0.1 Ω.

NOTE: For tee-connectors which do not impedance match the drop cable to the trunk cabling, the length of the stub cable should be 350 mm or less.

11.6.2 Characteristic Impedance. The characteristic impedance of the single-channel phase-continuous-FSK bus drop cable medium shall be 34 Ω to 51 Ω. The maximum VSWR at each of that medium's BNC-connectors shall be 1.5:1 or less when the BNC-connector is terminated with a 37.5 Ω resistive load, as measured over the entire single-channel phase-continuous-FSK bus cable spectrum of 3 MHz to 7 MHz.

11.6.3 Signal Level. When receiving the signal of a single station or regenerative repeater whose transmit level is as specified in 10.7.3.4, the single-channel phase-continuous-FSK bus medium shall present that signaling to the connected station or regenerative repeater at an amplitude of between +24 dB and +60 dB (1 mV, 37.5 Ω).

11.6.4 Distortion. The maximum group delay distortion shall be 25 ns or less over the frequency range of 3 MHz to 7 MHz.

11.6.5 Signal to Noise (S/N) Level. It is recommended that the in-band (3 MHz to 7 MHz) noise floor be 0 dB (1 mV, 37.5 Ω) or less. In no case shall it be worse than +4 dB (1 mV, 37.5 Ω) as measured at the point of connection to any station or regenerative repeater.

11.6.6 Power Handling Capability. The total power over the entire cable spectrum, as presented to the station or regenerative repeater, shall be less than 0.25 W.

11.6.7 Compatibility with the Stations and Regenerative Repeaters. An embodiment of a single-channel phase-continuous-FSK bus medium "layer" entity is deemed to support a specific single-channel phase-continuous-FSK bus local area network if the requirements of 11.6.1 through 11.6.6 (inclusive) are met when measured from each point of station connection to the medium, independent of which one of the points of station connection is chosen for test signal origination.

11.6.8 Redundancy Considerations. As implied by 10.7.10, redundant single-channel phase-continuous-FSK bus media are not precluded from this standard. Where redundant media are employed, the provisions of 11.6.1 to 11.6.7 shall apply separately and independently to each single nonredundant medium interface.

11.6.9 Reliability. All active (powered) medium "layer" equipment shall be designed so that the aggregate probability of that equipment causing a communication failure at more than one station connected to the medium is less than 10^{-4} per hour of continuous (or discontinuous) operation. Connectors and other passive components comprising the means of connecting the station to the coaxial cable medium shall be designed to minimize the probability of total network failure.

11.7 Environmental Specifications

{NOTE: Subsection 11.7 is not a part of the ISO standard. The subject of international standards in this area is under study by the International Electrotechnical Commission and other organizations.}

11.7.1 Safety Requirements. Recommendations and guidelines related to safety are given in this section. The list is incomplete; neither does it address all possible safety concerns. The designer is urged to consult the relevant local, national, and international safety codes and regulations to ensure compliance with the appropriate codes and standards. Additional guidance on many relevant regulatory requirements is provided in EIA CB8-1981[9].

Local area network cable systems as described in Section 11 are subject to at least four direct electrical safety hazards during their use, and designers of connecting equipment should be aware of these hazards. The hazards are

(1) Direct contact between local network components and power or lighting circuits

(2) Static charge buildup on local network cables and components

(3) High-energy transients coupled onto the local network cabling system

(4) Potential differences between safety grounds to which various network components are connected.

These electrical safety hazards, to which all similar cabling systems are subject, should be alleviated properly for a local area network to perform correctly. In addition to provisions for properly handling these faults in an operational system, special measures shall be taken to ensure that the intended safety features are not negated during installation of a new network or during modification of an existing network.

Proper implementation of the following provisions will decrease greatly the likelihood of shock hazards to persons installing and operating the local area network.

11.7.1.1 Sound installation practice, as defined by ANSI/NFPA 70-1984, Article 820, and applicable local codes and regulations shall be followed in every instance in which such practice is applicable.

11.7.1.2 The shields of the trunk coaxial cable segments and the housings of all attached tee-connectors are electrically in series in each branch of a properly installed single-channel phase-continuous-FSK bus medium. This connected conductive path shall be effectively grounded at more than one point along the length of the trunk cable, and at every point where the cable enters or leaves a building structure. The suggested practice is to effectively ground the cable shield at least once per hundred meters, but where large differences in ground potential exist between grounding points, other practices may be necessary. Effectively grounded means—permanently connected to earth through a ground connection of sufficiently low impedance and having sufficient ampacity to prevent the build-up of voltages that may result in undue hazard to connected equipment or to persons.

11.7.1.3 The shields of all drop coaxial cable segments shall be effectively grounded to the tee-connector housings to which they are attached.

11.7.1.4 Where there is reason to believe that the ground potential of an exposed shield of a coaxial cable, or housing of a connector differs from the ground potential in the vicinity of that component by more than a few volts, an insulating sleeve, boot, or cover should be affixed to that equipment in such a manner as to ensure that users (not installers) of the equipment will not inadvertently complete a circuit between the exposed shield or housing and the local ground through body contact.

11.7.1.5 Installation and Maintenance Guidelines. Installation and maintenance guidelines developed within the CATV industry for inter- and intra-facility installation of coaxial cable systems shall be followed where applicable. In addition the following caution shall be observed:

> **CAUTION:** At no time should the shield of any portion of the coaxial trunk cable be permitted to float without an effective ground. If a section of floating cable is to be added to an existing cable system, the installer shall take care not to complete the circuit between the shield of the floating cable section and the grounded cable section through body contact.

11.7.1.6 The installation instructions for single-channel phase-continuous-FSK bus coaxial cable networks shall contain language which familiarizes the installer with the caution and guidelines mentioned in 11.7.1.5.

11.7.2 Electromagnetic and Electric Environment. Sources of interference from the environment include electromagnetic fields, electrostatic discharge, transient voltages between earth connections, etc. Several sources of interference contribute to voltage build-up between the coaxial cable and the earth connection, if any, of the station.

The medium "layer" entity embodiment shall meet its specifications when operating in an ambient plane-wave field of

(1) 2 V/m from 10 kHz through 30 MHz
(2) 5 V/m from 30 MHz through 1 GHz.

11.7.3 Temperature and Humidity. Any embodiment of this standard is expected to operate over a reasonable range of environmental conditions related to temperature, humidity, and physical handling such as shock and vibration. Specific requirements and values for these parameters are considered to be beyond the scope of this standard. Manufacturers are requested to indicate in the literature associated with system components and equipment (and on the components if possible) the operating environment specifications to facilitate selection, installation, and maintenance of these components.

11.7.4 Regulatory Requirements. The following regulatory requirements may apply to local area network equipment and media:

ANSI/NFPA 70-1984[3] Articles 250, 800, and 820, ANSI/UL 94-1979[4] (see section on Flammability of Plastics), ANSI/UL 114-1982[5], ANSI/UL 478-1979[6], CSA Standard C22.2 No 154-M 1983[8], FCC Docket 20780-1980[10], Part 15, Subpart J, and IEC 716-1983[11].

In particular, the FCC requirements for radiation from the coaxial cable medium and connected equipment (Part 15) do apply, and shall be considered in any embodiment of the medium "layer" entity specified in this standard.

NOTE: Equipment designed for CATV use must comply with the relevant requirements of FCC Docket 20780-1980[10], Part 76, which generally are more stringent than FCC Docket 20780-1980[10], Part 15.

11.8 Transmission Path Delay Considerations. When specifying an embodiment of a medium "layer" which conforms to the specifications of this Section (11), a vendor shall state the Transmission Path Delay as the maximum <u>one-way</u> delay which the single-channel phase-continuous-FSK bus medium could be expected to induce on a transmission from any connected station through any intervening regenerative repeaters to any other station. The delays induced by the transmitting and receiving stations themselves should not be included in the Transmission Path Delay.

For each potentially worst-case path through the medium, a path delay is computed as the sum of the medium-induced delay and repeater-induced delay, if any, in propagating a signal from one station to another. The Transmission Path Delay used for determining the network's slot_time (see 6.1.9) shall be the largest of these path delays for the cable system.

These path delay computations shall take into account all circuitry delays in all relevant regenerative repeaters and medium "layer" splitters, etc, and all signal propagation delays within the cable segments. The regenerative repeater delays shall be determined as specified in 10.9 and 6.1.9.

The Transmission Path Delay shall be expressed in terms of the network's symbol signaling rate on the medium. When not an integral number of signaled symbols, it shall be rounded up to such an integral number. When uncertain of the exact value of the delay, vendors shall state an upper bound for the value.

11.9 Documentation. It is recommended that each vendor of an embodiment of a medium "layer" entity conformant to this standard provide to the user supporting documentation with at least these parameters

(1) Specific sections of the standards to which the embodiment conforms

(2) The transmission path delay, as specified in 11.10 and 6.1.9

(3) Data-rate capabilities in Mb/s, where regenerative repeaters are part of the medium and so constrain the supported data rates.

11.10 Network Sizing

11.10.1 Topology Considerations. Small to medium-sized systems can be constructed using only flexible coaxial cable and tee connectors. Larger systems require both semirigid and flexible trunk cable segments, or splitters, or regenerative repeaters, or any combination of the three. Branched topologies are achieved in this medium using CATV-like splitters and regenerative repeaters.

11.10.2 Signal Loss Budget Considerations. The placement of phase-continuous-FSK regenerative repeaters and splitters shall take into account

(1) Each station's minimum transmit level and receive level specifications (see 10.7.3.4 and 10.7.6)

(2) The desired current and anticipated future placement of station's and regenerative repeaters

(3) The presented signal level and noise floor specifications of 11.8.

Appendix

(This Appendix is not a part of this standard but is included for information only.)

11.11 Appendix—Guidelines for Configuring the Medium of a Single-Channel Phase-Continuous-FSK Bus LAN.

The following recommendations for designing and installing local area networks using phase-continuous-FSK transmission are the result of practical experience, and correspond to typical field conditions that are encountered.

11.11.1 Application. One of the first tasks in network design is the definition of both the current application and the possible future expanded or upgraded services. In typical situations where phase-continuous-FSK at 1 Mb/s is chosen, it is probable that planned (and unplanned) future changes will be limited to adding more drops on the existing trunk cable, and adding extensions at the ends of the cable. If the present network is small, and the possible future network is much larger, it probably will be more cost-effective, temporarily, to install a minimum network of low-cost flexible cable. Future requirements can then be based on current experience, but without any particular commitment to the current cable.

11.11.2 Network Size. Two important aspects of network size are overall length of the cable, and total number of drops. Since phase-continuous-FSK physical layer entities (modems) simply bridge the cable by a relatively loss-free tee connection, the loss per drop is small. Thus in typical practical networks the cable length is usually limited by cable attenuation rather than tap loss. The network's signal loss budget is then essentially equal to the dynamic range (difference between transmit and receive levels) specified in 10.7 (30 dB). Since cable loss increases with frequency, cable loss should be measured at 6.25 MHz, the highest frequency of interest.

Sections 10 and 11 recommend use of RG-6, RG-11, and semirigid (typical CATV trunk) types of 75 Ω cable. Many networks predating these specifications, but essentially conforming to them, are now installed and operating with cables of these types (and of various other 75 Ω cable types). Typical maximum network lengths achieved with several commercially-available cables are

Cable	Distance
RG-59	1280 m
RG-6	1600 m
RG-11 (foam)	2900 m
JT4412J	4600 m
JT4750J	7600 m

Although this specification includes the use of repeaters to extend the trunk cable beyond the length permitted by the loss budget, this has rarely been needed in practice, and such use may compromise the simplicity otherwise offered by the phase-continuous-FSK type of service.

The number of drops in the above networks has typically ranged from 2 to approximately 30. These numbers simply represent users' needs, not physical limitations. This specification does not constrain explicitly the maximum number of drops, nor is that number explicitly defined by cable parameters. The largest number of drops can be facilitated by minimizing the drop cable length.

11.11.3 Network Topology. The preferred network topology is a long unbranched trunk requiring a single trunk cable to be routed to every station site in turn. In principle, branches could be added by lossy nondirectional impedance-matching couplers, but this would usually lead to building a smaller network or requiring more expensive cable; such an approach is not recommended.

This specification does cover the use of active, regenerative repeaters for branching. Even so, the branch should be relatively long to justify its existence, and the evaluation of alternate unbranched routes is recommended first. The range of low-loss cables available makes it possible to meet most local area network needs with a completely passive medium.

11.11.4 Drop Cables. The maximum length of drop cables permitted for phase-continuous-FSK bus networks is 350 mm. Since it is not matched or terminated, the drop cable is an open stub much shorter than $\frac{1}{4}$ wavelength, and effectively presents a shunt capacitance to the trunk cable. (The purpose of the length limitation is to limit the shunt capacitance, which causes reflections, not to limit the length per se.)

Each drop causes a small reflection on the trunk. Since the size of the reflection is proportional to the stub length, it is beneficial to keep the stub length short. Only the maximum length is specified, and the length may be zero if convenient or desirable. This minimizes reflections and maximizes the number of drops possible in a given network.

11.11.5 Trunk Connection. The drop cable is usually coupled to the trunk cable through a simple tee connection. This is typically a matched 75 Ω connector for the trunk cable used, with a suitable adapter for the drop cable.

If use of a particular tap is permanently discontinued, the tee connector should be replaced with a corresponding straight-through (barrel) type, or the stub cable should be removed from the tee connector and replaced with a standard shielding tap.

NOTE: Since each tap introduces an impedance mismatch, spacing of taps can cause signal distortion due to accumulated reflections degrading signal-to-noise of the cable system. Network designers should consider the effects of tap placement.

11.11.6 Grounding. The trunk cable shield may be floating, single-point, or multiple-point grounded as far as signal transmission is concerned. Grounds thus may be installed in accordance with EMI and safety codes and other regulations applicable to the particular installation. This usually means grounding where the cable enters or leaves a building, and at intervals not exceeding approximately 100 m within the building. Grounds should be applied carefully by a clamp that does not crush or damage the cable, because such cable damage causes serious reflections. Suitable clamps are available from suppliers of CATV system hardware.

11.11.7 Surge Protection. It is good practice to protect the cable against ground surges due to lightning. Suitable surge protectors that meet the requirements of IEEE Std 472-1974 (R 1979)[12] should be used at each end of the cable. The capacitive loading of surge protectors shall be small to avoid affecting physical layer entity (modem) performance, and shall not exceed values permitted for a standard tap. For maximum surge protection, a low impedance, heavy-duty ground connection is required.

11.11.8 Termination. The trunk cable shall be properly terminated at both ends. Shielded 75 Ω coaxial terminations with good broadband characteristics are commercially available for most coaxial cables. Since transmit levels do not exceed 60 dB (1 mV, 37.5 Ω), power ratings of 0.25 W are sufficient.

Do not terminate any drop cable. Drop cables are short unmatched stubs on the trunk cable; they shall present a <u>high</u> dc shunt impedance to the tee connector.

11.11.9 Joining Cable Sections. In general, a trunk cable will consist of a number of separate sections of coaxial cable, each with a matched connector at each end. Some sections will be joined by the tee connectors used for taps, and others will be joined by straight-through (barrel) connectors. A good engineering practice is to maintain constant impedance between cable sections by using one cable type (such as RG-6 or RG-11) from one manufacturer for the entire trunk. This practice avoids significant reflections where cables are joined. When dissimilar types must be joined, it is suggested that a lossy (attenuating) impedance-matched connector, such as a tap, be employed to reduce repeated reflections.

11.11.10 Pretested Cable. It is a good practice to pretest all trunk cable before installation. The objectives are to ensure that the attenuation does not exceed the expected values at frequencies of interest, and to ensure that concealed (that is, internal) discontinuities that can cause reflections do not exist. For a nominal charge most cable suppliers will pretest or certify all cable before shipment.

On-site testing after installation is also recommended, since any damage may degrade operating margins or cause outright failure. A recommended method for testing the installed cable for damage, improper termination, shorts, or discontinuities is to use a time domain reflectometer, which is available from various instrument manufacturers.

12. Single-Channel Phase-Coherent-FSK Bus Physical Layer Specification

The functional, electrical, and mechanical characteristics of one specific form of physical layer (single-channel phase-coherent-FSK bus) of this standard are specified in this section. This specification includes the physical layer embodiments found in stations which could attach to the single-channel phase-coherent-FSK bus local area network. The relationship of this section to other sections of this standard and to LAN specifications is illustrated in Fig 12-1. The relationship of this section to the single-channel phase-coherent-FSK bus physical layer entity and medium is illustrated in Fig 12-2.

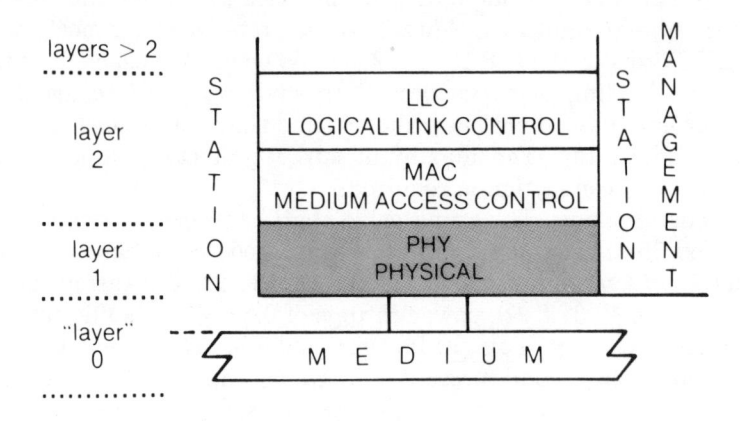

**Fig 12-1
Relation to LAN Model**

This standard specifies these physical layer entities only insofar as necessary to ensure

(1) The interoperability of implementations conforming to this specification
(2) The protection of the local area network and those using it.

12.1 Nomenclature. Terms used in this section whose meanings within the section are more specific than indicated in the glossary of Ref [1] are as follows:

single-channel FSK coaxial system. A system whereby information is encoded, frequency modulated onto a carrier, and impressed on the coaxial transmission medium. At any point on the medium, only one information signal at a time can be present in the channel without disruption.

TOKEN-PASSING BUS

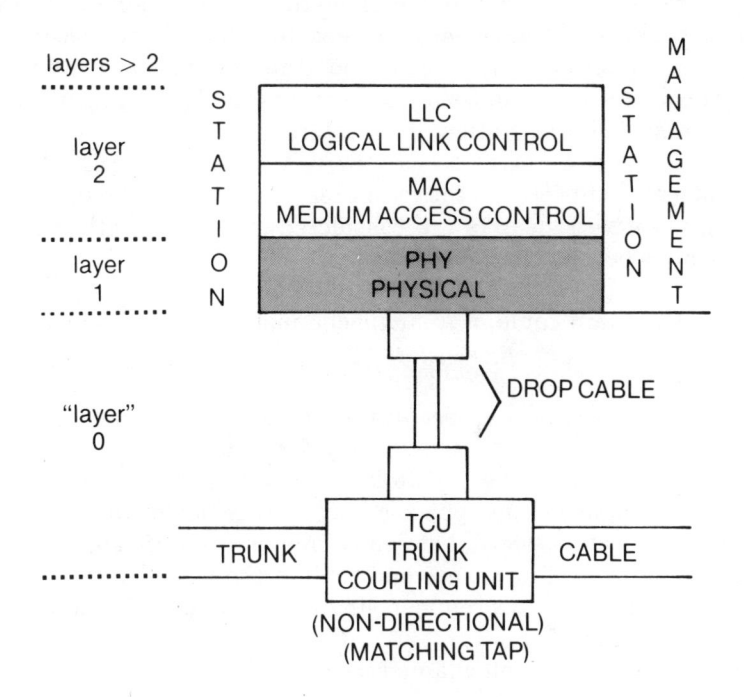

IEEE
Std 802.4-1985

**Fig 12-2
Physical Hardware Partitioning,
Token-Passing Bus Local Area Network**

drop cable. The smaller diameter flexible coaxial cable of the single-channel phase-coherent-FSK bus medium which connects to a station.

FSK, Frequency Shift Keying. A modulation technique whereby information is impressed upon a carrier by shifting the frequency of the transmitted signal to one of a small set of frequencies.

phase-coherent FSK. A particular form of FSK where the two signaling frequencies are integrally related to the data rate and transitions between the two signaling frequencies are made at zero crossings of the carrier waveform.

regenerative repeater. A device used to extend the length, topology, or interconnectivity of a local area network beyond that imposed by the minimum transmit and receive level specifications of the station and the connectivity restrictions of the medium. Regenerative repeaters perform the basic actions of restoring signal amplitude, waveform, and timing. They also prefix enough pad_idle symbols to a transmission to compensate for any symbols lost in transmission from the prior station or repeater.

station. Equipment connected to the local area network. For the purposes of this standard, regenerative repeaters are considered stations, whether or not they have functionality beyond that of a repeater.

trunk cable. The main cable of a single-channel phase-coherent-FSK coaxial cable system.

12.2 Object. The object of this specification is to
(1) Provide the physical means necessary for communication between local network stations employing the LAN token bus access method described in this standard using a single-channel phase-coherent-FSK bus medium.
(2) Define a physical interface that can be implemented independently among different manufacturers of hardware and achieve the intended level of compatibility when interconnected to a common single-channel phase-coherent-FSK bus local area network medium.
(3) Provide a communication channel capable of high bandwidth and low bit error rate performance. The resultant mean bit error rate at the MAC service interface (see Section 8) shall be less than 10^{-8}, with a mean undetected bit error rate of less than 10^{-9} at that interface.
(4) Provide for ease of installation and service in a wide range of environments.
(5) Provide for high network availability.
(6) Facilitate low-cost implementations.
(7) Facilitate upgrade to a broadband bus medium with corresponding physical layer entities.

12.3 Compatibility Considerations. This standard applies to physical layer entities which are designed to operate on a 75 Ω coaxial cable configured in a CATV-like trunk and drop cable structure. All single-channel phase-coherent-FSK bus coaxial cable systems that signal at the same data rate shall be compatible at the medium interface. Specific implementations based on this standard may be conceived in different ways provided compatibility at the medium is maintained.

12.4 Operational Overview of the Single-Channel Phase-Coherent-FSK Bus Medium. The communications medium specified in Section 13 consists of a CATV-like trunk and drop structure, with branching (splitters) possible in both the trunk and drop cables. The medium's trunk cable is connected to the drop cables by nondirectional passive impedance-matching networks (taps), and the drop cables in turn are connected to the stations. Extension of the topology or size of the local area network beyond that permitted by the transmitter and receiver specifications of this section is accomplished by way of active regenerative repeaters which are connected in series in the trunk cabling.

12.5 Overview of the Phase-Coherent-FSK Bus Physical Layer

12.5.1 General Description of Functions. The functions performed by the single-channel phase-coherent-FSK bus physical layer entity are described informally here. Jointly these functions provide a means whereby MAC-symbols presented at the MAC interface of one physical layer entity can be conveyed to all of the physical layer entities on the bus for presentation to their respective MAC interfaces.

12.5.1.1 Symbol Transmission and Reception Functions. Successive MAC-symbols presented to the physical layer entity at its MAC service interface are applied to an encoder which produces as output a three PHY-symbol code: {H}, {L}, {off}.

That output is then applied to a two-tone FSK modulator which represents each {H} as one full cycle of a tone whose period is exactly one-half of the MAC-symbol period, each {L} as one half cycle of a tone whose full-cycle period is exactly the MAC-symbol period, and each {off} as no tone for the same half MAC-symbol period. This modulated signal is then ac coupled to the single-channel phase-coherent-FSK bus medium and conveyed by the medium to one or more receivers.

Each receiver is also ac coupled to the bus medium. It bandpass filters the received signal to reduce received noise, demodulates the filtered signal, and then infers the transmitted PHY-symbol from the presence of carrier and the frequency of the received signal. It recovers the timing of the transmitted PHY-symbols directly from the representation of the PHY-symbols on the medium. It then decodes that inferred PHY-symbol by an inverse of the encoding process and presents the resultant decoded MAC-symbols at its MAC service interface.

For all MAC-symbols except pad_idle, this decoding process is an exact inverse of the encoding process in the absence of errors. The pad_idle symbols, which are referred to collectively as preamble, are transmitted at the start of each MAC frame, both to provide a training signal for receivers and to provide a nonzero minimum separation between consecutive frames. Since each transmission begins with pad_idle symbols, it is expected that some of these initial symbols may be "lost in transit" between the transmitter and receivers. Additionally, in phase-coherent FSK systems the encodings for the MAC-symbols pad_idle and one are identical, and receivers are permitted to decode the transmitted representation of pad_idle as one and report it as such to the MAC entity.

12.5.1.2 Regenerative Repeater Functions. Regenerative repeaters may be used to extend the network size beyond the maximum signal loss budget of an unassisted station. They do so by connecting two or more media segments and repeating anything "heard" on one segment to the other segments. For the purposes of this standard, regenerative repeaters are considered stations, whether or not they have functionality beyond that of a repeater.

12.5.1.3 Jabber-Inhibit Function. To protect the local area network from most faults in a station, each station contains a jabber-inhibit function. This function serves as a "watchdog" on the transmitter; if the station does not turn off its transmitter after a prolonged time (roughly one-half second), then the transmitter output shall be automatically disabled for at least the remainder of the transmission.

12.5.1.4 Local Administrative Functions. These are optional functions which select various modes of operation. They are activated either manually, or by way of the physical layer entity's station management interface, or both. They can include

(1) Enabling or disabling each transmitter output (A redundant medium configuration has two or more transmitter outputs.)

(2) Selecting the received signal source: either medium (if redundant media are present), or any available loopback point

NOTE: If a loopback point is selected, then all transmitter outputs shall be inhibited.

12.5.2 Model Used for the Functional Specification. The detailed functional specifications are modeled after CCITT V. series modem specifications Refs [16] and [17], particulary the V.36 specification, with additional detail added where necessary.

12.5.3 Basic Functions and Options. Symbol transmission and reception functions and jabber-inhibit functions are required in all implementations. All other functions are optional.

12.6 Detailed Application of Section 9, Generic Station Management to Physical Layer Interface Service Specification. The range of permissible values for the parameters specified in Section 9 are as follows:

LAN_topology_type parameter of PHY_RESET.confirmation primitive. The value of this parameter shall be token_bus.

PHY_role parameter of PHY_RESET.confirmation primitive. The value of this parameter shall be originate_and_repeat for bus repeater stations, and originate_only for all other stations.

Mode_class parameter of PHY_MODAL_CAPABILITY_QUERY and PHY_MODE_QUERY primitives. The mode_class parameter shall specify min_post_silence_preamble_length, transmitter_output_inhibits, or received_signal_sources. The value read for min_post_silence_preamble_length shall be equal to two octets at 5 Mb/s and three octets at 10 Mb/s. All other values of the mode_class parameter shall elicit an undefined_mode_class confirmation.

Mode_class parameter of PHY_MODE_SELECT primitives. The mode_class parameter shall specify transmitter_output_inhibits or received_signal_sources. All other values of the mode_class parameter shall elicit a failure confirmation.

12.7 Single-Channel Phase-Coherent-FSK Bus Physical Layer Functional, Electrical, and Mechanical Specifications. Unless otherwise stated, all voltage and power levels specified are in rms and dB (1 mV, 75 Ω) [dBmV]

rms, respectively, based on transmissions of arbitrary data patterns.

12.7.1 Data Signaling Rates. The standard data signaling rates for phase-coherent FSK systems are 5 Mb/s and 10 Mb/s. The permitted tolerance for each signaling rate is ±0.01% for an originating station, and is ±0.015% for a repeater station while repeating. When a composite physical layer entity is embodied in a regenerative repeater, it shall originate signaling on all trunks at exactly the same data rate.

12.7.2 Symbol Encoding. The physical layer entity transmits symbols presented to it at its MAC interface by the medium access control sublayer entity. The possible MAC-symbols are (see 8.2.1): zero, one, non_data, pad_idle, and silence. Each of these MAC-symbols is encoded into a pair of PHY-symbols from a different three-symbol {H}, {L}, {off} code and then transmitted. The encoding action to be taken for each of the input MAC-symbols is

(1) Silence —Each silence symbol shall be encoded as the sequence {off off}.
(2) Pad_idle—Each pad_idle symbol shall be encoded as the sequence {L L}.
(3) Zero —Each zero symbol shall be encoded as the sequence {H H}.
(4) One —Each one symbol shall be encoded as the sequence {L L}.
(5) Non_data—Non_data symbols are transmitted by the MAC sublayer entity in pairs. Each such pair of consecutive non_data symbols shall be encoded as the sequence {H L} {L H}. Thus the (start frame delimiter) subsequence

non_data non_data zero non_data non_data zero

shall be encoded as the sequence
{H L} {L H} {H H} {H L} {L H} {H H},

and the (end frame delimiter) subsequence

non_data non_data one non_data non_data one

shall be encoded as the sequence
{H L} {L H} {L L} {H L} {L H} {L L}.

12.7.3 Line Signal (at the line output of the station). The PHY-symbols resulting from the encoding of 12.7.2 shall be converted directly to their line representations, as described in 12.7.3.1, and the resultant signaling shall be coupled to the single-channel phase-coherent-FSK bus medium as specified in 12.7.5.

12.7.3.1 The line signal representations of the {H}, {L} and {off} PHY-symbols shall be as follows:

(1) An {H} shall be represented as one full cycle of a signal, starting and ending with a nominal zero amplitude, whose period is equal to half the period of MAC-symbol delivery to the MAC entity at the MAC interface

(2) An {L} shall be represented as one half cycle of a signal, starting and ending with a nominal zero amplitude, whose period is equal to the period of MAC-symbol delivery to the MAC entity at the MAC interface, with the phase of the representing half cycle changing at each successive {L}

(3) An {off} shall be represented by no signal for a period equal to one half of the period of MAC-symbol delivery to the MAC entity at the MAC interface.

Table 12-1 summarizes this relationship

Table 12-1
Data Rate Versus Signaling Frequencies

Data Rate (Mb/s)	Frequency of Lower Tone (MHz)	Frequency of Higher Tone (MHz)
5	5.0	10.0
10	10.0	20.0

The maximum jitter in the period of any {L} or half-cycle of any {H} shall be no more than ±2% of the period of MAC-symbol delivery to the MAC entity at the MAC interface.

12.7.3.2 The output level of the transmitted signal into a 75 Ω resistive load shall be between +60 dB and +63 dB (1 mV) [dBmV].

12.7.3.3 The residual or leakage transmitter-off output signal shall be no more than −28 dB (1 mV, 75 Ω) [dBmV].

12.7.4 Jabber Inhibit. Each physical layer entity shall have a self-interrupt capability to inhibit modulation from reaching the local area network medium. Hardware within the physical layer (with no external message other than the prolonged detection of an output-on condition within the transmitter) shall provide a nominal window of one-half second ± 25% during which time a normal data link transmission may occur. If a transmission is in excess of this duration, the jabber-inhibit function shall operate to inhibit any further output from reaching the medium. Reset of this jabber inhibit function shall occur upon receipt of a station management PHY_RESET.request (see 9.2.1). Additional resetting means are permitted.

12.7.5 Coupling to the Medium. The physical layer functions are intended to operate satisfactorily over a medium consisting of a 75 Ω bidirectional coaxial trunk cable, nondirectional impedance matching taps, and 75 Ω drop cables. The mechanical coupling of the station to the medium shall be to a drop cable by way of a 75 Ω female F-series connector on the station, as specified in Section 13. The maximum VSWR at that F-connector shall be 1.5:1 or less when that connector is terminated with a 75 Ω resistive load, as measured over the spectral range of 2 MHz to 30 MHz.

Both the transmitter and the receiver shall be ac coupled to the center conductor of the drop cable of the 75 Ω single-channel phase-coherent-FSK bus coaxial cable medium, and the breakdown voltage of that ac coupling means shall be at least 500 V ac rms. In addition to this coupling, the shield of the coaxial cable medium shall be connected to chassis ground, and the impedance of that connection shall be less than 0.1 Ω.

12.7.6 Receiver Sensitivity and Selectivity. The physical layer entity shall be capable of providing an undetected bit error rate of 10^{-9} or lower, and a detected bit error rate of 10^{-8} or lower, when receiving signals with a level of -15 dB to $+66$ dB (1 mV, 75 Ω) [dBmV], in a system with an in-band noise floor of -25 dB (1 mV, 75 Ω) [dBmV] or less, as measured at the point of connection to the station.

12.7.7 Symbol Timing. Each physical layer entity shall recover the PHY-symbol timing information contained within the waveform of the received signal, and shall use this recovered timing information to determine the precise rate at which MAC-symbols should be delivered to the MAC interface. The jitter in this reported MAC-symbol timing relative to the PHY-symbol timing actually within the received signaling shall be 5% or less. When receiving silence from the medium, it shall be reported at the MAC interface at a rate determined by 12.7.1.

12.7.8 Symbol Decoding. After demodulation and determination of each received signaled PHY-symbol, that PHY-symbol shall be decoded by the process inverse to that described in 12.7.2, and the decoded MAC-symbols shall be reported at the MAC interface. (As noted in 12.5.1.1, receivers are permitted to decode the transmitted representation of pad_idle as one.) Whenever a signaled PHY-symbol sequence is received for which the encoding process has no inverse, those PHY-symbols shall be decoded as an appropriate number of bad_signal MAC-symbols and reported as such at the MAC interface. In such cases, the receiving entity should resynchronize the decoding process as rapidly as possible.

12.7.9 Transmitter Enable/Disable and Received Signal Source Selection. [OPTIONAL] The ability to enable and disable the transmission of modulation onto the single-channel phase-coherent-FSK bus medium as directed by the station management entity is recommended but optional.

The ability to select the source of received signaling, either a loopback point within the physical layer entity or (one of) the (possibly redundant) media, as directed by the station management entity, is recommended but optional. When such an option is invoked and the selected source is other than (one of) the media, transmission to all connected single-channel phase-coherent-FSK bus media shall be disabled automatically while such selection is in force.

12.7.10 Redundant Media Considerations. Embodiments of this standard which can function with redundant media are not precluded, provided that the embodiment as delivered functions correctly in a nonredundant single-cable environment. Where redundant media are employed, the provisions of 12.7.4 and 12.7.9 shall apply separately and independently to each single medium interface, and much of 12.7.9 shall be mandatory. Specifically, separate jabber inhibit monitoring shall exist for each medium (although common inhibition is permissible), receiver signal source selection shall be provided capable of selecting any one of the redundant media, and it shall be possible to enable or disable each single transmitter independently of all other redundant transmitters when the source of received signaling is one of the redundant media.

12.7.11 Reliability. The physical layer entity shall be designed so that its probability of causing a communication failure among other stations connected to the medium is less than 10^{-6} per hour of continuous (or discontinuous) operation. For regenerative repeaters this requirement is relaxed to a probability of 10^{-5} per hour of operation. Connectors and other passive components comprising the means of connecting the station to the coaxial cable medium shall be designed to minimize the probability of total network failure.

12.7.12 Regenerative Repeater Considerations. The physical layer entity of a regenerative repeater can be considered to be a composite entity, with separate electrical and mechanical low-level transmit and receive functions for each connected trunk segment (that is, each port), all under a common encoding, decoding, timing-recovery and control function.

The basic mode of operation, originating or repeating, shall be determined by the superior MAC entity and conveyed by the PHY_MODE.request primitive (see 8.2.3). When originating, the repeater physical layer entity shall originate the symbol timing provided to the MAC entity and transmit the encoded MAC-symbols onto all connected trunk segments. It shall use either internal loopback or any one of the attached trunks as the source of PHY-symbols which are decoded and reported by way of the PHY_DATA.indicate primitive.

When switching to repeating, the repeater physical layer entity shall delay for an implementation-dependent amount of time (typically a few symbol-durations) to prevent repeating the end of the just-prior transmission, and shall then scan the connected ports for one on which signaling is being received. During the delay period, and while this scan for signal is unsuccessful, the repeater physical layer entity shall indicate <u>silence</u> symbols to its MAC-entity using its locally-originated symbol timing. Upon detecting signaling at one or more ports, the repeater entity shall select one of those active ports as the source of its received signaling. It shall then temporarily disable that selected port's low-level transmitter function, decode the received signaling, retime that signaling before or after decoding so that the implementation-determined constant phase relationship between PHY_DATA.indicate and PHY_DATA.request is maintained (see 8.2), and indicate the decoded MAC-symbols to its associated MAC entity. It should then vary the frequency of the MAC-symbol timing, within the bounds of this subsection (12.7), as necessary to maintain the proper relationship with the frequency of the received PHY-symbol timing.

When repeating, after decoding the MAC-symbol <u>silence</u> received from the active port, the repeater physical layer entity shall await the MAC-entity's transmission of <u>silence</u> by way of a PHY_DATA.request, shall then re-enable the temporarily-disabled low-level transmitter function, and shall then again follow the procedure outlined in the prior paragraph just as if the MAC entity had just switched to repeating.

In summary, when the MAC entity is originating

(1) The physical layer entity alone shall determine the MAC-symbol timing

(2) Transmission occurs on all attached trunks (unless disabled by the provisions of 12.7.9)

(3) Internal loopback or any one of the attached trunks can be used as the source of PHY-symbols which are decoded and reported by way of the PHY_DATA.indicate primitive.

When the MAC entity is repeating

(a) The physical layer entity first delays long enough to ensure that the prior transmission is not repeated, then scans all attached trunks for signaling and selects one of those trunks with signaling as the source of received signaling

(b) Transmission to the selected trunk is temporarily inhibited

(c) The received signaling from the selected trunk is decoded and indicated to the MAC entity

(d) The frequency of MAC-symbol timing is varied as necessary (at most ±0.015%) to track the frequency of the peer transmitter's MAC-symbol timing

(e) Upon detecting a loss of signaling (that is, receiving silence) from the selected trunk, the physical layer entity first waits until the MAC entity requests transmission of silence, and then repeats the whole procedure.

12.8 Environmental Specifications

{NOTE: Subsection 12.8 is not a part of the ISO standard. The subject of international standards in this area is under study by the International Electrotechnical Commission and other organizations.}

12.8.1 Safety Requirements. A number of recommendations and guidelines related to safety are given in this subsection. The list is incomplete; neither does it address all possible safety concerns. The designer is urged to consult the relevant local, national, and international safety regulations to ensure compliance with the appropriate standards. Additional guidance on many relevant regulatory requirements is provided in EIA CB8-1981[9].

Local area network cable systems as described in Section 13 are subject to at least four direct electrical safety hazards during their use, and designers of connecting equipment should be aware of these hazards. The hazards are

(1) Direct contact between local network components and power or lighting circuits

(2) Static charge buildup on local network cables and components

(3) High-energy transients coupled onto the local network cabling system

(4) Potential differences between safety grounds to which various network components are connected.

These electrical safety hazards, to which all similar cabling systems are subject, should be alleviated properly for a local network to perform properly. In addition to provisions for properly handling these faults in an operational system, special measures shall be taken to ensure that the intended safety features are not negated when attaching or detaching equipment from the local area network medium of an existing network.

Sound installation practice, as defined by ANSI/NFPA 70-1984[3], Article 820 and applicable local codes and regulations shall be followed in every instance in which such practice is applicable.

12.8.2 Electromagnetic and Electric Environment. Sources of interference from the environment include electromagnetic fields, electrostatic discharge, transient voltages between earth connections, etc. Several sources of interference contribute to voltage build-up between the coaxial cable and the earth connection, if any, of the station.

The physical layer entity embodiment shall meet its specifications when operating in an ambient plane-wave field of

(1) 2 V/m from 10 kHz through 30 MHz
(2) 5 V/m from 30 MHz through 1 GHz.

12.8.3 Temperature and Humidity. Any embodiment of this standard is expected to operate over a reasonable range of environmental conditions related to temperature, humidity, and physical handling such as shock and vibration. Specific requirements and values for these parameters are considered to be beyond the scope of this standard. Manufacturers are requested to indicate in the literature associated with system components and equipment (and on the components if possible) the operating environment specifications to facilitate selection, installation, and maintenance of these components.

12.8.4 Regulatory Requirements. The following regulatory requirements may apply to local area network equipment and media:
ANSI/NFPA 70-1984[3] Articles 250, 800, and 820, ANSI/UL 94-1979[4] Rated under V-0, ANSI/UL 114-1982[5], ANSI/UL 478-1979[6], CSA Standard C22.2 No 154-M 1983[8], FCC Docket 20780-1980[10], Part 15, Subpart J and Part 76, Subpart K, and IEC 716-1983[11].

12.9 Labeling. It is recommended that each embodiment (and supporting documentation) of a physical layer entity conformant to this standard be labeled in a manner visible to the user with at least these parameters

(1) Specific sections of the standards to which the equipment conforms

(2) Data rate capabilities in Mb/s

(3) Worst-case round-trip delay (for nonrepeaters) or one-way delay (for repeaters) which this equipment induces on a two-way transmission exchange between stations, as specified in 6.1.9

(4) Operating modes and selection capabilities as defined in 12.7.9 and 12.7.10.

Additionally, when the station has multiple F-connectors (for example, for redundant media), the role of each such connector shall be designated clearly by markings on the station in the vicinity of that connector.

13. Single-Channel Phase-Coherent-FSK Bus Medium "Layer" Specification

The functional, electrical, and mechanical characteristics of one specific form of medium "layer" (single-channel phase-coherent-FSK bus) of this standard are specified in this section. This specification includes the medium "layer" embodiments of a single-channel phase-coherent-FSK bus local area network. The relationship of this section to other sections of this standard and to LAN

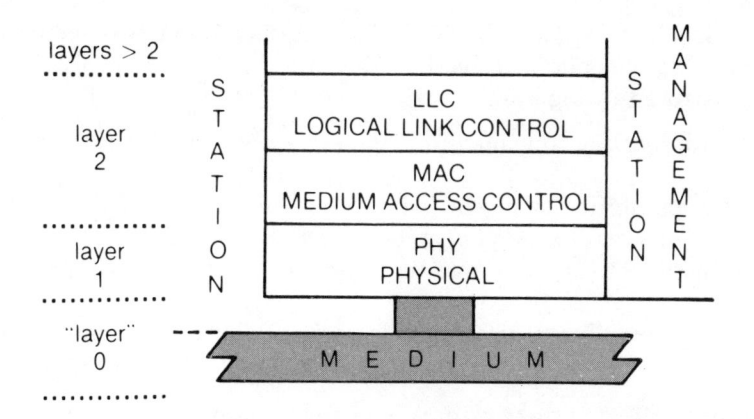

**Fig 13-1
Relation to LAN Model**

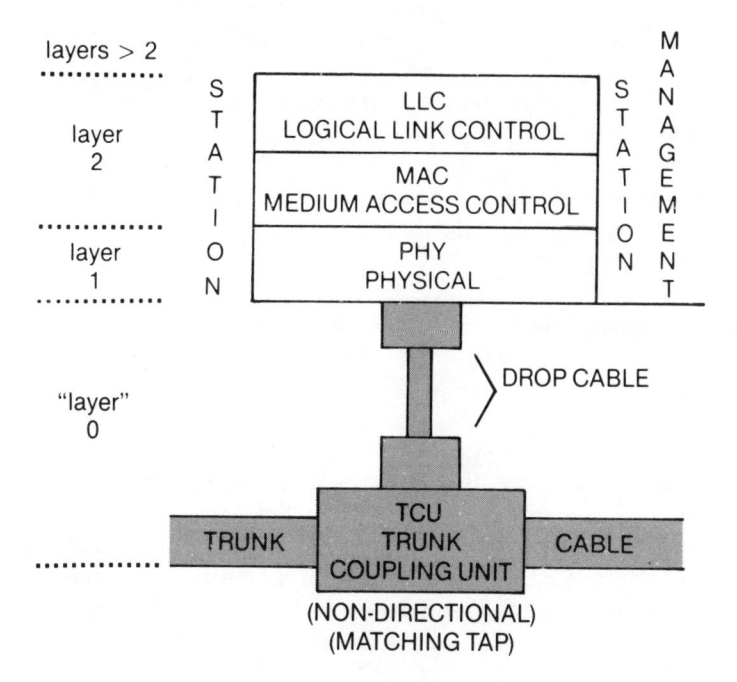

**Fig 13-2
Physical Hardware Partitioning,
Token-Passing Bus Local Area Network**

specifications is illustrated in Fig 13-1. The relationship of this section to the single-channel phase-coherent-FSK bus physical layer and medium "layer" entities is illustrated in Fig 13-2.

This standard specifies the medium "layer" only insofar as necessary to ensure

(1) The interoperability of physical layer entities conforming to Section 12 when connected to a medium layer conformant to this section

(2) The protection of the local area network itself and those using it

13.1 Nomenclature. Terms used in this section whose meanings within the section are more specific than indicated in the glossary of Ref [1] are as follows:

single-channel FSK coaxial system. A system whereby information is encoded, frequency modulated onto a carrier, and impressed on the coaxial transmission medium. At any point on the medium, only one information signal at a time can be present in the channel without disruption.

drop cable. The smaller diameter flexible coaxial cable of the single-channel phase-coherent-FSK medium which connects to a station.

F-connector. A 75 Ω F-series coaxial cable connector (of the kind commonly found on consumer television and video equipment).

FSK, Frequency Shift Keying. A modulation technique whereby information is impressed upon a carrier by shifting the frequency of the transmitted signal to one of a small set of frequencies.

phase-coherent FSK. A particular form of FSK where the two signaling frequencies are integrally related to the data rate and transitions between the two signaling frequencies are made at zero crossings of the carrier waveform.

(impedance-matching) power splitter. A small module which electrically and mechanically couples one large diameter trunk cable to other large diameter trunk cables, providing a branching topology for the single-channel phase-coherent-FSK trunk. A power splitter combines signal energy received at its ports, splitting any signal energy received from a trunk symmetrically among the other trunks. It passes low frequency (< 1 kHz) ac power between the trunk cables. It contains only passive electrical components (R, L, C).

regenerative repeater. A device used to extend the length, topology, or interconnectivity of a single-channel phase-coherent-FSK bus local area network beyond the limits imposed by the minimum transmit and receive level specifications of the station. Regenerative repeaters perform the basic actions of restoring signal amplitude, waveform, and timing. They also prefix enough preamble signaling to a transmission to compensate for any lost in transmission from the prior station or repeater.

TOKEN-PASSING BUS

IEEE
Std 802.4-1985

(impedance-matching) splitter. A smaller version of the power splitter used to couple drop cables together symmetrically. It does not pass low-frequency ac power between the drop cables.

station. Equipment connected to the local area network. For the purposes of this standard, regenerative repeaters are considered stations, whether or not they have functionality beyond that of a repeater.

(impedance-matching) tap. A small module which electrically and mechanically couples the large diameter trunk cable to smaller diameter drop cables, passes low-frequency (< 1 kHZ) ac power between trunk cable sections, and isolates that ac power from drop cable sections. It splits the signal energy received from each trunk cable very asymmetrically, with the bulk of that signal energy passed to the other trunk cable and only a small percentage passed to the drop cables. It combines any signal energy received from the drop cables, splits a small part of that signal energy equally among the trunk cables, and passes most of the rest of that combined signal energy back to the drop cables. It contains only passive electrical components (R, L, C).

trunk cable. The main (larger-diameter), usually semirigid, coaxial cable of a single-channel phase-coherent-FSK bus coaxial cable system. Both ac power and signaling are carried on semirigid cables; only signaling is carried on flexible cables.

13.2 Object. The object of this specification is to
  (1) Provide the physical medium necessary for communication between local network stations employing the token bus access method defined in this standard and a single-channel phase-coherent-FSK bus physical "layer"
  (2) Provide for high network availability
  (3) Provide for ease of installation and service in a wide range of environments
  (4) Provide for upgrading the single-channel phase-coherent-FSK bus medium to a broadband medium as specified in Section 15, by replacement of tap components and installation of amplifiers and a head-end remodulator, without replacing the coaxial cable itself
  (5) Permit use of components similar to, and in some cases identical with, those mass produced for the cable TV industry, and of a similar set of installation practices

13.3 Compatibility Considerations. This standard applies to medium "layer" entities which are designed to operate as CATV-like but nondirectional single-channel phase-coherent-FSK bus coaxial cable systems. Such systems generally use nondirectional taps in standard CATV tap housings, and standard CATV connectors, power supplies, and coaxial cable. This specification applies to a single trunk system in which two-way communication is accomplished through the use of nondirectional taps and splitters and, in large systems, multidirectional regenerative repeaters.

All implementations of medium "layer" entities conformant to this standard shall be compatible at their station interfaces. Specific implementations based on this standard may be conceived in different ways provided compatibility at the actual station interfaces is maintained.

13.4 Overview of the Phase-Coherent-FSK Bus Medium "Layer"

13.4.1 General Description of Functions. The functions performed by the single-channel phase-coherent-FSK bus medium "layer" entity are described informally here. Jointly these functions provide a means whereby signaling presented at the station interfaces of drop cables can be combined and conveyed to all of the stations on all of the medium's drop cables. Thus stations connected to these drop cables can communicate.

13.4.1.1 Operational Overview of the Single-Channel Phase-Coherent-FSK Bus Medium. Stations are connected to the larger-diameter trunk coaxial cable(s) of single-channel phase-coherent-FSK bus systems by smaller-diameter drop cables and impedance-matching taps. These taps are passive devices which are nondirectional (that is, omnidirectional) with regard to signal propagation, and which block any flow of ac trunk power to the drop cables. The nondirectional characteristics of the taps permit the station's signal to propagate in both directions along the trunk cable. The taps also minimize the effects of reflections due to any impedance mismatches along the trunk or on other drop cables.

The topology of the single-channel phase-coherent-FSK bus system is that of a highly branched tree without a root, with the stations connected as leaves to the tree's branches. Branching is accomplished in the trunk itself by way of regenerative repeaters (described below) and power splitters, which provide nondirectional coupling of the signaling carried on the trunk cables similar to that of the just-described taps, and also nondirectional coupling of ac power which may be carried on the trunk cables. Like the taps, the power splitters also employ only passive electrical components (R, L, C only).

Branching in the drop cables is provided by (drop cable) splitters (which also block ac power flow among their ports). They also employ only passive electrical components.

Regenerative repeaters provide both branching and the ability to extend a system topology beyond that permitted by the minimum transmit and receive level specifications of an unassisted station. The regenerative repeaters of the single-channel phase-coherent-FSK bus system may be connected to trunk cables by taps and drop cables, or they may be placed in special housings at the juncture of trunk cables and powered from the trunk cables themselves. Low-voltage (30 V or 60 V) ac power may be carried on the center conductor and grounded shield of the trunk cable at a nominal frequency of 50 Hz or 60 Hz; connected regenerative repeaters use some of that power and pass the rest to the connected trunk cables. Standard CATV power supplies and power-combining, and power-blocking components similar to those found in CATV systems, permit the power to be supplied to the trunk cabling at one or more points in the system.

13.4.1.2 Regenerative Repeater Functions. In an actual single-channel phase-coherent-FSK bus system, regenerative repeaters may be used to connect trunk segments into a highly branched topology, or to extend the length of, or number of taps on, a trunk beyond that which the unassisted station's minimum transmit and receive level specifications would allow. The repeater which performs these functions may be connected directly to the trunk coaxial cables in a manner akin to that of a CATV amplifier or power splitter, or it may be connected to the trunks by way of taps and flexible drop cables. For the purposes of this standard, regenerative repeaters are considered stations, whether or not they have functionality beyond that of a repeater.

In performing its repeating functions, the regenerative repeater (see 12.7.12) serves as a relay station, with a composite physical-layer entity (one sub-entity per connected trunk) and one medium-access entity monitoring and repeating the received composite signaling. When not transmitting for itself, the repeater's medium-access entity interprets the symbols received from the composite physical-layer entity. When a PHY-symbol other than {off} is received, the composite physical-layer entity determines which trunk carried the PHY-symbol, and it then selects that trunk as the source of reported signaling. Concurrently, the medium access entity begins to retransmit all MAC-symbols reported (onto the other trunks). When a collision or noise is detected (for example, bad_signal reported), the repeater's MAC entity sends an abort sequence (see 4.1.8) in lieu of the received MAC-symbols.

13.4.2 Model Used for the Functional Specification. The detailed functional specifications are modeled after CCITT H. series media specifications Refs [18] and [19], particularly the H.14 specification, with additional detail added where necessary.

13.4.3 Basic Characteristics and Options. All signal-conveyance characteristics and station-interface characteristics are mandatory. All other characteristics are optional.

13.5 Bibliography

GENERAL MOTORS UNIFIED COMMUNICATIONS SYSTEMS TASK FORCE OF MCC/CMC COMPUTERS IN MANUFACTURING SUBCOMMITTEE, General Specifications: Broadband Co-axial Cable Networks for Digital, Video, and Audio Transmission, General Motors, Detroit, Michigan, May 1978.

RHEINFELDER, W. CATV Circuit Engineering, TAB Books, Blue Ridge Summit, PA, 1975.

RHEINFELDER, W. CATV System Engineering, TAB Books, Blue Ridge Summit, PA, 1962.

Design and Construction of CATV Systems, RCA / Cablevision Systems, Van Nuys, CA.

Basic CATV Concepts, THETA-COM CATV / TEXSCAN, Phoenix, Arizona.

13.6 Single-Channel Phase-Coherent-FSK Bus Medium "Layer" Functional, Electrical and Mechanical Specifications. The single-channel phase-coherent-FSK bus medium "layer" entity is an entity whose sole function (relative to this standard) is signal transport between the stations of a single-channel phase-coherent-FSK bus local area network. Consequently only those characteristics of the medium "layer" entity which impinge on station to station signal transport, or on human and equipment safety, are specified in this standard.

An implementation of the medium "layer" entity shall be deemed conformant to this standard if it provides the specified signal transport services and characteristics for the stations of a single-channel phase-coherent-FSK bus local area network, and if it meets the relevant safety and environmental codes.

All measurements specified in 13.6 are to be made at the point of station or regenerative repeater connection to the medium. Unless otherwise stated, all voltage and power levels specified are in rms and dB (1 mV, 75 Ω) [dBmV] rms, respectively, based on transmissions of arbitrary data patterns.

13.6.1 Coupling to the Station. The connection of the single-channel phase-coherent-FSK bus medium to the station shall be by way of a flexible 75 Ω drop cable terminated in a male F-series 75 Ω connector; this combination shall mate with a female F-series 75 Ω connector mounted on the station.

In addition to this coupling, the shield(s) of the coaxial drop cable medium shall be connected to the shell of the terminating male F-connector and the impedance of that connection shall be less than 0.1 Ω. Also, the impedance of a connection between the shell of that male F-series connector and the outer barrel of a mated female F-series connector shall be less than 0.1 Ω.

13.6.2 Characteristic Impedance. The characteristic impedance of the single-channel phase-coherent-FSK bus medium shall be 75 ±3 Ω. The maximum VSWR at each of the medium's F-connectors shall be 1.5:1 or less when the F-connector is terminated with a 75 Ω resistive load, as measured over the entire single-channel phase-coherent-FSK cable spectrum of 2 MHz to 30 MHz.

13.6.3 Signal Level. When receiving the signal of a single station or regenerative repeater whose transmit level is as specified in 12.7.3.2, the single-channel phase-coherent-FSK bus medium shall present that signaling to the connected station or regenerative repeater at an amplitude of between −15 dB and +60 dB (1 mV, 75 Ω) [dBmV].

13.6.4 Distortion. The maximum group delay distortion shall fall within the limits specified by Eq 13-1 and Fig 13-3.

$$\text{PGD} = \begin{cases} \pm 2.5, & 1 \leq \frac{f}{B} \leq 2 \\ \pm 5.0 \left(\frac{f}{B} - 1.5\right), & 0.5 \leq \frac{f}{B} \leq 1 \text{ and } 2 \leq \frac{f}{B} \leq 2.5 \end{cases}$$

(Eq 13-1)

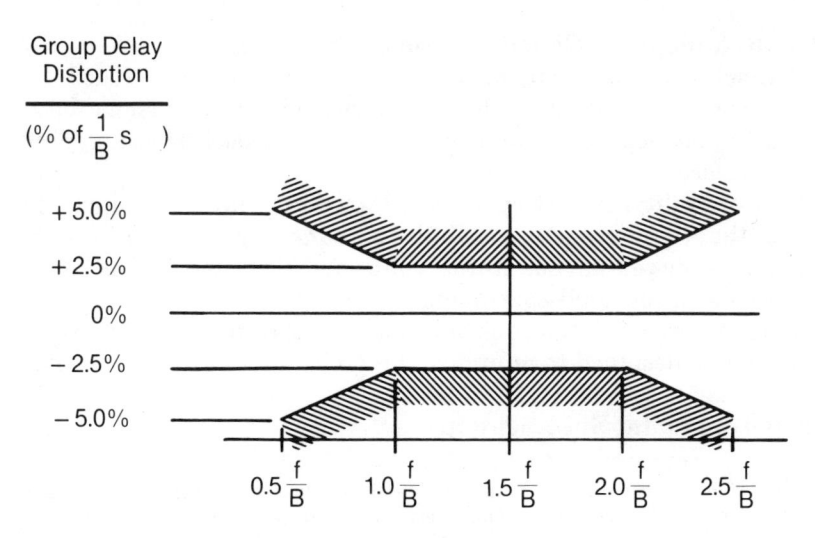

**Fig 13-3
Limits for Group-Delay Distortion**

where

    B   denotes the MAC-symbol signaling rate in bits/s
    f   denotes the frequency, Hz
    PGD denotes the maximum permissible group delay distortion as a <u>percent</u> of 1/B seconds.

13.6.5 Signal to Noise (S/N) Level. It is recommended that the in-band (2 MHz to 30 MHz) noise floor be −30 dB (1 mV, 75 Ω) [dBmV] or less. In no case shall it be less than -25 dB (1 mV, 75 Ω) [dBmV] (as measured at any point of station or regenerative repeater connection to the medium).

13.6.6 Power Handling Capability. The 50 Hz or 60 Hz ac power commonly carried on single-channel phase-coherent-FSK bus trunk cables shall not be carried on the (drop-cable) medium which connects directly to the station or regenerative repeater. The total power over the entire cable spectrum, as presented to the station or regenerative repeater, shall be less than 0.25 W.

13.6.7 Compatibility with the Stations and Regenerative Repeaters. An embodiment of a single-channel phase-coherent-FSK bus medium "layer" entity is deemed to support a specific single-channel phase-coherent-FSK bus local area network if the requirements of 13.6.1 through 13.6.6 (inclusive) are met when measured from each point of station connection to the medium, independent of which one of the points of station connection is chosen for test signal origination.

13.6.8 Redundancy Considerations. As implied by 12.7.10, redundant single-channel phase-coherent-FSK bus media are not precluded from this standard. Where redundant media are employed, the provisions of 13.6.1 to 13.6.7 shall apply separately and independently to each single nonredundant medium interface.

13.6.9 Reliability. All active (powered) medium "layer" equipment shall be designed so that the aggregate probability of that equipment causing a communication failure at more than one station connected to the medium is less than 10^{-4} per hour of continuous (or discontinuous) operation. Connectors and other passive components comprising the means of connecting the station to the coaxial cable medium shall be designed to minimize the probability of total network failure.

13.7 Environmental Specifications

{NOTE: Subsection 13.7 is not a part of the ISO standard. The subject of international standards in this area is under study by the International Electrotechnical Commission and other organizations.}

13.7.1 Safety Requirements. A number of recommendations and guidelines related to safety are given in this subsection. The list is incomplete; neither does it address all possible safety concerns. The designer is urged to consult the relevant local, national, and international safety codes and regulations to ensure compliance with the appropriate codes and standards. EIA CB 8-1981[9] provides additional guidance on many relevant regulatory requirements.

Local area network cable systems as described in Section 13 are subject to at least four direct electrical safety hazards during their use, and designers of connecting equipment should be aware of these hazards. The hazards are

(1) Direct contact between local network components and power or lighting circuits

(2) Static charge build-up on local network cables and components

(3) High-energy transients coupled onto the local network cabling system

(4) Potential differences between safety grounds to which various network components are connected

These electrical safety hazards, to which all similar cabling systems are subject, should be alleviated properly for a local area network to perform correctly. In addition to provisions for properly handling these faults in an operational system, special measures shall be taken to ensure that the intended safety features are not negated when attaching or detaching equipment from the local area network medium of an existing network.

13.7.1.1 Sound installation practice, as defined by ANSI/NFPA 70-1984[3], Article 820 and applicable local codes and regulations shall be followed in every instance in which such practice is applicable.

13.7.1.2 The shields of the trunk coaxial cable segments and the tap housings of all connected taps are connected in series in each branch of a properly installed single-channel phase-coherent-FSK bus medium. This connected conductive path shall be effectively grounded at more than one point along the length of the trunk cable, and at every point where the cable enters or leaves a building structure. The suggested practice is to effectively ground each tap housing, and to effectively ground the cable shield at least once per hundred meters on long cable runs between tap housings, but where large differences in ground potential exist between grounding points, other practices may be necessary. Effectively grounded means—permanently connected to earth through a ground connection of sufficiently low impedance and having sufficient ampacity to prevent the build-up of voltages that may result in undue hazard to connected equipment or to persons.

13.7.1.3 The shields of all drop coaxial cable segments shall be effectively grounded to the tap housings to which they connect.

13.7.1.4 Where there is reason to believe that the ground potential of an exposed shield of a coaxial cable, or housing of a connector or tap differs from the ground potential in the vicinity of that component by more than a few volts, an insulating sleeve, boot, or cover should be affixed to that equipment in such a manner as to ensure that users (not installers) of the equipment will not inadvertently complete a circuit between the exposed shield or housing and the local ground through body contact.

13.7.1.5 Installation and Maintenance Guidelines. Installation and maintenance guidelines developed within the CATV industry for inter- and intra-facility installation of coaxial cable systems shall be followed where applicable. In addition the following caution shall be observed:

> **CAUTION:** At no time should the shield of any portion of the coaxial trunk cable be permitted to float without an effective ground. If a section of floating cable is to be added to an existing cable system, the installer shall take care not to complete the circuit between the shield of the floating cable section and the grounded cable section through body contact.

13.7.1.6 The installation instructions for single-channel phase-coherent-FSK bus coaxial cable networks shall contain language which familiarizes the installer with the caution and guidelines of 13.7.1 through 13.7.1.5.

13.7.2 Electromagnetic and Electric Environment. Sources of interference from the environment include electromagnetic fields, electrostatic discharge, transient voltages between earth connections, etc. Several sources of interference contribute to voltage build-up between the coaxial cable and the earth connection, if any, of the station.

The medium "layer" entity embodiment shall meet its specifications when operating in an ambient plane-wave field of

(1) 2 V/m from 10 kHz through 30 MHz
(2) 5 V/m from 30 MHz through 1 GHz

13.7.3 Temperature and Humidity. Any embodiment of this standard is expected to operate over a reasonable range of environmental conditions related to temperature, humidity, and physical handling such as shock and vibration. Specific requirements and values for these parameters are considered to be beyond the scope of this standard. Manufacturers are requested to indicate in the literature associated with system components and equipment (and on the components if possible) the operating environment specifications to facilitate selection, installation, and maintenance of these components.

13.7.4 Regulatory Requirements. The following regulatory requirements may apply to local area network equipment and media:
ANSI/NFPA 70-1984[3], Articles 250, 800, and 820, ANSI/UL 94-1979[4], Rated under V-0, ANSI/UL 114-1982[5], ANSI/UL 478-1979[6], CSA Standard C22.2 No 154-M 1983[8], FCC Docket 20780-1980(Part 15)[10], and IEC 716-1983[11].

In particular, the FCC requirements for radiation from the coaxial cable medium and connected equipment [10], Part 15 do apply, and shall be considered in any embodiment of the medium "layer" entity specified in this standard.

NOTE: Equipment designed for CATV use must comply with the relevant FCC requirements [10], Part 76, which generally are more stringent than [10], Part 15.

13.8 Transmission Path Delay Considerations. When specifying an embodiment of a medium "layer" which conforms to the specifications of this Section (13), a vendor shall state the Transmission Path Delay as the maximum one-way delay which the single-channel phase-coherent-FSK bus medium could be expected to induce on a transmission from any connected station through any intervening regenerative repeaters to any other station. The delays induced by the transmitting and receiving stations should not be included in the Transmission Path Delay.

For each potentially worst-case path through the medium, a path delay is computed as the sum of the medium-induced delay and repeater-induced delay, if any, in propagating a signal from one station to another. The Transmission Path Delay used for determining the network's slot_time (see 6.1.9) shall be the largest of these path delays for the cable system.

These path delay computations shall take into account all circuitry delays in all relevant regenerative repeaters and medium "layer" splitters, etc, and all signal propagation delays within the cable segments. The regenerative repeater delays shall be determined as specified in 12.9 and 6.1.9.

The Transmission Path Delay shall be expressed in terms of the network's symbol signaling rate on the medium. When not an integral number of signaled symbols, it shall be rounded up to such an integral number. When uncertain of the exact value of the delay, vendors shall state an upper bound for the value.

13.9 Documentation. It is recommended that each vendor of an embodiment of a medium "layer" entity conformant to this standard provide to the user supporting documentation with at least these parameters
  (1) Specific sections of standards to which the embodiment conforms
  (2) The transmission path delay, as specified in 13.8 and 6.1.9.

13.10 Network Sizing
  13.10.1 Topology Considerations. Very small systems can be constructed

using only flexible coaxial cable and passive impedance-matching networks. Larger systems require semirigid trunk cable and flexible drop cables, or regenerative repeaters, or both. Highly branched topologies are achieved in this medium using CATV-like components.

13.10.2 Signal Loss Budget Considerations. The placement of phase-coherent-FSK regenerative repeaters and taps should take into account

(1) Each station's minimum transmit level and receive level specifications (see 12.7.3.2 and 12.7.6)

(2) The desired current and anticipated future placement of station's and regenerative repeaters, and

(3) The presented signal level and signal to noise specifications of 13.6.

Appendix

(This Appendix is not a part of this standard but is included for information only.)

13.11 Appendix—Guidelines for Configuring the Medium for a Single-Channel Phase-Coherent-FSK Bus Local Area Network.

The following recommendations for designing and installing local area networks using phase-coherent-FSK transmission are the result of practical experience, and correspond to typical field conditions that are encountered.

13.11.1 Application. When implemented with semirigid coaxial cable, phase coherent FSK networks may be converted to the CATV-like configuration of multilevel duobinary AM/PSK networks (Section 15) by making relatively simple hardware changes. It is equally possible to implement the network with lower-cost flexible cable and tap housings that are not convertible, thus permitting practical and economic installation in networks of a temporary nature, or of shorter overall length. It is necessary to decide at the outset whether the network is likely to be upgraded, so that an appropriate coaxial cable may be selected.

When semirigid cable is used, it is recommended that the tap housings compatible with the multilevel duobinary AM/PSK specifications of Section 15 be used. Upgrading then consists of the following simple steps:

(1) Remove any regenerative repeaters and replace them (at least conceptually) with N-port power splitters

(2) Determine the placement on the cable of the head-end remodulator and the bidirectional broadband amplifiers. Cut the cable and install them

(3) Replace each nondirectional matching network in the phase-coherent-FSK tap with a corresponding CATV-like directional matching network

(4) Replace each phase-coherent FSK physical layer entity (modem) with a multilevel duobinary AM/PSK physical layer entity (modem) and install in accordance with the specifications of Section 14.

13.11.2 Network Size. Both overall length of cable and number of taps should be explicitly combined in the system signal loss budget. Each tap is matched at all ports, and the attenuation between all ports is specified. Thus each tap makes a known contribution to the network loss budget, as does each length of the trunk cable. In addition, each tap includes a definite tap loss between the trunk and the drop, which should also be included in the loss budget.

Insertion loss and tap loss values are not determined by this specification. However, typical values for commercially available taps conforming to this specification are 0.5 dB insertion loss, and 14 dB drop loss, over a frequency range of 0.1 MHz to 30 MHz. An example calculation of the signal loss budget for a simple, unbranched network, including 32 such drops might look like this:

```
Drop loss at first tap:                    14 dB
Insertion loss of 30 intervening taps:     15 dB
Drop loss at 32nd tap:                     14 dB

Total lumped losses:                       43 dB
```

The transmit level and receive sensitivity specified in Section 12 are +60 dB and −15 dB (1 mV, 75 Ω) [dBmV] respectively. Thus, the cable loss in this example network should not exceed 32 dB. Given the actual intended length of the installed trunk cable, one should select a suitable cable based on attenuation at the highest frequency component for the particular data rate planned or anticipated.

13.11.3 Network Topology. The simplest network topology is a long unbranched trunk, requiring the trunk cable to be routed to each station site in turn. Branched topologies may be implemented by impedance-matched nondirectional splitters, which are three-port passive networks that divide the signal incident at one port into two equal parts that are transmitted to the other two ports. The insertion loss between any two ports of a typical, commercially available nondirectional splitter, is 6.1 dB. When branches are implemented by way of such splitters, a separate loss budget should be calculated for each possible end-to-end path, so that the highest loss path can be used to select the trunk cable.

13.11.4 Repeaters. Regenerative repeaters are specified in these sections (12 and 13) for the purposes of branching and the extension of the network beyond the basic signal loss budget. Note that simply cascading 96 taps in an unbranched trunk configuration (at 0.5 dB insertion loss for each of 94 taps, and 14 dB drop loss for each of the other two) consumes the entire dynamic range specified in 12.7, and repeaters may be necessary on larger networks even when end-to-end cable lengths are relatively short.

13.11.5 Drop Cables. The drop cables specified in this section are variable lengths of flexible 75 Ω cable, typically not to exceed 30 m in length, so that loss in the drop cable is less than 1 dB and almost may be ignored. This length of cable permits relative freedom in routing the trunk cable and locating the station. Since the drop cable length is not negligible, the drop cable shall be terminated in its characteristic impedance of 75 Ω to preserve the impedance-matched conditions at the tap.

13.11.6 Trunk Connection. The drop cable is coupled to the trunk cable through a passive, nondirectional, coupling network that is impedance matched at all ports. A fixed small fraction of the signal traveling in either direction on the trunk cable is transfered to the drop cable, while a signal on the drop cable is attenuated and then propagates out in both directions on the trunk.

Insertion losses essentially represent the way the incident power is divided between the ports; they are not due to dissipation in the network. Typical values, mentioned earlier in connection with network sizing, are 0.5 dB between the trunk ports, and 14 dB between the trunk and drop ports. Other ratios are possible, and more complex networks providing more than one drop connection are available. In every case, all ports should be matched for proper operation. This means that a 75 Ω termination should be connected to every unused port, and that the cable attached to any port should be properly terminated.

The coupling networks consist only of passive R, L, and C elements. Power connections are not required.

The coupling networks are enclosed by sealed housings to provide both environmental protection and electrical shielding. The housings, typically metal castings, include integral connectors for the trunk cable and drop cable(s). Housings designed for flexible trunk cables typically use type-F connectors for all ports, while those designed for semirigid trunk cables use type-F connectors for the drop cable, and special connectors that mate directly with properly prepared ends of the trunk cable. The housings for semirigid cable are designed so that the coupling network may be removed from the housing without disturbing the trunk connections, and replaced with a directional coupling network appropriate for the CATV-like multilevel duobinary AM/PSK transmission method specified in Sections 14 and 15.

13.11.7 Grounding. The trunk cable shield may be floating, single-point, or multiple-point grounded as far as signal transmission is concerned. Grounds thus may be installed in accordance with EMI and safety codes and other regulations applicable to the particular installation. This usually means grounding where the cable enters or leaves a building, and at intervals not exceeding approximately 100 m within the building. Grounds should be applied carefully by a clamp that does not crush or damage the cable, because such cable damage causes serious reflections. Suitable clamps are available from suppliers of CATV system hardware.

13.11.8 Surge Protection. It is good practice to protect the cable against ground surges due to lightning. Suitable surge protectors that meet the requirements of IEEE Std 472-1974(R 1979)[12] should be used at each end of the cable. The capacitive loading of surge protectors should be small to avoid affecting physical layer entity (modem) performance, and should not exceed values permitted for a standard tap. For maximum surge protection, a low-impedance, heavy-duty ground connection is required.

13.11.9 Termination. The trunk cable should be properly terminated at both ends. All drop cables should be properly terminated at the station end. All unused tap ports should be properly terminated. Shielded 75 Ω coaxial terminations with good broadband characteristics are commercially available for most coaxial cables. Since transmit levels are approximately 60 dB (1 mV, 75 Ω) [dBmV], power ratings of 0.25 W are sufficient.

13.11.10 Joining Cable Sections. In general, the trunk cable will consist of a number of separate sections of coaxial cable. Some sections may be joined by connections to tap housings, while others may be joined by splicing connectors (for semirigid cable) or straight-through connectors (for flexible cable). Flexible cables will be fitted with matched connectors at each end, while semirigid cables will simply have their ends properly prepared to mate with corresponding connectors.

A good engineering practice is to maintain constant impedance between cable sections by using one cable type from one manufacturer for the entire trunk. This practice avoids significant reflections where cables are joined. When dissimilar types must be joined, it is suggested that a lossy (attenuating) impedance-matched connector, such as a tap, be employed to reduce repeated reflections.

13.11.11 Pretested Cable. It is a good practice to pretest all trunk cable before installation. The objectives are to ensure that the attenuation does not exceed the expected values at frequencies of interest, and to ensure that concealed (that is, internal) discontinuities that can cause reflections do not exist. For a nominal charge most cable suppliers will pretest or certify all cable before shipment.

On-site testing after installation is also recommended, since any damage may degrade operating margins or cause outright failure. A recommended method for testing the installed cable for damage, improper termination, shorts, or discontinuities is to use a time domain reflectometer, which is available from various instrument manufacturers.

14. Broadband Bus Physical Layer Specification

The functional, electrical, and mechanical characteristics of one specific form of physical layer (broadband bus) of this standard are specified in this section. This specification includes

(1) The physical layer embodiments found in stations which could attach to the broadband bus local area network

(2) The physical layer embodiments of head-end remodulators which are part of the broadband bus local area network.

The relationship of this section to other sections of this standard and to LAN specifications is illustrated in Fig 14-1. The relationship of this section to the broadband physical layer entity and medium is illustrated in Fig 14-2.

TOKEN-PASSING BUS

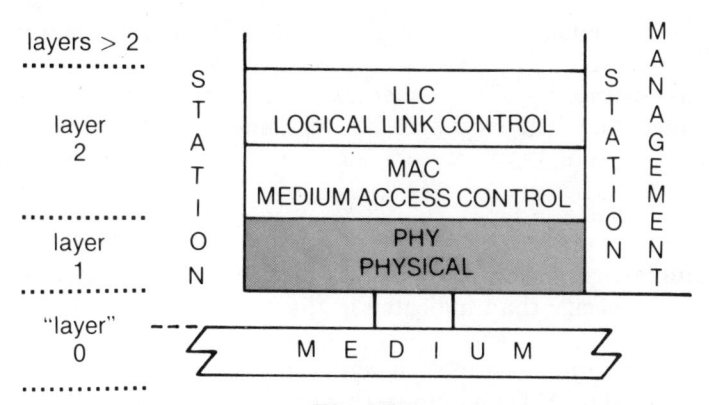

IEEE
Std 802.4-1985

**Fig 14-1
Relation to LAN Model**

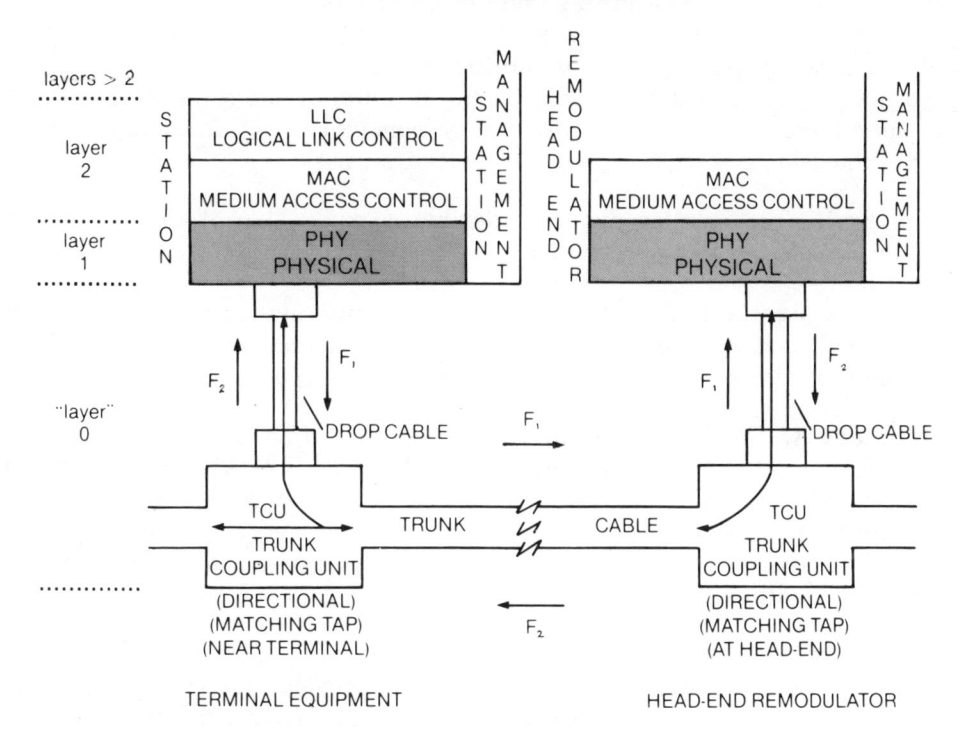

NOTE: On single (bidirectional) cable systems, $F_1 < F_2$ and both F_1 and F_2 are carried on common trunk and drop cables. On dual (unidirectional) cable systems, F_1 and F_2 are carried on separate trunk and drop cables.

**Fig 14-2
Physical Hardware Partitioning,
Token-Passing Broadband Bus Local Area Network**

This standard specifies these physical layer entities only in so far as necessary to ensure
 (1) The interoperability of implementations conforming to this specification
 (2) The protection of the local area network and those using it.

14.1 Nomenclature. Terms used in this section whose meanings within the section are more specific than indicated in the glossary of Ref [1] are as follows:

AM/PSK modulation. A form of modulation in which an rf carrier is both amplitude modulated (AM) and phase-shifted (PSK, Phase Shift Keyed).

broadband coaxial system. A system whereby information is encoded, modulated onto a carrier, and band-pass filtered or otherwise constrained to occupy only a limited frequency spectrum on the coaxial transmission medium. Many information signals can be present on the medium at the same time without disruption provided that they all occupy nonoverlapping frequency regions within the cable system's range of frequency transport.

drop cable. The smaller diameter flexible coaxial cable of the broadband medium which connects to a station.

duobinary signaling. A method of representing information to be transmitted by pulses shaped so as to reduce the frequency spectrum required to signal the information. Also known as Class 1 Partial Response coding.

duobinary AM/PSK modulation. As used in this section, a form of modulation in which data is precoded and signaled as duobinary pulses AM/PSK modulated onto an rf carrier. The particular precoding used is such that receivers can demodulate the modulated signal without having to recover the phase of that signal. In essence, the PSK component of the modulation is used to reduce the rf signal bandwidth, not to carry additional data.

head-end remodulator. As depicted in Fig 14-3 the unit located at the head-end of a broadband bus local area network which demodulates the F_1-frequency signals transmitted by other network stations and rebroadcasts them as F_2-frequency signals back to those stations. In this standard, it transmits continuously and in doing so specifies the precise data-rate at which all stations shall transmit.

multilevel duobinary AM/PSK. A form of duobinary AM/PSK modulation which uses more than two distinct amplitude levels (in this specification, independent of phase) to represent information. This section specifies a three-level duobinary AM/PSK system capable of signaling at one MAC-symbol/Bd; an Appendix discusses extensions capable of signaling at two MAC-symbols/Bd and four MAC-symbols/Bd.

station. Equipment connected to the local area network. For the purposes of this standard, head-end remodulators are considered stations, whether or not they have functionality beyond that of a remodulating repeater.

trunk cable. The main (larger-diameter) cable of a broadband coaxial cable system.

14.2 Object. The object of this specification is to

(1) Provide the physical means necessary for communication between local network stations employing the token bus access method defined in this standard and a broadband bus medium

(2) Define a physical interface that can be implemented independently among different manufacturers of hardware and achieve the intended level of compatibility when interconnected to a common broadband bus local area network medium

(3) Provide a communication channel capable of high bandwidth and low bit error rate performance. The resultant mean bit error rate at the MAC service interface (defined in Section 8) shall be less than 10^{-8}, with a mean undetected bit error rate of less than 10^{-9} at that interface

(4) Provide for ease of installation and service in a wide range of environments

(5) Provide for high network availability

(6) Use a medium which can be shared by totally unrelated applications (such as voice, data, and analog video), and conserve the capacity of that medium where reasonable.

14.3 Compatibility Considerations. This standard applies to physical layer entities which are designed to operate on conventional bidirectional (split frequency) CATV-like broadband coaxial cable systems, or on similar unidirectional (split cable) dual-cable systems, or both. Such networks use standard CATV taps, connectors, amplifiers, power supplies, and coaxial cable.

The use of a coaxial broadband system permits the assignment of different frequency bands to multiple simultaneous applications. For example, a portion of the cable spectrum can be used by local area networks while other portions are used for point-to-point or multipoint data links, and others are used to convey television and audio signals. With the proper selection of signal levels and proper equipment design all of the applications can be supported simultaneously.

All implementations of broadband bus coaxial cable systems that occupy the same transmit and the same receive channels (both center frequency and bandwidth), and that signal data at the same rate(s) and on the same number of cables, shall be compatible at the medium interface. Specific implementations based on this standard may be conceived in different ways provided compatibility at the medium is maintained.

14.4 Operational Overview of a Single-Cable Broadband Bus Medium. The use of a coaxial cable operating as a broadband medium introduces special system considerations which are not encountered in single-channel transmission systems. A conventional CATV-like system uses bidirectional amplifiers to achieve two-way transmission on a single coaxial cable. The amplifier actually consists of two independent unidirectional amplifiers, together with the appropriate crossover filters, so that one amplifier transmits the upper portion of the cable spectrum in the forward direction, outbound from the head-end, while the other amplifier transmits the lower portion in the reverse direction, toward the head-end. Therefore the physical layer entity requires an rf transmitter and receiver each operating in a different portion of the cable spectrum.

At the head-end, where forward direction signals originate and reverse direction signals converge, a remodulator receives the lower-frequency reverse channel signal and retransmits it as the higher-frequency forward channel signal to the "downstream" stations.

Stations are connected to the trunk coaxial cable in such systems by smaller-diameter drop cables and impedance-matching taps. These taps are passive devices which are highly directional with regard to signal propagation as shown in Fig 14-2. The directional characteristics of the taps improve the impedance matching at the ports of the tap and minimize the effects of reflections due to any impedance mismatches along the trunk or on other drop cables.

The directionality of the tap is such that the transmission loss between the station and the reverse direction trunk is considerably less than that between the station and the forward direction trunk. Hence communication between devices connected to different taps along the coax occurs through the transmission of a frequency F_1 in the low-band toward the head-end, reception at the head-end and retransmission in the forward direction at a high-band frequency F_2, and reception by the "listening" stations.

14.5 Operational Overview of a Dual-Cable Broadband Bus Medium. Dual-cable systems are similar to single-cable systems except that bidirectionality is provided by separate cables, rather than by separate portions of the frequency spectrum on the same cable. Consequently, amplifiers only need be unidirectional and, with respect to Fig 14-2, F_1 need not be a lower frequency than F_2.

14.6 Overview of the Broadband Bus Physical Layer

14.6.1 General Description of Functions. The functions performed by the broadband bus physical layer entity are described informally here. Some of these functions are common to all stations of a broadband bus local area network; others are found only in the head-end remodulator station. Jointly they provide a means whereby symbols presented at the MAC interface of one physical layer entity can be conveyed to all of the physical layer entities on the bus for presentation to their respective MAC interfaces.

14.6.1.1 Symbol Transmission and Reception Functions. Successive MAC-symbols presented to the physical layer entity at its MAC service interface are applied to an encoder which produces as output PHY-symbols from the set: {0} {2} {4}. The encoder includes a scrambler which is applied to consecutive zero and one input MAC-symbols to reduce the autocorrelation of the encoder's output. The output is then applied to a modulator which uses a duobinary signal shaping process to produce a multilevel AM/PSK signal within the designated rf channel, where the amplitude of each output pulse corresponds directly with the relative numeric value of the associated PHY-symbol. This rf signal is then ac coupled to the broadband bus medium and conveyed by the medium to one or more receivers.

NOTE: Except for the head-end remodulator, sequences of the MAC-symbol silence are conveyed by turning off the transmitter.

Each receiver is also ac coupled to the broadband bus. It bandpass filters the received signal to eliminate noise from other channels and then infers the transmitted PHY-symbol from the amplitude of the received signal. It then decodes that inferred PHY-symbol by an approximate inverse of the encoding process and presents the resultant decoded MAC-symbols at its MAC service interface.

For all MAC-symbols except pad_idle, this decoding process is an exact inverse of the encoding process in the absence of errors. The pad_idle symbols, which are referred to collectively as preamble, are transmitted at the start of each MAC frame, both to provide a training signal for receivers and to provide a nonzero minimum separation between consecutive frames. Since each transmission begins with pad_idle symbols, it is expected that some of these initial symbols may be "lost in transit" between the transmitter and the head-end remodulator. Additionally, in broadband bus systems the encoding for the sequence of pad_idle MAC-symbols is identical to the encoding for a particular sequence of one and zero MAC-symbols, and receivers are permitted to decode the transmitted representation of pad_idle as a one or zero MAC-symbol, descramble it if desired, and report it as such to the MAC entity.

As alluded to above, the head-end remodulator actively transmits sequences of the MAC-symbol silence as a specific repeating signaling sequence known as pseudo-silence. This sequence is used to provide a continuous signal for the AGC and carrier and data recovery circuitry of the local area network's other stations, and to indicate the signaling type (one MAC-symbol/Bd, or an extended type as defined in 14.12) currently in use on the local area network. When received by the other stations in the network, pseudo-silence is decoded and reported to their local MAC entities as the MAC-symbol silence.

14.6.1.2 Head-End Remodulator Functions. In an actual single-cable broadband bus system, stations do not transmit and receive on the same frequency channel. One central station, designated the head-end remodulator, receives on a low-frequency channel and transmits on a high-frequency channel. All of the other stations transmit on the low-frequency channel and receive on the high-frequency channel. Thus the system really consists of a pair of directional channels, with the low-frequency (reverse) channel having many transmitters and one receiver, and the high-frequency (forward) channel having one transmitter and many receivers. To allow stations to communicate, the head-end remodulator serves as a relay station; when not transmitting for itself, its medium access sublayer entity interprets the MAC-symbols received in the reverse channel and retransmits them (in some form) in the forward channel.

NOTE: The head-end remodulator may also function like any other station and source transmissions of its own.

During normal operation the head-end remodulator transmits continuously. The other stations in the local area network determine the exact transmit and receive data rate from that continuously on, forward-channel signal and the type of signaling (one MAC-symbol/Bd, or an extended type as defined in 14.12) from the transmitted pseudo-silence pattern.

In a dual-cable system, the forward channel is carried by the forward-direction cable, the reverse channel by the reverse-direction cable, and the reverse channel frequency does not need to be less than the forward channel frequency. In other respects dual-cable operation is similar to single-cable operation.

14.6.1.3 Jabber-Inhibit Function. To protect the local area network from most faults in a station, each station other than the head-end remodulator contains a jabber-inhibit function. This function serves as a "watchdog" on the transmitter; if the station does not turn off its transmitter after a prolonged time (roughly one-half second), then the transmitter output shall be disabled automatically for at least the remainder of the transmission.

14.6.1.4 Local Administrative Functions. These are optional functions which select various modes of operation. They are activated either manually, or by way of the physical layer entity's station management interface, or both. They can include

(1) Selecting the transmit and receive channels (frequencies and bandwidth)

(2) Enabling or disabling each transmitter output (A redundant medium configuration would have two or more transmitter outputs.)

(3) Adjusting the transmitted power level of each transmitter output

(4) Selecting the received signal source: any medium (if redundant media are present), or any available loopback point

NOTE: If a loopback point is selected, then all transmitter outputs shall be inhibited.

(5) Reporting the level of the received rf signal

(6) Selecting the signaling type (one MAC-symbol/Bd, or an extended type as defined in 14.12) at the head-end remodulator.

14.6.2 Model Used for the Functional Specification. The detailed functional specifications are modeled after CCITT V. series modem specifications Refs [16] and [17] particulary the V.36 specification, with additional detail added where necessary.

14.6.3 Basic Functions and Options. Symbol transmission and reception functions and jabber-inhibit functions are required in all implementations. Within the symbol transmission and reception functions, three-symbol signaling (one MAC-symbol/Bd) capability is mandatory. All other functions are optional.

14.7 Bibliography

LENDER, A., author, & FEHER, K., ed, Digital Communications: Microwave Applications, Prentice-Hall, Inc, Englewood Cliffs, NJ, 1981, pp 144-182.

KABAL, P. and PASUPATHY, S., Partial Response Signaling, IEEE Transactions on Communications, vol COM-23, Sept 1975, pp 921-934.

DAVIES, D. and BARBER, D., Communication Networks for Computers, John Wiley & Sons, Ltd., London, England, 1973, pp 143-145 & ff.

14.8 Detailed Application of Section 9, Generic Station Management to Physical Layer Interface Service Specification. The range of permissible values for the parameters specified in Section 9 are as follows:

LAN_topology_type parameter of PHY_RESET.confirmation primitive. The value of this parameter shall be token_bus.

PHY_role parameter of PHY_RESET.confirmation primitive. The value of this parameter shall be originate_and_repeat for head-end remodulator stations, and originate_only for all other stations.

Mode_class parameter of PHY_MODAL_CAPABILITY_QUERY and PHY_MODE_QUERY primitives. The mode_class parameter shall specify

(1) min_post_silence_preamble_length
(2) channel_assignments
(3) transmitted_power_level_adjustments
(4) transmitter_output_inhibits
(5) received_signal_sources
(6) signaling_mode
(7) received_signal_level_reporting

The value read for min_post_silence_preamble_length shall be equal to the number of octets that produce 32 PHY-symbols. See 14.9.2.1(2). (For 1b/Hz signaling this value is four octets.) All other values of the mode_class parameter shall elicit an undefined_mode_class confirmation.

Mode_class parameter of PHY_MODE_SELECT primitives. The mode_class parameter shall specify

(a) channel_assignments
(b) transmitted_power_level_adjustments
(c) transmitter_output_inhibits
(d) received_signal_sources
(e) signaling_mode
(f) received_signal_level_reporting

All other values of the mode_class parameter shall elicit a failure confirmation.

14.9 Broadband Bus Physical Layer Functional, Electrical, and Mechanical Specifications. Unless otherwise stated, all voltage and power level specifications are in rms and dB (1 mV, 75 Ω) [dBmV] rms, respectively, based on transmissions of random data patterns. Measurements for voltage levels and power ratios may be made using a data pattern of unscrambled ones, with a correction factor of +3 dB over equivalent measurements using random data.

14.9.1 Data Signaling Rates. The standard data signaling rates are 1 Mb/s, 5 Mb/s, and 10 Mb/s. The permitted tolerance for each signaling rate is ±0.005%. The exact rate in any given local area network shall be determined by that network's head-end remodulator.

14.9.2 Symbol Encoding. The physical layer entity transmits symbols presented to it at its MAC interface by the medium access control sublayer entity.

IEEE
Std 802.4-1985
LOCAL AREA NETWORKS:

The possible MAC-symbols are zero, one, non_data, pad_idle, and silence. Each of these MAC-symbols is encoded into a different code of PHY-symbols {0} {2} {4} and then transmitted.

14.9.2.1 Three-Symbol Encoder. The encoding action to be taken for each of the input MAC-symbols when three-symbol (one MAC-symbol/Bd) encoding is employed is

(1) Silence—

(a) The head-end remodulator shall encode successive silence symbols as successive PHY-symbols of the repeating sequence {2} {2} {0} {4}, always restarting with the first {2} of the sequence for each new period of transmitted pseudo-silence. (It is permissible to terminate the sequence after any PHY-symbol.)

(b) All stations other than the head-end remodulator shall encode the first MAC-symbol of silence after non-silence, and the last MAC-symbol of silence before non-silence, as the PHY-symbol {2}. Such stations shall encode all other MAC-symbols of silence as the PHY-symbol {0} and shall cease transmission while transmitting only such {0} symbols representing silence.

(2) Pad_idle—Consecutive pad_idle symbols shall be encoded as successive PHY-symbols of the repeating sequence {4} {0}, always restarting the sequence with the {4} for each new period of pad_idle. When sending pad_idle MAC-symbols immediately after sending silence MAC-symbols, the MAC-sublayer entity shall send at least as many octets of pad_idle MAC-symbols as are required to result in a minimum of 32 PHY-symbols.

NOTE: For 1b/Bd signaling, this minimum is four octets of pad_idle MAC-symbols.

(3) Non_data—The scrambler described in 14.9.2.3 shall be reinitialized (preset to all ones) at each non_data symbol. Each non_data symbol shall be encoded as a {2}, and the eight-symbol (frame delimiter) sequence of 8.2.1 shall be encoded as follows; each

non_data non_data data$_1$ non_data non_data data$_2$ data$_3$ data$_4$

sequence shall be encoded as the sequence

{2} {2} {d$_1$} {2} {2} {d$_2$} {d$_3$} {d$_4$},

where each data$_i$ is either a zero or a one, and each d$_i$ is the corresponding encoding of the MAC-symbol data$_i$, either a {0} or a {4} as described below.

After each such eight-symbol (frame delimiter) sequence, as defined in 8.2.1, the encoder shall start to maintain a sense of PHY-octet alignment, with the next output PHY-symbol considered to be the first of a new PHY-octet.

NOTE: This physical-layer sense of PHY-octet alignment is coincidentally identical to the MAC entity's sense of MAC-octet alignment.

(4) Zero and one—Each zero and one symbol shall be encoded as follows:

(a) The MAC-symbol shall be applied as input to the scrambler described in 14.9.2.3, resulting in a "scrambled" zero or one MAC-symbol

(b) The scrambled MAC-symbol shall be converted to one of the PHY-symbol output codes as follows:

zero —> {0̲}
one —> {4̲}

This is the data̲$_i$ to {d̲$_i$} mapping referred to in 14.9.2.1(3).

(c) The following procedure shall be performed on each resultant PHY-octet of {0̲} and {4̲} PHY-symbol codes. Each such octet of these PHY-symbol codes shall be compared with the immediately prior octet of PHY-symbols as transmitted (that is, after execution of this procedure on that prior octet, if applicable). If both PHY-octets consist solely of the identical PHY-symbol code (that is, either sixteen {0̲}s or sixteen {4̲}s), then the last three codes in the PHY-octet under examination shall be altered before transmission as follows:

```
{0̲} {0̲} {0̲} shall be replaced by {4̲} {2̲} {2̲}
{4̲} {4̲} {4̲} shall be replaced by {0̲} {2̲} {2̲}.
```

NOTES: (1) This procedure can alter at most every other octet of PHY-symbols, and the second octet after the encoded (frame delimiter) sequence of 8.2.1 is the first such octet that can be altered. This procedure has no effect on the scrambler described in 14.9.2.3 and in the previous sub-section.

(2) The constraints on the occurrence of non_data and pad_idle MAC-symbols imposed by 8.2.1 and 8.2.2, and the resulting constraints on the occurrence of {2̲} PHY-symbols imposed by 14.9.2.1, may be used in post-detection processing to decrease the error rate of the receiving physical-layer entity's PHY-symbol to MAC-symbol decoding process.

14.9.2.2 Pseudo-Silence Provisions for Enhanced Encoders. Three additional pseudo-Silence sequences (other than that of 14.9.2.1) have been reserved for two MAC-symbol/Bd and four MAC-symbol/Bd enhancements to the basic signaling method. The enhancements themselves are described in 14.12, and are for further study.

The pseudo-silence sequence of 14.9.2.1 is

{2̲} {2̲} {0̲} {4̲}   — one MAC-symbol/Bd three-symbol signaling

The three reserved pseudo-silence sequences are

{2̲} {0̲} {4̲}   — two MAC-symbol/Bd five-symbol signaling
{2̲} {2̲} {4̲} {0̲}   — two MAC-symbol/Bd three-symbol quadrature signaling
{2̲} {4̲} {0̲}   — four MAC-symbol/Bd five-symbol quadrature signaling

14.9.2.3 Data Scrambler. To reduce the probability of long transmitted sequences of identical PHY-symbol codes and to randomize spectral components of the transmitted modulation, the symbolic binary data transmitted as zero and one MAC-symbols for the MAC entity shall be pseudo-randomized by dividing the equivalent message polynomial by the generating polynomial $1+X^{-6}+X^{-7}$. The coefficients of the quotient of this division are taken in descending order as the MAC-symbol sequence to be coded in step (2) of 14.9.2.1. The logical arrangements of such a scrambler and corresponding descrambler is described in 14-13.

As specified in 14.9.2.1, this scrambler (or the corresponding descrambler) is reinitialized at each non_data symbol requested by (or indicated to, respectively) the associated MAC entity. After reinitialization, which is presetting to all ones, the scrambler polynomial guarantees that the next five MAC-symbols output will

Table 14-1
Baseband Pulse Coding Rules

2nd Prior Pulse	Prior Pulse	Desired PHY-symbol	Required Pulse	MAC-symbol usage (post-scrambler)
—	+2	{0}	−2	zero,
—	−2	{0}	+2	second pad_idle (of pair)
—	0	{0}	0	other silence (transmitter off)
—	+2	{2}	0	first non_data (of pair),
—	−2	{2}	0	first silence
+2	0	{2}	+2	second non_data (of pair)
−2	0	{2}	−2	
—	0	{2}	+2	last silence
—	0	{2}	−2	
—	+2	{4}	+2	one, first pad_idle
—	−2	{4}	−2	(of pair)

be unaffected by the scrambling process. Thus the zeros and ones within the frame delimiter octets of 8.2.1 are unaffected by the scrambling process, even though in a technical sense they have been scrambled.

The alteration in the transmitted PHY-symbol codes described in the last paragraphs of 14.9.2.1 has no effect on this scrambler or the corresponding descrambler, as the alteration is made subsequent to scrambling and is reversed prior to descrambling.

14.9.3 Baseband Modulation. The PHY-symbol coded signal shall be converted to an appropriately-shaped pulse whose phase and amplitude are chosen from the set of pulses of phase and relative amplitude −2, 0, and +2 as determined by the output PHY-symbol code and by the phase and amplitude of the immediately prior one or two pulses as specified by Table 14-1.

The equivalent baseband signal shaping function shall be based upon the partial response pulse often referred to as duobinary or Class I partial response, whose time and spectral functions are defined by Eq 14-1, Eq 14-2, and Eq 14-3.

This shaping process shall be effected in such a way that the decoding can be achieved by full wave rectification of the demodulated line signal (that is, without recovery or reconstruction of the phase of the transmitted equivalent baseband signal).

NOTE: The pulse-coding rules of Table 14-1, when combined with the above duobinary signal-shaping function, give rise to a combined signal whose amplitude, when sampled at the correct intervals, corresponds directly to the coded PHY-symbol as follows (where MAX is the maximum such amplitude)

$\quad\quad\quad\quad$ {0} —> 0/4 of MAX (= 0)
$\quad\quad\quad\quad$ {2} —> 2/4 of MAX (= MAX/2)
$\quad\quad\quad\quad$ {4} —> 4/4 of MAX (= MAX)

The reference to equivalent baseband signals recognizes that the physical layer implementation may be such that the MAC-symbols encoded as in 14.9.2 are converted to and from the line signals without appearing as actual baseband signals.

$$g(t) = \frac{4}{\pi} \cdot \frac{\cos(\pi \frac{t}{T})}{1 - (2\frac{t}{T})^2} \quad \text{(Eq 14-1)}$$

$$|G(f)| = \begin{cases} 2T \cos(\pi f T), & |f| \leq \frac{1}{2T} \\ 0, & |f| > \frac{1}{2T} \end{cases} \quad \text{(Eq 14-2)}$$

$$\lfloor G(f) = \begin{cases} -\pi f T, & |f| \leq \frac{1}{2T} \\ 0, & |f| > \frac{1}{2T} \end{cases} \quad \text{(Eq 14-3)}$$

respectively, where
    f denotes the frequency (Hz)
    $1/T$ denotes the PHY-symbol signaling rate (symbols/second)

14.9.4 Recommended Frequency Allocation / Channel Spacing.

(1) This standard recommends a communication medium configuration that is known in the CATV industry as a single-cable mid-split configuration. In this configuration, the unidirectional forward and reverse channels are paired to provide bidirectional channels. This standard recommends a frequency offset of 192.25 MHz between paired forward and reverse channels in both mid-split and high-split configurations. Other configurations, including dual-cable where forward and reverse channels are on separate unidirectional cables, also are permitted.

(2) The relationship between data signaling rate and minimum channel bandwidth is: A data rate of 1 Mb/s requires 1.5 MHz of channel bandwidth. A data rate of 5 Mb/s requires 6 MHz of channel bandwidth. A data rate of 10 Mb/s requires 12 MHz of channel bandwidth. Higher data rates for a given channel bandwidth are for future study.

{NOTE: The remainder of 14.9.4 is not part of the ISO Standard. Frequency allocations are a subject for national standardization.}

(3) Table 14-2 shows the preferred pairing for the usual North American 6 MHz channels. The conventional North American CATV nomenclature has been used for the channel names, and the frequency specified is that of the lower band edge.

Table 14-2
**Usual North American 6 MHz Mid-split Channels
—Nomenclature and Pairing**

Reverse Channel	Frequency (MHz)		Forward Channel	Frequency (MHz)
T10	23.75		J	216
T11	29.75		K	222
T12	35.75		L	228
T13	41.75		M	234
T14	47.75		N	240
2'	53.75	————	O	246
3'	59.75	*	P	252
4'	65.75	—*—	Q	258
4A'	71.75	*	R	264
5'	77.75	—*—	S	270
6'	83.75	*	T	276
FM1'	89.75	—*—	U	282
FM2'	95.75		V	288
FM3'	101.75		W	294

* These channel pairings are recommended for use with this standard.

' The primed reverse-direction channels are offset from the conventional forward-direction channels of the same (un-primed) name.

The 1.5 MHz channels are formed by equally subdividing any given 6 MHz channel. The 12 MHz channels are composed of adjacent 6 MHz channels, paired as indicated by the lines in the center column of Table 14-2.

The preferred channel assignments for dual-frequency mid-split and high-split North American system configurations are

(1) For a 10 Mb/s data rate, a 12 MHz channel pair should be used, with reverse channels 3' and 4' paired with forward channels P and Q.

(2) For a 5 Mb/s data rate, a 6 MHz channel pair should be used, with reverse channel 3' paired with forward channel P, or reverse channel 4' paired with forward channel Q.

(3) For a 1 Mb/s data rate, a 1.5 MHz channel pair should be used, chosen from one of the eight equally-spaced 1.5 MHz subchannels of reverse channels 3' and 4', paired with corresponding forward channels P and Q.

For dual-cable single-frequency systems, either the forward channel frequencies or the reverse channel frequencies specified can be used on both forward- and reverse-direction cables.

Where multiple channel assignments are needed for multiple local area networks on a single shared broadband medium, it is suggested that they be assigned different channel pairs in accordance with these recommendations.

14.9.5 Line Signal in RF Band (at the line output of the terminal equipment). The equivalent baseband modulation of 14.9.3 shall be applied to an rf carrier centered in the assigned channel (for example, 3 MHz from each channel edge of a 6 MHz channel), and the resultant modulated carrier shall be coupled to the broadband bus medium as specified in 14.9.7.

14.9.5.1 In the appropriate 1.5 MHz wide, 6 MHz wide, or 12 MHz wide rf channel, the line signal shall correspond to a double-sideband signal with its carrier frequency at the channel mid-point frequency ±0.01%.

14.9.5.2 The relationship between the multilevel signals at the real or hypothetical output of the multisymbol signal coder and the transmitted line signal shall be such that the amplitude of the modulated signal at the proper sampling intervals is directly proportional to the numeric symbol of the coded signal.

In a practical case this means that the voltage which results from the full wave rectification of the demodulated line signal corresponds at the proper sampling intervals with the numeric value of the coded signal symbol, with the maximum amplitude corresponding to a coded {4}, a zero amplitude corresponding to a coded {0}, and intermediate amplitudes corresponding proportionately.

14.9.5.3 The amplitude of the theoretical line signal pulse spectrum, corresponding to an isolated maximum-amplitude pulse appearing at the output of the multisymbol signal coder, is to be cosine shaped in the frequency domain, as indicated in Eq 14-2, with maxima at the carrier frequency and zeros at ± 0.5 MHz, ± 2.5 MHz, or ± 5.0 MHz from that carrier frequency for 1.5 MHz, 6 MHz, and 12 MHz channel bandwidths, respectively.

14.9.5.4 The output level of the transmitted signal into a 75 Ω resistive load shall be adjustable over the range specified in Table 14-3, with adjustment performed either manually, or upon command through the physical layer entity's

Table 14-3
Required Transmit Level Range

Channel Bandwidth (MHz)	Required Transmit Level Range in dB (1 mV, 75 Ω) [dBmV]	
	Minimum	Maximum
1.5	+24	+44
6	+30	+50
12	+33	+53

station management interface (see 14.8), or both. The granularity (step-size) of this adjustment shall be at most 2 dB, and once set, the actual long-term variance from the set transmitter level shall be at most ±2 dB. The maximum variance of the transmitter amplitude for any coded symbol, measured over one transmission or one second, shall be at most 0.5 dB.

When installed in an operational local area network, the output level of the head-end remodulator's transmitter shall be adjusted as specified by the supplier of the medium (see 15.9); the output level of each of the other stations' transmitters shall be adjusted so that its signal, as presented to the network's head-end remodulator by the broadband medium, is within ±2 dB of the nominal signal level specified in Table 14-7.

14.9.5.5 In the 1 MHz, 5 MHz, or 10 MHz signaling band centered at the actual rf carrier frequency, the amplitude distortion of the real spectrum relative to the theoretic spectrum as defined under 14.9.3 above shall fall within the limits specified by Table 14-4 and Fig 14-3, and the group-delay distortion relative to the center of the band shall fall within the limits specified by Eq 14-4. At the signaling band edges, where the theoretic spectrum has zeros (infinite attenuation), the actual signal amplitude shall be attenuated at least 20 dB with respect to the signal amplitude at the center of the band.

14.9.5.6 In the modulated output spectrum, relative to the output level of 14.9.5.4 and independent of the data transmitted, the transmitted power in that portion of the output spectrum that is outside the channel bandwidth shall meet or exceed the relative attenuation specified in Fig 14-4 and Eq 14-5.

14.9.5.7 The residual or leakage transmitter-off output signal shall be at least 70 dB below that of the modulated signal.

14.9.5.8 When ending a period of (passively-"transmitted") silence by transmitting the PHY-symbol {2} representing the final silence symbol, the physical layer entity shall sequence the transmitter from a transmitter-off to transmitter-on state immediately prior to the transmission of that {2} PHY-symbol. That transmitter-on state shall be reached before the transmitter energy, averaged over the period of one PHY-symbol, has increased to a level of 26 dB below the level of the modulated signal.

At the end of transmission, when beginning a period of (passively-"transmitted") silence by transmitting the PHY-symbol {2} representing the initial silence symbol, the physical layer entity shall sequence the transmitter from a transmitter-on to transmitter-off state immediately subsequent to the transmission of that {2} PHY-symbol. That transmitter-off state shall be reached after the transmitter energy, averaged over the period of one PHY-symbol, has decreased to a level of 26 dB below the level of the modulated signal.

14.9.5.9 Where separate input and output physical couplings to the medium exist (for example, in dual-cable systems), the leakage output into the input coupling

(1) During transmitter-off periods shall be the same as that specified for the output coupling in 14.9.5.7

(2) During transmitter-on periods shall be the same as the maximal out-of-band attenuation specified for the output coupling in 14.9.5.6.

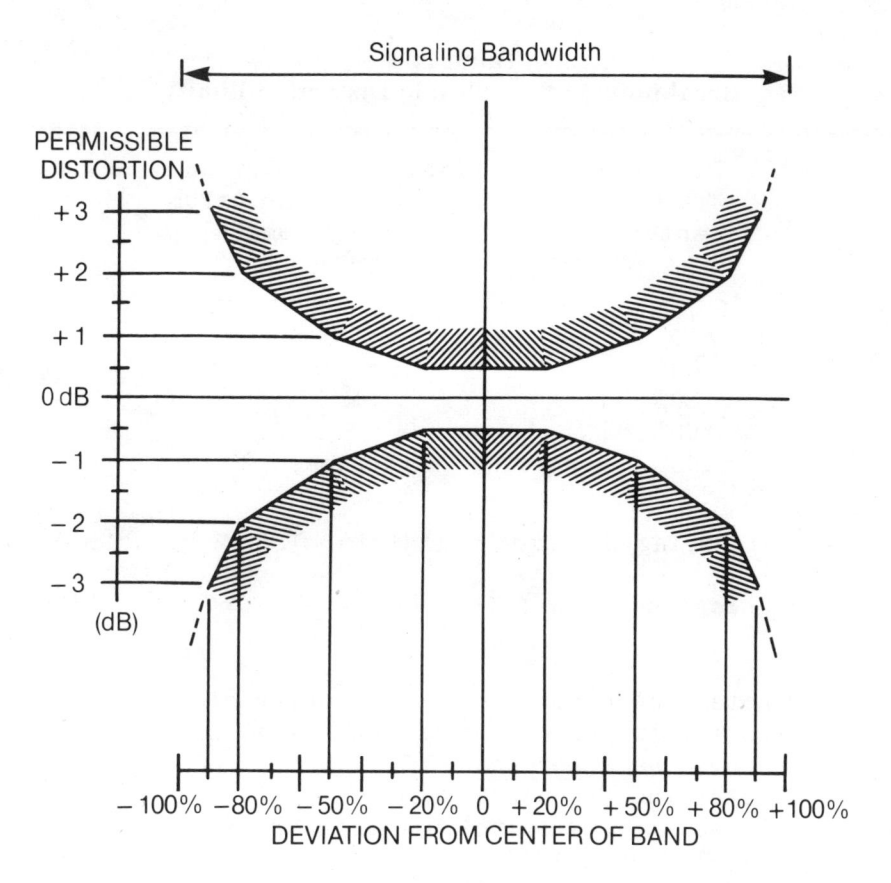

**Fig 14-3
Limits for Amplitude Distortion**

Table 14-4
Breakpoints of Amplitude Distortion Limits

Distance from band center (% of HBW)	Permissible Distortion from Theoretic Spectrum (in frequency domain) (dB)
±20%	±0.5
±50%	±1.0
±80%	±2.0
±90%	±3.0
±100%	(at least 20 dB attenuation)

where
  HBW = $\frac{1}{2}$ signaling bandwidth, that is, 0.5, 2.5, or 5 MHz

$$\text{PGD} = \pm 90 \log_{10} \cos(\pi f T), \quad |f| \leq \frac{1}{2T} \qquad \text{(Eq 14-4)}$$

where
  PGD denotes the permissible group delay distortion relative to the center of the signaling band, measured as a <u>percent</u> of T
  f   denotes the frequency (Hz)
  1/T denotes the PHY-symbol signaling rate (symbols/second).

$$\text{RA} = \min\left(60,\ 35 + 10 \log_{10} B + 80 \left|\frac{MF-NCEF}{B}\right|\right) \qquad \text{(Eq 14-5)}$$

where
  RA   is the attenuation relative to total transmitted power in dB measured in any 30 kHz band
  B   is the channel bandwidth (MHz)
  MF   is the measurement frequency (MHz)
  NCEF is the frequency (MHz) of the nearest edge of the channel.

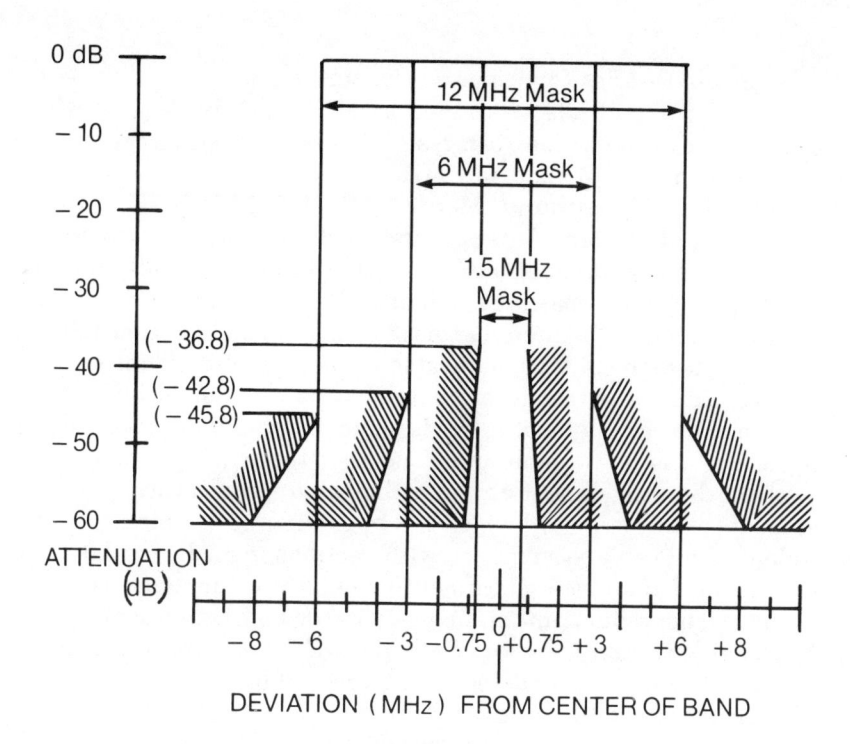

**Fig 14-4
Transmit Spectrum Mask**

14.9.6 Jabber Inhibit. Each physical layer entity other than a head-end remodulator (which transmits continuously) shall have a self-interrupt capability to inhibit modulation from reaching the local area network medium. Hardware within the physical layer (with no external message other than the prolonged detection of an output-on condition within the transmitter) shall provide a nominal window of one-half second ±25% during which time a normal data link transmission may occur. If a transmission is in excess of this duration, the jabber-inhibit function shall operate to inhibit any further output from reaching the medium. Reset of this jabber-inhibit function shall occur upon receipt of a station management PHY_RESET.request (see 9.2.1). Additional resetting means are permitted.

14.9.7 Coupling to the Medium. The physical layer functions are intended to operate satisfactorily over 75 Ω CATV-like bidirectional broadband cable installations employing mid-split, sub-split, or high-split line amplifiers and filters, or dual unidirectional cables employing (no-split) line amplifiers.

Both the transmitter and the receiver shall be ac coupled to the center conductor of the 75 Ω broadband medium, and the breakdown voltage of that ac coupling means shall be at least 500 V ac rms. In addition to this coupling, the shield of the coaxial cable medium shall be connected to chassis ground, and the impedance of that connection shall be less than 0.1 Ω.

The mechanical coupling of the station to the medium shall be to a drop cable by way of a female F-series connector on the station, as specified in Section 15. The maximum VSWR at that F-connector shall be 1.5:1 or less when that F-connector is terminated with a 75 Ω resistive load, as measured over the entire broadband spectrum of 5 MHz to 450 MHz.

14.9.8 Alternate Broadband Media. [OPTIONAL] Sections 14 and 15 specify the standard (preferred) broadband medium configuration as a single trunk cable and single drop cable, bidirectional by frequency, midsplit CATV-like configuration with channel pairings as indicated in 14.9.4. Other configurations are possible which meet the intent of this standard, including alternate channel pairings, sub-split, high-split, or dual-cable media, and redundant media.

Any channel pairing or range of channel pairings compatible with any of mid-split, sub-split, or high-split single-cable operation, or with dual-cable operation, or both, is permissible, provided that the pairing(s) is (are) clearly labeled both on the embodiment and in accompanying literature.

Embodiments of this standard which can be configured to function with either single-cable or dual-cable systems, or with redundant media, or both, are not precluded, provided that the embodiment as delivered functions correctly in a minimal (that is, nonredundant, or single-cable, or both) environment.

14.9.9 Receiver Sensitivity and Selectivity. The physical layer entity shall be capable of providing an undetected bit error rate of 10^{-9} or lower, and a detected bit error rate of 10^{-8} or lower, while

(1) Receiving in-band signals of average amplitude level in the range specified by Table 14-5, transmitted by a physical layer entity conforming to the requirements of Section 14, and

(2) The in-band signal-to-noise level of the medium is +30 dB (V rms /(V rms)) or greater, as measured at the F-connector.

NOTE: Specifications of signal power, both out of band and in band due to adjacent channels, are for future study. It is anticipated that the specification format will be to include an unweighted signal power over the total bandwidth (5 MHz to 450 MHz), and a weighted signal power over the same bandwidth. The specification of unweighted power is to constrain the maximum power presented to the receiver. The specification of weighted power is to constrain the noise power contribution by all other signal sources as presented to a receiver's demodulator.

Table 14-5
Required Noise Floor and In-band Signal Level

Channel Bandwidth (MHz)	Max In-band Noise Floor in dB (1 mV, 75 Ω) [dBmV]	Received Signal Amplitude in dB (1 mV, 75 Ω) [dBmV] Minimum	Maximum
1.5	−46	−16	+4
6.0	−40	−10	+10
12.0	−37	−7	+13

Table 14-6
Minimum Length of Pad_idle Preamble

Data Rate (Mb/s)	At Start of Transmission — Minimum # of MAC Symbols	At Start of Transmission — Minimum Time (μs)	Between Frames — Minimum # of MAC Symbols	Between Frames — Minimum Time (μs)
1	32	32.0	8	8.0
5	32	6.4	16	3.2
10	32	3.2	24	2.4

14.9.10 Automatic Gain Control. The physical layer entity shall monitor the level of the received signaling in general, and the signaling of pad_idle symbols at the start of a transmission in particular, and adjust its receiver gain as necessary based upon that monitoring. For receivers connected to the forward channel, this adjustment may be based upon long-term observation of the received signal. For the head-end remodulator (which is receiving the reverse channel), the initial adjustment shall be made rapidly during the initial pad_idle sequence which begins each transmission, and shall be completed at least four pad_idle symbols before the end of that sequence (see 8.2.2). The minimum length of that pad_idle sequence is a function of both the data rate and whether that pad_idle sequence follows silence or other non-silence symbols. Table 14-6 expresses that relationship in both microseconds and signaled MAC-symbols for three-symbol (one MAC-symbol/Bd) signaling.

14.9.11 Symbol Timing. Each physical layer entity whose receiver is connected to the forward channel shall recover the PHY-symbol timing information contained within the received signaling, and shall use this recovered timing information to determine the precise rate of symbol transmission. The instantaneous transmit and receive data rates of each such entity shall be identical, with exactly one MAC-symbol (possibly silence) transmitted for each MAC-symbol received. (This relationship usually is termed loopback timing.) The jitter of the transmitted PHY-symbol timing relative to the PHY-symbol timing within the received signaling shall not exceed a total excursion of 5% of the period of one PHY-symbol.

The head-end remodulator shall originate its own transmit symbol timing. The jitter of the transmitted symbol timing shall not exceed 0.1% of the period of one PHY-symbol. The head-end remodulator may use the known loopback timing arrangement of the other stations in the local area network (as specified in the preceding paragraph) in determining the PHY-symbol timing of any received signaling. In a practical case this means that the head-end remodulator may determine the phase difference between its transmitted and received PHY-symbol timings upon first receipt of a transmission, and then use its self-generated transmit timing plus that measured phase delay to infer the PHY-symbol timing of the received signaling.

The head-end remodulator shall retime the received signaling, either before or after the symbol decoding process of 14.9.13, so that the received MAC-symbols reported at the MAC interface have a constant phase relationship with the to-be-transmitted MAC-symbols which the MAC sublayer entity provides at that interface. In a practical case this means that the receiver may have a FIFO (first-in first-out) symbol buffer to provide for this retiming.

14.9.12 Signaling Type Determination. The head-end remodulator shall determine the type of signaling (one MAC-symbol/Bd, or an extended type as defined in 14.12) to be employed in the local area network before commencing transmission in the forward channel and shall convey that determination to all connected stations by means of the pseudo-silence signaling sequence used in lieu of "transmitted" silence as specified in 14.9.2.1 and 14.9.2.2. The head-end remodulator may change this determination at any time, either due to manually invoked command, or upon command through the physical layer entity's station management interface (see 14.8), or both; when so doing it shall cease all transmissions for a minimum period of 5 ms before making such a redetermination. (As a practical case, this may be used to fallback from extended signaling to one MAC-symbol/Bd signaling in an extended-capability system which is experiencing unusually high noise, as inferred from error rates.)

14.9.13 Symbol Decoding. After demodulation and determination of each received signaled PHY-symbol, that PHY-symbol shall be decoded to a corresponding MAC-symbol by the process inverse to that described in 14.9.2, and the decoded MAC-symbols shall be reported at the MAC interface at a data rate determined jointly by the provisions of 14.9.11 and 14.9.12. Whenever a signaled PHY-symbol sequence is received for which the encoding process has no inverse, those PHY-symbols shall be decoded as an appropriate number of bad_signal MAC-symbols and reported as such at the MAC interface. In such cases, the receiving entity should resynchronize the decoding process as rapidly as possible.

NOTE: Receivers are permitted to decode each transmitted pad_idle MAC-symbol, which was encoded as a {0} or a {4} PHY-symbol, as a zero or a one MAC-symbol.

14.9.14 Received Signal Level Assessment. [OPTIONAL] To assist in determining the identity of reverse channel transmitters which are not properly adjusted, the head-end remodulator may be able to assess the level of the received signal and report by way of its station management interface whether that received signal level is within the bounds specified by Table 14-7, exceeds the upper bound, or falls below the lower bound. The accuracy of this assessment need be no greater than ±2 dB. Better resolution or finer assessment (for example, actual measurement of received signal amplitude in dB (1 mV, 75 Ω) [dBmV]) is optional.

**Table 14-7
Desired Head-end Received Signal Levels**

Channel Bandwidth (MHz)	Signal Levels in dB (1 mV, 75 Ω) [dBmV] Minimum	Nominal	Maximum
1.5	−13	−6	+1
6	−7	0	+7
12	−4	+3	+10

14.9.15 Transmitter Enable/Disable and Received Signal Source Selection. The ability to enable and disable the transmission of modulation onto the broadband medium as directed by the station management entity is mandatory in head-end remodulators, where signaled silence does not turn off the transmitter, and recommended but optional in all other equipments.

The ability to select the source of received signaling, either a loopback point within the physical layer entity or (one of) the (possibly redundant) media, as directed by the station management entity, is recommended but optional. When such an option is invoked and the selected source is other than (one of) the media, transmission to all connected broadband media shall be disabled automatically while such selection is in force.

14.9.16 Transmit and Receive Channel Selection. [OPTIONAL] The determination of a physical layer entity's transmit and receive channels, either channel center frequencies or channel bandwidth or both, may be alterable. In such cases the alteration may be accomplished either manually, or upon command through the physical layer entity's station management interface (see 14.8), or both. All transmissions to the medium shall be inhibited while such changes are being effected, and any signaling received during such a period of change shall be discarded and not reported to the MAC interface.

14.9.17 Redundant Media Considerations. As implied by 14.9.8, redundant broadband media are not precluded from this standard. Where redundant media are employed, the provisions of 14.9.5.4, 14.9.6, and 14.9.15 shall apply separately and independently to each single medium interface, and much of 14.9.15 shall be mandatory. Specifically, the transmitted signal level adjustment of 14.9.5.4 shall be made separately and independently for each connected medium, separate jabber-inhibit monitoring shall exist for each medium (although common inhibition is permissible), receiver signal source selection shall be provided capable of selecting any one of the redundant media, and it shall be possible to enable or disable each single transmitter independently of all other redundant transmitters when the source of received signaling is one of the redundant media.

14.9.18 Reliability. The physical layer entity shall be designed so that its probability of causing a communication failure among other stations connected to the medium is less than 10^{-6} per hour of continuous (or discontinuous) operation. For head-end remodulators this requirement is relaxed to a probability of 2×10^{-5} per hour of operation. Connectors and other passive components comprising the means of connecting the station to the coaxial cable medium shall be designed to minimize the probability of total network failure.

14.9.19 Head-End Remodulator Considerations. A head-end remodulator can be considered to be a specialized form of regenerative repeater, which either repeats signaling from the reverse channel on the forward channel or originates signaling of its own on the forward channel. In either case, the head-end remodulator originates the symbol timing provided to its local MAC entity and to all the other stations on the local area network.

The basic mode of operation, originating or repeating, shall be determined by the remodulator's associated MAC entity and conveyed by the PHY_MODE.request primitive (see 8.2.3). When originating, the remodulator's physical layer entity shall use internal loopback as the source of the PHY-symbols which it reports to its associated MAC entity by way of the PHY_DATA.indicate primitive.

When repeating, the head-end remodulator shall decode the signaling received on the reverse channel, retime that signaling before or after decoding so that the implementation-determined constant phase relationship between PHY_DATA.indicate and PHY_DATA.request is maintained (see 8.3), and indicate the decoded MAC-symbols to its associated MAC entity.

In summary, when the MAC entity is originating, internal loopback is used as the source of PHY-symbols which are reported by way of the PHY_DATA.indicate primitive. When the MAC entity is repeating, the received signaling from the reverse channel is decoded and reported by way of the PHY_DATA.indicate primitive.

In either case the following apply:

(1) The head-end remodulator determines its own MAC-symbol timing and the exact PHY-symbol signaling rate for itself and for all other stations on the local network (see 14.9.1 and 14.9.11)

(2) The head-end remodulator determines the signaling type (one MAC-symbol/Bd, or an extended type as defined in 14.12) for the entire network, and may optionally change that signaling type after disabling its transmitter(s) for a period of at least five ms (see 14.9.12)

(3) The head-end remodulator transmits a specific repeating sequence (pseudo-silence) during periods when its MAC entity requests the repeated transmission of the MAC-symbol <u>silence</u> (see 14.9.2 and 14.9.12). This pseudo-silence sequence is used

   (a) To provide a continuous signal for the AGC and carrier and data recovery circuitry of the local area network's other stations

   (b) To indicate the signaling type (one MAC-symbol/Bd, or an extended type as defined in 14.12) currently in use on the local area network (see 14.9.2.2)

(4) The head-end remodulator can use the known exact signaling rate of the

other stations (that is, its own exact signaling rate as retransmitted by those other stations, see 14.9.11) and the probable reduced range of received signals at the head-end (see 14.9.14) to minimize the time required to train on a new transmission and be able to report the received signaling at the specified bit error rates (see 14.9.9)

NOTE: Designers are cautioned that the head-end remodulator shall be designed to achieve these bit error rates at least four MAC-symbol times (see 8.2.2) before the end of reception of a minimum-length preamble (see 14.9.10) when the transmission originates from a station whose transmitter output, as measurable at the remodulator's F-connector, falls within the bounds of Table 14-7.

(5) The receive levels of Tables 14-5 and 14-7 may be exceeded during periods when the distributed token bus protocol has more than one station transmitting. A head-end remodulator should be designed to tolerate at least a +30 dB increase in the received signal level over the maximum specified in Table 14-5. Furthermore, the remodulator shall report the presence of received signaling, perhaps as bad_signal, and shall not report silence, to the MAC sublayer during such periods of overload.

The same phenomenon may occur in any other channel which employs a distributed protocol with potential collisions. Thus a head-end remodulator should be designed to sharply reject signaling in other channels.

14.10 Environmental Specifications

{NOTE: Subsection 14.10 is not a part of the ISO standard. The subject of international standards in this area is under study by the International Electrotechnical Commission and other organizations.}

14.10.1 Safety Requirements. Recommendations and guidelines related to safety are given here. The list is incomplete; neither does it address all possible safety concerns. The designer is urged to consult the relevant local, national, and international safety codes and regulations to ensure compliance with the appropriate codes and standards. EIA CB 8-1981[9] provides additional guidance on many relevant regulatory requirements.

Local area network cable systems as described in Section 15 are subject to at least four direct electrical safety hazards during their use, and designers of connecting equipment should be aware of these hazards. The hazards are

(1) Direct contact between local network components and power or lighting circuits

(2) Static charge buildup on local network cables and components

(3) High-energy transients coupled onto the local network cabling system

(4) Potential differences between safety grounds to which various network components are connected.

These electrical safety hazards, to which all similar cabling systems are subject, should be alleviated properly for a local network to perform properly. In addition to provisions for properly handling these faults in an operational system, special measures shall be taken to ensure that the intended safety features are not negated when attaching or detaching equipment from the local area network medium of an existing network.

Sound installation practice, as defined by ANSI/NFPA 70-1984[3], Article 820 and applicable local codes and regulations shall be followed in every instance in which such practice is applicable.

14.10.2 Electromagnetic and Electric Environment. Sources of interference from the environment include electromagnetic fields, electrostatic discharge, transient voltages between earth connections, etc. Several sources of interference contribute to voltage buildup between the coaxial cable and the earth connection, if any, of the station.

The physical layer entity embodiment shall meet its specifications when operating in an ambient plane-wave field of

(1) 2 V/m from 10 kHz through 30 MHz
(2) 5 V/m from 30 MHz through 1 GHz.

14.10.3 Temperature and Humidity. Any embodiment of this standard is expected to operate over a reasonable range of environmental conditions related to temperature, humidity, and physical handling such as shock and vibration. Specific requirements and values for these parameters are considered to be beyond the scope of this standard. Manufacturers are requested to indicate in the literature associated with system components and equipment (and on the components if possible) the operating environment specifications to facilitate selection, installation, and maintenance of these components.

14.10.4 Regulatory Requirements. The following regulatory requirements may apply to local area network equipment and media:

ANSI/NFPA 70-1984[3], Articles 250, 800, and 820, ANSI/UL 94-1979[4], rated under V-0, ANSI/UL 114-1982[5], ANSI/UL 478-1979[6], CSA Standard C22.2 No 154-M 1983[8], FCC Docket 20780-1980 (Part 15, Subpart J)[10], and IEC 716-1983[11].

14.11 Labeling. It is recommended that each embodiment (and supporting documentation) of a physical layer entity conformant to this standard be labeled in a manner visible to the user with at least these parameters

(1) Specific sections of the standards to which the equipment conforms
(2) Data rate capabilities in Mb/s
(3) Types of signaling—one MAC-symbol/Bd only, or one MAC-symbol/Bd plus specific extensions as described in 14.11
(4) Transmit and receive channel assignments, both frequency and bandwidth
(5) Worst-case one-way repeater delay (for head-end remodulators) or round-trip delay (for other stations) which this equipment induces on a two-way transmission exchange between stations, as specified in 6.1.9
(6) Operating modes and selection capabilities as defined in 14.9.14 through 14.9.17.

Additionally, when the station has multiple F-connectors (for example, for dual cables, or redundant media, or both), the role of each F-connector shall be designated clearly by markings on the station in the vicinity of that F-connector.

Appendix

(This Appendix is not a part of this standard but is included for information only.)

14.12 Appendix —Provisions for Two MAC-symbol/Bd and Four MAC-symbol/Bd Signaling.

This Appendix gives preliminary considerations for methods of enhancing the basic three-symbol multilevel duobinary AM/PSK signaling to higher data rates within the same signaling bandwidth. Three such methods are described. The first method adds two more symbols (with corresponding amplitude levels) to the multilevel modulation, at an implementation-dependent S/N penalty of between 6 dB and 12 dB over the basic three-symbol system. The second method transmits two three-symbol channels in quadrature (that is, on carriers that are in phase-quadrature to each other), at a S/N penalty of approximately 5 dB, but with a requirement for coherent or quasi-coherent detection within receivers. The third method combines both of the other two methods to achieve four MAC-symbol/Bd signaling, and also combines the S/N penalties and implementation disadvantages of the other two methods. All three methods are for further study.

In systems where the head-end remodulators and other stations support one or more of these extended signaling methods (in addition to the required one MAC-symbol/Bd method of 14.9.2.1 and 14.9.3), additional requirements for interoperability will be needed. The following requirements are proposed; each is for further study.

(1) Each physical layer entity (including a head-end remodulator) conforming to the provisions of 14.12.1 or 14.12.2 should be able to fall back to half-speed under the provisions of 14.9.2.1 and 14.9.3. A station conforming to the provisions of 14.12.3 should be able to fall back to half-speed under the provisions of 14.12.1, and independently under the provisions of 14.12.2, and should be able to fall back to quarter-speed under the provisions of 14.9.2.1 and 14.9.3. Such fallback should be under station management control (see 14.8).

In diagram form, this states

```
                         2 b/Bd (5-symbol)
1 b/Bd (3-symbol)                           4 b/Bd (quad 5-symbol)
                       2 b/Bd (quad 3-symbol)
```

(2) Each physical layer entity (other than a head-end remodulator) capable of signaling by way of one or more of the extended methods of 14.12 should be able to recognize and differentiate between the pseudo-silence sequences (see 14.9.2.2) of all of its supported signaling methods.

(3) When the signaling method of the network, as determined by the active head-end remodulator, is one of the types supported by the physical layer entity, then that entity should infer the type of signaling then being employed in the local area network from the pseudo-silence signaling sequence used in lieu of "transmitted" silence in the forward channel, as specified in 14.9.2.1 and 14.9.2.2. This determination should be remade after any period in which

continuous silence (lack of modulation) has been detected in the forward channel for at least 2 ms, or after any loopback mode has been deselected and the broadband medium reselected as the source of received symbols (as described in 14.9.15).

If the inferred network signaling type differs from the current signaling type of the physical layer entity, then that entity should report the new signaling type to station management (see 9.2.9) and should inhibit transmission while those types differ.

14.12.1 Five-symbol (two MAC-symbol/Bd) Signaling

14.12.1.1 Symbol Encoding. The encoding action to be taken for each of the input MAC-symbols when five-symbol (two MAC-symbol/Bd) encoding is employed is

(1) Silence. All stations other than the head-end remodulator shall encode pairs of silence as the PHY-symbol {0} and shall cease transmission while transmitting only silence. The head-end remodulator shall encode successive pairs of silence symbols as successive PHY-symbols of the repeating sequence {2} {0} {4}, always restarting with the first {2} of the sequence for each new period of transmitted pseudo-silence. (It is permissible to terminate the sequence after any PHY-symbol.)

(2) Pad_idle. Consecutive pairs of pad_idle symbols shall be encoded as successive symbols of the repeating sequence {4} {0}, always restarting the sequence with the {4} for each new period of pad_idle.

(3) Non_data—The scrambler described in 14.9.2.3 shall be reinitialized (preset to all ones) at each non_data symbol. Each pair of non_data symbols shall be encoded as a {2}, and the eight-symbol (frame delimiter) sequence of 8.2.1 shall be encoded as follows; each

non_data non_data data$_1$ non_data non_data data$_2$ data$_3$ data$_4$

sequence shall be encoded as the sequence:

{2} {d$_{12}$} {2} {d$_{34}$},

where each data$_i$ is either a zero or a one, and each d$_{ij}$ is the corresponding encoding of the MAC-symbol pair data$_i$ and data$_j$, either a {0}, a {1}, a {3}, or a {4}, as described below.

After each such eight-symbol (frame delimiter) sequence, as defined in 8.2.1, the encoder shall start to maintain a sense of PHY-octet alignment, with the next output PHY-symbol considered to be the first of a new PHY-octet. (Notice that this physical-layer sense of PHY-octet alignment coincidentally corresponds to the MAC entity's sense of pairs of MAC-octets.)

NOTE: Since non_data symbols occur only in frame delimiters (see 8.2.1), the physical layer may infer that the MAC sublayer is outputting a frame delimiter sequence upon receipt of its first non_data symbol.

(4) Zero and one —Each zero and one symbol shall be encoded as follows:

(a) The MAC-symbol shall be applied as input to the scrambler described in 14.9.2.3, resulting in a "scrambled" zero or one symbol;

(b) Each successive pair of scrambled MAC-symbols shall be converted to one of the PHY-symbol output codes by way of the following correspondence:

```
+------first scrambled symbol of pair
|
zero, zero --> {0}
zero, one  --> {1}
one,  zero --> {3}
one,  one  --> {4}
```

This is the ($\underline{data}_i$, $\underline{data}_j$) to $\{\underline{d}_{ij}\}$ mapping referred to in 14.12.1.1(3).

(c) The following procedure shall be performed on each resultant PHY-octet of $\{\underline{0}\}$, $\{\underline{1}\}$, $\{\underline{3}\}$, and $\{\underline{4}\}$ PHY-symbol codes. Each such octet of these PHY-symbol codes shall be compared with the immediately prior octet of PHY-symbols as transmitted (that is, after execution of this procedure on that prior octet, if applicable). If both PHY-octets consist solely of the identical PHY-symbol code (that is, either sixteen $\{\underline{0}\}$s, or sixteen $\{\underline{1}\}$s, or sixteen $\{\underline{3}\}$s, or sixteen $\{\underline{4}\}$s), then the last code in the PHY-octet under examination shall be replaced by a $\{\underline{2}\}$ before transmission.

NOTE: This procedure can alter at most every other octet of PHY-symbols, and the second octet after the encoded (frame delimiter) sequence of 8.2.1 is the first such octet that can be altered. This procedure has no effect on the scrambler described in 14.9.2.3 and in the previous subsection.

14.12.1.2 Baseband Modulation. The PHY-symbol coded signal shall be converted to an appropriately-shaped pulse whose amplitude is determined by the output symbol code as follows (where MAX is the amplitude of the largest pulse):

$\{\underline{0}\}$ —> 0/4 of MAX (= 0)
$\{\underline{1}\}$ —> 1/4 of MAX
$\{\underline{2}\}$ —> 2/4 of MAX
$\{\underline{3}\}$ —> 3/4 of MAX
$\{\underline{4}\}$ —> 4/4 of MAX (= MAX)

14.12.1.3 Signal and Noise Levels. Some adjustment in the transmitted or received signal levels or the required in-band noise floor may be necessary. The most likely adjustment is an increase in the required in-band signal-to-noise level.

14.12.2 Three-symbol Quadrature (two MAC-symbol/Bd) Signaling

14.12.2.1 Symbol Encoding. For this encoding, two separate baseband signals are formed and independently modulated onto in-phase and quadrature carriers for transmission. These are referred to in the following discussion as the in-phase and quadrature subchannels, respectively. Successively encoded MAC-symbols are transmitted alternately in the in-phase and quadrature subchannels.

The encoding action to be taken for each of the input MAC-symbols when three-symbol quadrature (two MAC-symbol/Bd) encoding is employed is

(1) <u>Silence</u> —All stations other than the head-end remodulator shall encode <u>silence</u> as the PHY-symbol $\{\underline{0}\}$ and shall cease transmission while transmitting only <u>silence</u>. The head-end remodulator shall encode successive <u>silence</u> symbols

as successive PHY-symbols of the repeating sequence {2} {0} {2} {0} {4} {0} {0} {0}, always restarting with the first {2} of the sequence for each new period of transmitted pseudo-silence, and always with the first {2} transmitted in the in-phase subchannel. (Thus the in-phase subchannel transmission sequence is {2} {2} {4} {0} and the quadrature subchannel transmission sequence is {0} {0} {0} {0}. Also, it is permissible to terminate the sequence after any even number of PHY-symbols.)

(2) Pad_idle —Consecutive pad_idle symbols shall be encoded as successive PHY-symbols of the repeating sequence {4} {0} {0} {0}, always restarting the sequence with the {4} for each new period of pad_idle, and always with the {4} transmitted in the in-phase subchannel. (Thus the in-phase subchannel transmission sequence is {4} {0} and the quadrature subchannel transmission sequence is {0} {0}.)

(3) Non_data —The scrambler described in 14.9.2.3 shall be reinitialized (preset to all ones) at each non_data symbol. Each non_data symbol shall be encoded as a {2}, and the eight-symbol (frame delimiter) sequence of 8.2.1 shall be encoded as follows; each

non_data non_data data$_1$ non_data non_data data$_2$ data$_3$ data$_4$

sequence shall be encoded as the sequence

{2} {2} {2} {2} {d$_1$} {d$_2$} {d$_3$} {d$_4$},

where each data$_i$ is either a zero or a one, each d$_i$ is the corresponding encoding of the MAC-symbol data$_i$, either a {0} or a {4} as described below, and always with the first {2} transmitted in the primary channel. (Thus the in-phase subchannel transmission sequence is

{2} {2} {d$_1$} {d$_3$}

and the quadrature subchannel transmission sequence is

{2} {2} {d$_2$} {d$_4$}.)

After each such eight-symbol (frame delimiter) sequence, as defined in 8.2.1, the encoder shall start to maintain a sense of PHY-octet alignment, with the next output PHY-symbol considered to be the first of a new PHY-octet. (Notice that this physical-layer sense of PHY-octet alignment is coincidentally identical to the MAC entity's sense of MAC-octet alignment.)

NOTE: Since non_data symbols occur only in frame delimiters (see 8.2.1), the physical layer may infer that the MAC sublayer is outputting a frame delimiter sequence upon receipt of its first non_data symbol.

(4) Zero and one —Each zero and one symbol shall be encoded as follows

(a) The MAC-symbol shall be applied as input to the scrambler described in 14.9.2.3, resulting in a "scrambled" zero or one MAC-symbol;

(b) The scrambled MAC-symbol shall be converted to one of the PHY-symbol output codes as follows:

zero ---> {0}
one ---> {4}

This is the $\underline{\text{data}}_i$ to $\{\underline{d}_i\}$ mapping referred to in 14.12.2.1(3).

(c) The following procedure shall be performed on each resultant PHY-octet of $\{\underline{0}\}$ and $\{\underline{4}\}$ PHY-symbol codes. Each such octet of these PHY-symbol codes shall be compared with the immediately prior octet of PHY-symbols <u>as transmitted</u> (that is, after execution of this procedure on that prior octet, if applicable). If the pair of PHY-octets is identical to a single ordered pair of PHY-symbol codes repeated eight times (that is, $(\{\underline{0}\}\ \{\underline{0}\})^8$, $(\{\underline{0}\}\ \{\underline{4}\})^8$, $(\{\underline{4}\}\ \{\underline{0}\})^8$, or $(\{\underline{4}\}\ \{\underline{4}\})^8$), so that the in-phase and quadrature subchannel transmission sequences each consist of a single PHY-symbol code, possibly different in each subchannel, repeated eight times, then the last three codes in the PHY-octet under examination shall be altered as follows:

$\{\underline{0}\}\ \{\underline{0}\}\ \{\underline{0}\}$ shall be replaced by $\{\underline{2}\}\ \{\underline{4}\}\ \{\underline{2}\}$
$\{\underline{0}\}\ \{\underline{4}\}\ \{\underline{0}\}$ shall be replaced by $\{\underline{2}\}\ \{\underline{0}\}\ \{\underline{2}\}$
$\{\underline{4}\}\ \{\underline{0}\}\ \{\underline{4}\}$ shall be replaced by $\{\underline{2}\}\ \{\underline{4}\}\ \{\underline{2}\}$
$\{\underline{4}\}\ \{\underline{4}\}\ \{\underline{4}\}$ shall be replaced by $\{\underline{2}\}\ \{\underline{0}\}\ \{\underline{2}\}$

In other words, the last code of the in-phase subchannel transmission sequence is altered before transmission as follows:

$\{\underline{0}\}$ is replaced by $\{\underline{4}\}$
$\{\underline{4}\}$ is replaced by $\{\underline{0}\}$

and the last two codes of the quadrature subchannel transmission sequence are changed to $\{\underline{2}\}\ \{\underline{2}\}$ before transmission.

NOTE: This procedure can alter at most every other octet of PHY-symbols, and the second octet after the encoded (frame delimiter) sequence of 8.2.1 is the first such octet that can be altered. This procedure has no effect on the scrambler described in 14.9.2.3 and in the prevous subsection.

14.12.2.2 Baseband Modulation. The PHY-symbol coded signals shall be converted to appropriately-shaped pulses whose amplitude at the correct sampling intervals is determined by the output PHY-symbol codes as follows (where MAX is the amplitude of the largest pulse):

$\{\underline{0}\}$ ---> 0/4 of MAX (= 0)
$\{\underline{2}\}$ ---> 2/4 of MAX
$\{\underline{4}\}$ ---> 4/4 of MAX (= MAX)

The sequence of pulses corresponding to the first, third, and so forth (odd numbered) PHY-symbols of each transmission sequence shall be shaped for transmission in the in-phase subchannel, as described in 14.9.3, so that their decoding can be achieved by full-wave rectification of the demodulated in-phase component of the line signal. This sequence is known as the baseband in-phase modulation.

The sequence of pulses corresponding to the second, fourth, and so forth (even numbered) PHY-symbols of each transmission sequence shall be shaped for transmission in the quadrature subchannel, as described in 14.9.3, so that their decoding can be achieved by full-wave rectification of the demodulated quadrature component of the line signal. This sequence is known as the baseband quadrature modulation.

14.12.2.3 Line Signal in RF Band (at the line output of the terminal equipment). The equivalent baseband in-phase modulation of 14.12.2.2 shall be applied to an (in-phase) rf carrier centered in the assigned channel, the equivalent baseband quadrature modulation of 14.12.2.2 shall be applied to an rf carrier in phase-quadrature with the preceding (in-phase) rf carrier, and the resultant modulated carriers shall be combined and coupled to the broadband bus medium as specified in 14.9.7.

NOTE: Any equivalent method of impressing in-phase and quadrature components on the rf carrier is acceptable.

14.12.2.4 Signal and Noise Levels. It is unlikely that adjustment of the transmitted or received signal levels or the required in-band noise floor will be necessary.

14.12.3 Five-symbol Quadrature (four MAC-symbol/Bd) Signaling

14.12.3.1 Symbol Encoding. For this encoding, two separate baseband signals are formed and independently modulated onto in-phase and quadrature carriers for transmission. These are referred to in the following discussion as the in-phase and quadrature subchannels, respectively. Successively encoded MAC-symbols are transmitted alternately in the in-phase and quadrature subchannels.

The encoding action to be taken for each of the input MAC-symbols when five-symbol quadrature (four MAC-symbol/Bd) encoding is employed is

(1) Silence —All stations other than the head-end remodulator shall encode pairs of silence as the PHY-symbol {0} and shall cease transmission while transmitting only silence. The head-end remodulator shall encode successive pairs of silence symbols as successive PHY-symbols of the repeating sequence {2} {0} {4} {0} {0} {0}, always restarting with the first {2} of the sequence for each new period of transmitted pseudo-silence, and always with the first {2} transmitted in the in-phase subchannel. (Thus the in-phase subchannel transmission sequence is {2} {4} {0} and the quadrature subchannel transmission sequence is {0} {0} {0}. Also, it is permissible to terminate the sequence after any even number of PHY-symbols.)

(2) Pad_idle. Consecutive pairs of pad_idle symbols shall be encoded as successive symbols of the repeating sequence {4} {0} {0} {0}, always restarting the sequence with the {4} for each new period of pad_idle. (Thus the in-phase subchannel transmission sequence is {4} {0} and the quadrature subchannel transmission sequence is {0} {0}.)

(3) Non_data—The scrambler described in 14.9.2.3 shall be reinitialized (preset to all ones) at each non_data symbol. Each pair of non_data symbols shall be encoded as a {2}, and the eight-symbol (frame delimiter) sequence of 8.2.1 shall be encoded as follows; each

non_data non_data data$_1$ non_data non_data data$_2$ data$_3$ data$_4$

sequence shall be encoded as the sequence

{2} {2} {d$_{12}$} {d$_{34}$},

where each data$_i$ is either a zero or a one, and each d$_{ij}$ is the corresponding encoding of the MAC-symbol pair data$_i$ and data$_j$, either a {0}, a {1}, a {3}, or a {4}, as described below. (Thus the in-phase subchannel transmission sequence is {2} {d$_{12}$} and the quadrature subchannel transmission sequence is {2} {d$_{34}$}.)

After each such eight-symbol (frame delimiter) sequence, as defined in 8.2.1, the encoder shall start to maintain a sense of PHY-octet alignment, with the next output PHY-symbol considered to be the first of a new PHY-octet. (Notice that this physical-layer sense of PHY-octet alignment coincidentally corresponds to the MAC entity's sense of pairs of MAC-octets.)

NOTE: Since non_data symbols occur only in frame delimiters (see 8.2.1), the physical layer may infer that the MAC sublayer is outputting a frame delimiter sequence upon receipt of its first non_data symbol.

(4) Zero and one —Each zero and one symbol shall be encoded as follows:

(a) The MAC-symbol shall be applied as input to the scrambler described in 14.9.2.3, resulting in a "scrambled" zero or one symbol

(b) Each successive pair of scrambled MAC-symbols shall be converted to one of the PHY-symbol output codes by way of the following correspondence

```
        +------ scrambled symbol of pair
        |
   zero,   zero  --> {0}
   zero,   one   --> {1}
   one,    zero  --> {3}
   one,    one   --> {4}
```

This is the (data$_i$, data$_j$) to {d$_{ij}$} mapping referred to in 14.12.3.1(3).

(c) The following procedure shall be performed on each resultant PHY-octet of {0}, {1}, {3}, and {4} PHY-symbol codes. Each such octet of these PHY-symbol codes shall be compared with the immediately prior octet of PHY-symbols as transmitted (that is, after execution of this procedure on that prior octet, if applicable). If the pair of PHY-octets is identical to a single ordered pair of PHY-symbol codes repeated eight times (that is, ({M} {N})^8, where {M} and {N} are each chosen independently from the set ({0}, {1}, {3}, and {4}), so that the in-phase and quadrature subchannel transmission sequences each consist of a single PHY-symbol code, possibly different in each subchannel, repeated eight times, then the last code in the PHY-octet under examination shall be replaced by a {2} before transmission.

In other words, the in-phase subchannel transmission sequence is unchanged and the last code of the quadrature subchannel transmission sequence is changed to a {2} before transmission.

NOTE: This procedure can alter at most every other octet of PHY-symbols, and the second octet after the encoded (frame delimiter) sequence of 8.2.1 is the first such octet that can be altered. This procedure has no effect on the scrambler described in 14.9.2.3 and in the previous subsection.

14.12.3.2 Baseband Modulation. The PHY-symbol coded signals shall be converted to appropriately-shaped pulses whose amplitude at the correct sampling intervals is determined by the output PHY-symbol codes as follows (where

MAX is the amplitude of the largest pulse):

$\{0\}$ --> 0/4 of MAX (= 0)
$\{1\}$ --> 1/4 of MAX
$\{2\}$ --> 2/4 of MAX
$\{3\}$ --> 3/4 of MAX
$\{4\}$ --> 4/4 of MAX (= MAX)

The sequence of pulses corresponding to the first, third, and so forth (odd numbered) PHY-symbols of each transmission sequence shall be shaped for transmission in the in-phase subchannel, as described in 14.9.3, so that their decoding can be achieved by full-wave rectification of the demodulated in-phase component of the line signal. This sequence is known as the baseband in-phase modulation.

The sequence of pulses corresponding to the second, fourth, and so forth (even numbered) PHY-symbols of each transmission sequence shall be shaped for transmission in the quadrature subchannel, as described in 14.9.3, so that their decoding can be achieved by full-wave rectification of the demodulated quadrature component of the line signal. This sequence is known as the baseband quadrature modulation.

14.12.3.3 Line Signal in RF Band (at the line output of the terminal equipment). The equivalent baseband in-phase modulation of 14.12.2.2 shall be applied to an (in-phase) rf carrier centered in the assigned channel, the equivalent baseband quadrature modulation of 14.12.2.2 shall be applied to an rf carrier in phase-quadrature with the preceding (in-phase) rf carrier, and the resultant modulated carriers shall be combined and coupled to the broadband bus medium as specified in 14.9.7.

NOTE: Any equivalent method of impressing in-phase and quadrature components on the rf carrier is acceptable.)

14.12.3.4 Signal and Noise Levels. Some adjustment in the transmitted or received signal levels or the required in-band noise floor may be necessary. The most likely adjustments are an increase in the required in-band signal-to-noise level from +30 dB to +35 dB and a smaller increase in transmitter output levels.

TOKEN-PASSING BUS

IEEE
Std 802.4-1985

Appendix

(This Appendix is not a part of this standard but is included for information only.)

14.13 Appendix —Detailed Scrambling and Descrambling Process.

14.13.1 Scrambling. The message polynomial is divided by the generating polynomial $1+X^{-6}+X^{-7}$. (See Fig 14-5) The coefficients of the quotient of this division are taken in descending order from the data sequence to be transmitted.

14.13.2 Descrambling. At the receiver the incoming bit sequence is multiplied by the generating polynomial $1+X^{-6}+X^{-7}$ to form the recovered message polynomial. The coefficients of the recovered polynomial, taken in descending order, form the output data sequence.

14.13.3 Elements of the Scrambling Process. The factor $1+X^{-6}+X^{-7}$ randomizes the transmitted data over a sequence length of 127 bits. Fig 14-6 is given as an indication only, since with another technique the logical arrangement might take another form.

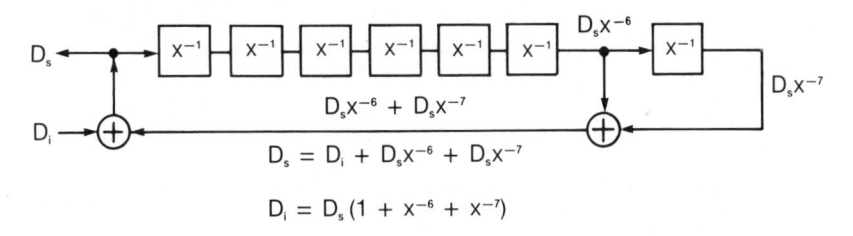

Fig 14-5
$1+X^{-6}+X^{-7}$ **Scrambler**

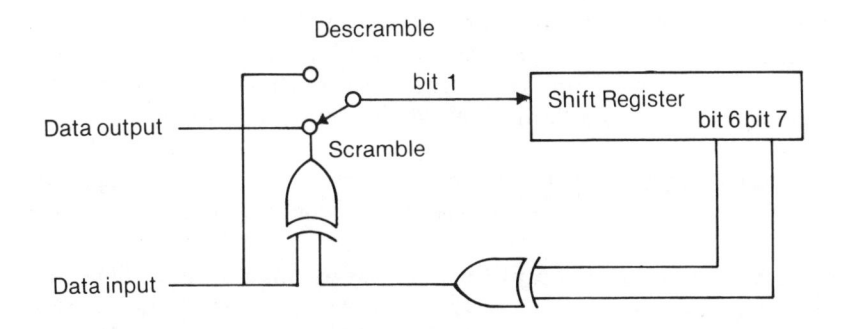

Fig 14-6
Examplary Scrambler / Descrambler Circuitry

15. Broadband Bus Medium "Layer" Specification

The functional, electrical, and mechanical characteristics of one specific form of medium "layer" (broadband bus) of this standard are specified in this section. This specification includes the medium "layer" embodiments of a broadband bus LAN. The relationship of this section to other sections of this standard and to LAN specifications is illustrated in Fig 15-1. The relationship between this specification and the broadband bus physical layer and medium "layer" entities is illustrated in Fig 15-2.

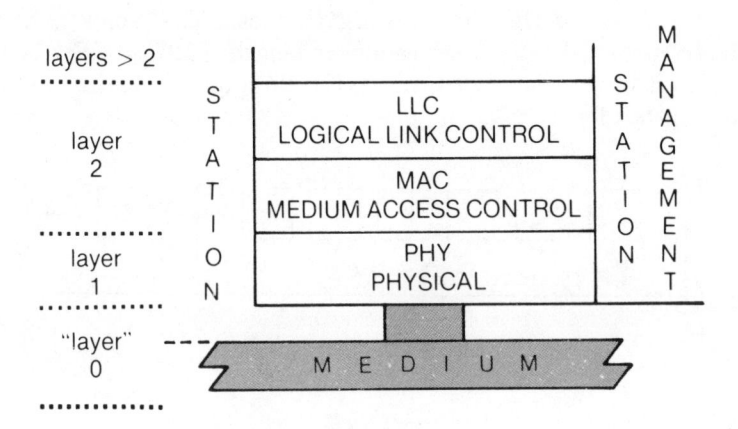

**Fig 15-1
Relation to LAN Model**

This standard specifies the medium "layer" only insofar as necessary to ensure
(1) The interoperability of physical layer entities conforming to Section 14 when connected to a medium layer conformant to this section, and
(2) The protection of the local area network and those using it.

15.1 Nomenclature. Terms used in this section whose meanings within the section are more specific than indicated in the glossary of Ref [1] are as follows:

bidirectional broadband amplifier. An assemblage of amplifiers and filters which amplifies and re-equalizes in the forward direction all signals received in the higher frequency portion of the broadband spectrum, and simultaneously amplifies and re-equalizes in the reverse direction all signals received in the lower frequency portion of the broadband spectrum.

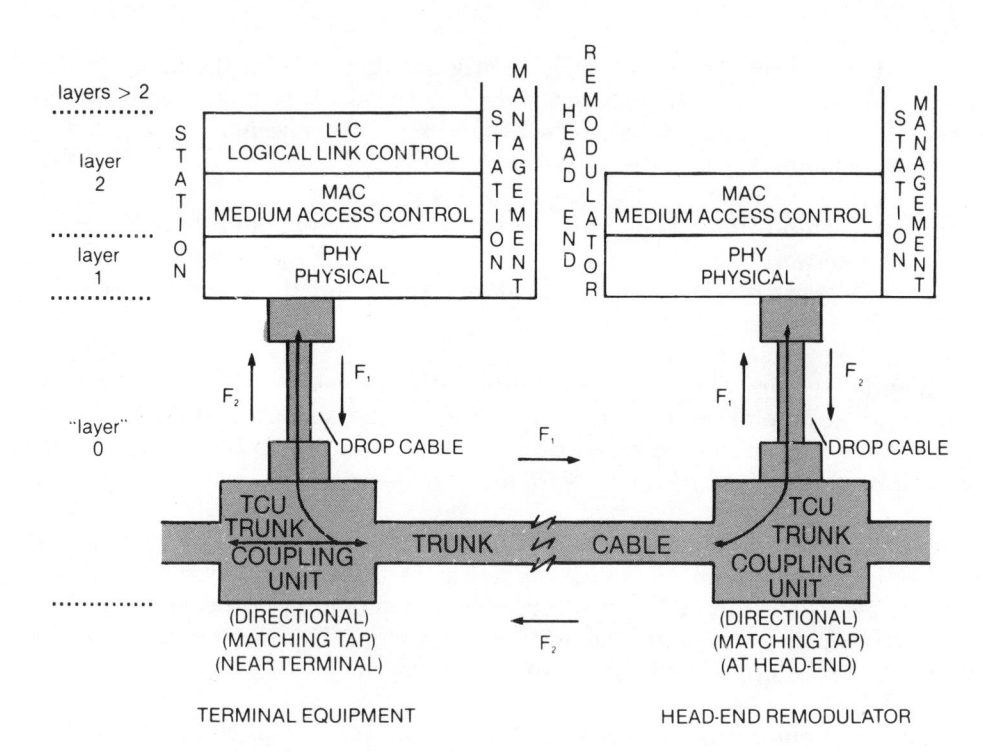

TOKEN-PASSING BUS

IEEE
Std 802.4-1985

**Figure 15-2
Physical Hardware Partitioning,
Token-Passing Broadband Bus Local Area Network**

NOTE: On single (bidirectional) cable systems, $F_1 < F_2$ and both F_1 and F_2 are carried on common trunk and drop cables. On dual (unidirectional) cable systems, F_1 and F_2 are carried on separate trunk and drop cables.

broadband coaxial system. A system whereby information is encoded, modulated onto a carrier, and band-pass filtered or otherwise constrained to occupy only a limited frequency spectrum on the coaxial transmission medium. Many information signals can be present on the medium at the same time without disruption provided that they all occupy nonoverlapping frequency regions within the cable system's range of frequency transport.

drop cable. The smaller diameter flexible coaxial cable of the broadband medium which connects to a station.

dual-cable. A broadband coaxial cable system in which separate coaxial cables are used for the forward and reverse directions of signal transmission. Connection of a dual-cable system to a station requires dual F-connectors at the station—one for transmission and one for reception.

F-connector. A 75 Ω F-series coaxial cable connector (of the kind commonly found on consumer television and video equipment).

forward. The direction of transmission originating at the head-end of a broadband cable system and relayed "outbound" by the system's bidirectional broadband amplifiers to the system's "subscribers". Transmission on the higher-frequency channels is supported in this direction.

head-end remodulator. The unit located at the head-end of a broadband bus local area network which receives in a reverse channel the signals transmitted by other network stations, and rebroadcasts those signals back to those other stations in a corresponding forward channel.

high-split. The broadband system configuration, as determined by the system's bidirectional amplifiers, in which signaling in the spectrum from 5 MHz to 174 MHz is relayed in the reverse direction and signaling in the spectrum from 234 MHz up is relayed in the forward direction.

mid-split. The broadband system configuration, as determined by the system's bidirectional amplifiers, in which signaling in the spectrum from 5 MHz to 108 MHz is relayed in the reverse direction and signaling in the spectrum from 162 MHz up is relayed in the forward direction. This is the configuration preferred in the broadband portion of this standard.

(impedance-matching) power splitter. A small module which electrically and mechanically couples one large diameter trunk cable to other large diameter trunk cables, providing a branching topology for the broadband trunk. A power splitter splits the signal energy received in the forward direction among the outgoing trunks, and combines any signal energy received in the reverse direction. It passes low-frequency (< 1 kHz) ac power between the trunk cables. It contains only passive electrical components (R, L, C).

reverse. The direction of transmission originating at the "subscribers" of a broadband cable system, terminating at the head-end and relayed "inbound" by the system's bidirectional broadband amplifiers. Transmission on the lower-frequency channels is supported in this direction.

(impedance-matching) splitter. A smaller version of the power splitter used to couple drop cables together. It does not pass low-frequency ac power between the drop cables.

sub-split. The broadband system configuration, as determined by the system's bidirectional amplifiers, in which signaling in the spectrum from 5 MHz to 30 MHz is relayed in the reverse direction and signaling in the spectrum from 54 MHz up is relayed in the forward direction. (This configuration is commonly found in community residential cable TV systems.)

(impedance-matching) tap. A small module which electrically and mechanically couples the large diameter trunk cable to smaller diameter drop cables, passes low-frequency (< 1 kHz) ac power between input and output trunk cable sections, and isolates the power from drop cable sections. It splits the signal energy received in the forward direction very asymmetrically, with the bulk of that signal energy passed to the outgoing trunk cable and only a small percentage going to the drop cables, and combines with similar asymmetry any signal energy received in the reverse direction. It contains only passive electrical components (R, L, C).

trunk cable. The main (larger-diameter) semirigid coaxial cable of a broadband coaxial cable system. Both ac power and rf signaling are carried on the cable.

15.2 Object. The object of this specification is to
(1) Provide the physical medium necessary for communication between local network stations employing the token bus access method defined in this standard and a broadband bus physical layer.
(2) Provide a medium which can be shared by multiple local area networks and by totally unrelated applications (such as voice, data, and analog video).
(3) Provide for high network availability.
(4) Provide for ease of installation and service in a wide range of environments.
(5) Permit use of existing components mass produced for the cable TV industry, and of the corresponding set of installation practices, where feasible.

15.3 Compatibility Considerations. This standard applies to medium "layer" entities which are designed to operate as conventional bidirectional (by frequency) CATV-like broadband coaxial cable systems. Such systems generally use standard CATV taps, connectors, amplifiers, power supplies, and coaxial cable. This specification primarily applies to a single trunk system in which two-way communication usually is accomplished through the use of bidirectional amplifiers whose filters permit differing parts of the available cable spectrum to be transmitted in each direction. Dual-trunk systems in which each trunk is used unidirectionally are also permitted, but require both stations and the head-end remodulator to have the necessary dual-cable connector fittings.

The use of a coaxial broadband system permits the assignment of different frequency bands to multiple simultaneous applications. For example, a portion of the cable spectrum can be used by LANs while other portions are used for point-to-point or multipoint data links, and others are used to convey television and audio signals. With the proper selection of signal levels and proper equipment design all of the applications can be propagated without deleterious interference.

All implementations of medium "layer" entities conformant to this standard shall be compatible at their station interfaces. Specific implementations based on this standard may be conceived in different ways provided compatibility at the actual station interfaces is maintained.

15.4 Overview of the Broadband Bus Medium "Layer"

15.4.1 General Description of Functions. The functions performed by the broadband bus medium "layer" entity are described informally here. Jointly these functions provide a means whereby signaling in the reverse-direction spectrum presented at the station interfaces of drop cables can be combined and conveyed as corresponding forward-channel spectrum signaling (with the assistance of head-end remodulators functioning as relay entities) to all of the stations on all of the medium's drop cables. Thus stations connected to these drop cables can communicate.

15.4.1.1 Operational Overview of the Broadband Bus Medium. The use of a coaxial cable operating as a broadband medium introduces special system considerations which are not encountered in single-channel transmission systems. A conventional CATV-like system uses bidirectional amplifiers to achieve two-way transmission on a single coaxial cable. The amplifier actually consists of two independent unidirectional amplifiers, together with the appropriate crossover filters, so that one amplifier transmits the upper portion of the cable spectrum in the forward direction, outbound from the head-end, while the other amplifier transmits the lower portion in the reverse direction, toward the head-end. (Therefore each station requires an rf transmitter and receiver each operating in a different portion of the cable spectrum.)

At the head-end, where forward direction signals originate and reverse direction signals converge, a remodulator receives the lower-frequency reverse channel signal and retransmits it as the higher-frequency forward channel signal to the "downstream" stations. One remodulator is needed for each separate channel pair used as a broadband bus local area network.

Stations are connected to the trunk coaxial cable in such systems by smaller-diameter drop cables and impedance-matching taps. These taps are passive devices which are highly directional with regard to signal propagation as shown in Fig 15-2. The directional characteristics of the taps improve the impedance matching at the ports of the tap and minimize the effects of reflections due to any impedance mismatches along the trunk or on other drop cables.

The directionality of the tap is such that the transmission loss between the station and the reverse direction trunk is considerably less than that between the station and the forward direction trunk. Hence communication between devices connected to different taps along the coax occurs through the transmission of a frequency F_1 in the low-band toward the head-end, reception at the head-end and retransmission in the forward direction at a high-band frequency F_2, and reception by the "listening" stations.

NOTE: Head-end taps are connected with forward and reverse directions interchanged to support the remodulator's role as a relay entity.

The topology of the broadband system is that of a highly branched tree, with the head-end equipment located at the tree's roots, and the other equipment connected as leaves to the tree's branches. Branching is accomplished in the trunk itself by way of power splitters, which provide nondirectional coupling of the ac power carried on the trunk cables, and directional coupling of the rf power similar to that of the just-described taps. Like the taps, the power splitters also employ only passive electrical components (R, L, C only).

Branching in the drop cables is provided by (drop cable) splitters which block ac power flow among their ports. They also employ only passive electrical components.

The amplifiers of the broadband system are powered from the trunk cable itself. Low-voltage (30 V or 60 V) ac power usually is carried on the center conductor and grounded shield of the cable at a nominal frequency of 50 Hz or 60 Hz; the amplifiers use some of that power and pass the rest to the connected "downstream" trunk cable. Standard CATV-like power supplies and power-combining and power-blocking components permit the power to be supplied to the trunk cabling at one or more points in the system.

15.4.1.2 Head-End Remodulator Functions. In an actual broadband bus system, stations do not transmit and receive on the same frequency channel. For each broadband bus local area network, one central station, designated the head-end remodulator, receives on a low-frequency channel and transmits on a high-frequency channel. All of the other stations of that particular network receive on the high-frequency channel and transmit on the low-frequency channel. Thus any one network really uses a pair of directional channels, with the low-frequency (reverse) channel having many transmitters and one receiver, and the high-frequency (forward) channel having one transmitter and many receivers.

To allow stations to communicate, the head-end remodulator (see 14.9.19) serves as a relay station; when not transmitting for itself, its medium access sublayer entity interprets the symbols received in the reverse channel and retransmits them (in some form) in the forward channel. When a collision or noise is detected (for example, bad_signal reported), the head-end remodulator's medium access entity sends an Abort sequence (see 4.1.8) in lieu of the received symbols. When silence is detected, the head-end remodulator sends a pseudo-silence pattern which the other stations report to their medium access entities as silence. Thus during normal operation the head-end remodulator transmits continuously.

To support its functioning as a relay, the head-end remodulator is located at the "root" of the tree-like structure of the medium, and is connected to the trunk by way of a tap so installed that the remodulator receives signaling originating "downstream" from it, and also transmits its signal "downstream".

15.4.2 Model Used for the Functional Specification. The detailed functional specifications are modeled after CCITT H.series media specifications Refs [18] and [19], particularly the H.14 specification, with additional detail added where necessary.

15.4.3 Basic Characteristics and Options. All signal-conveyance characteristics and station-interface characteristics are mandatory. All other characteristics are optional.

15.5 Bibliography

CCIR Recommendation 567, Performance Characteristics of Television Circuits Designed for use in International Connections, vol XII, ITU, Geneva, 1978.

CCIR Recommendation 570, Standard Test Signal for Conventional Loading of a Television Channel, vol XII, ITU, Geneva, 1978.

CCIR Report, Characteristics of Television Systems, vol XI, Report 624-1, ITU, Geneva, 1978.

GENERAL MOTORS UNIFIED COMMUNICATIONS SYSTEMS TASK FORCE OF MCC/CMC COMPUTERS IN MANUFACTURING SUBCOMMITTEE, General Specifications: Broadband Co-axial Cable Networks for Digital, Video, and Audio Transmission, General Motors, Detroit, Michigan, May 1978.

RHEINFELDER, W. CATV Circuit Engineering, TAB Books, Blue Ridge Summit, PA, 1975.

RHEINFELDER, W. CATV System Engineering, TAB Books, Blue Ridge Summit, PA, 1962.

Design and Construction of CATV Systems, RCA / Cablevision Systems, Van Nuys, CA.

Basic CATV Concepts, THETA-COM CATV / TEXSCAN, Phoenix, Az.

NCTA 008-0477, Standards of Good Engineering Practices for Measurements on Cable Television Systems.

15.6 Broadband Bus Medium "Layer" Functional, Electrical, and Mechanical Specifications.

The broadband bus medium "layer" entity is an entity whose sole function (relative to this standard) is signal transport between the stations and head-end remodulator of a broadband bus local area network. Consequently only those characteristics of the medium "layer" entity which impinge on station to remodulator and remodulator to station signal transport, or on human and equipment safety, are specified in this standard.

An implementation of the medium "layer" entity shall be deemed conformant to this standard if it provides the specified signal transport services and characteristics for the stations and remodulator of a broadband bus local area network, and if it meets the relevant safety and environmental codes.

All measurements specified in the following paragraphs are to be made at the point of station or remodulator connection to the medium. Unless otherwise indicated, these measurements shall be made across that central portion of the 1.5 MHz, 6 MHz, or 12 MHz channel actually used for signaling, that is, the central 1 MHz, 5 MHz, or 10 MHz, respectively. Unless otherwise stated, all voltage and power levels specified are in rms and dB (1 mV, 75 Ω) [dBmV] rms, respectively, based on transmissions of random data patterns. (See the NOTE in 14.9 for more details.)

15.6.1 Coupling to the Station / Head-End Remodulator. The connection of the broadband medium to the station or head-end remodulator shall be by way of a flexible 75 Ω drop cable terminated in a male F-series 75 Ω connector; this combination shall mate with a female F-series 75 Ω connector mounted on the station or remodulator.

In addition to this coupling, the shield(s) of the coaxial drop cable medium shall be connected to the shell of the terminating male F-connector and the impedance of that connection over the range from dc to 450 MHz shall be less than 0.1 Ω. Also, the impedance of a connection between the shell of that male F-series connector and the outer barrel of a mated female F-series connector over the range from dc to 450 MHz shall be less than 0.1 Ω.

15.6.2 Characteristic Impedance. The characteristic impedance of the broadband medium shall be 75 ±3 Ω. The maximum VSWR at each of the medium's F-connector shall be 1.5:1 or less when the F-connector is terminated with a 75 Ω resistive load, as measured over the entire broadband cable frequency spectrum supported by the medium. (Note that this spectrum shall include both the forward and reverse channels in use in the network.)

15.6.3 Signal Level. When receiving the signal of a single station or head-end remodulator whose transmit level has been adjusted properly (as in 14.9.5.4), the broadband medium shall present that signaling to the connected remodulator or station, respectively, at an amplitude as specified in Table 15-1. The maximum short-term variation of that amplitude level with respect to a reference signal of constant mean amplitude provided at any remodulator or station site shall be no more than ±1 dB/min.

15.6.4 Distortion. Broadband amplifiers and diplexing filters are the primary cause of amplitude and phase distortion on the broadband medium. Over any directional channel used for a broadband bus local area network, the

**Table 15-1
Delivered In-band Signal Level**

Channel Bandwidth (MHz)	Delivered Signal Amplitude in dB (1 mV, 75 Ω) [dBmV]	
	Minimum	Maximum
1.5	−16	+4
6.0	−10	+10
12.0	−7	+13

PERMISSIBLE DISTORTION

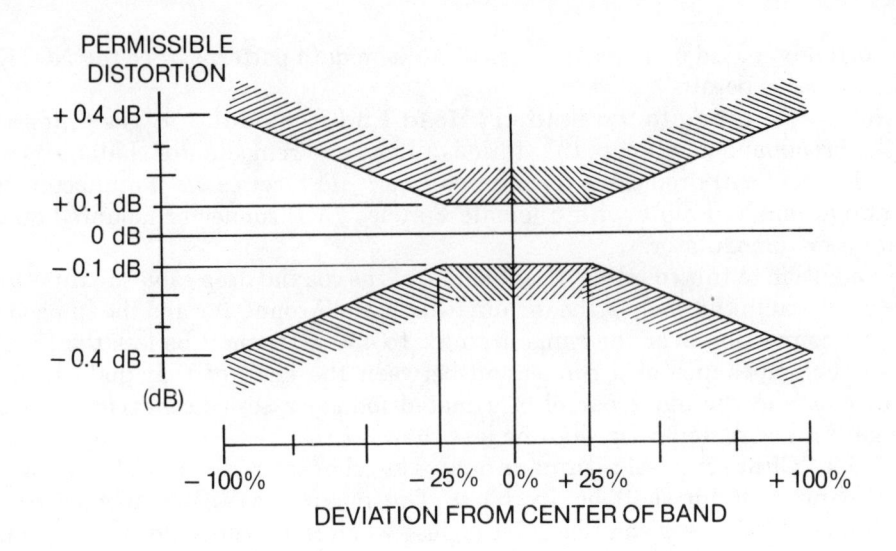

**Fig 15-3
Limits for Amplitude Distortion**

amplitude distortion shall fall within the limits specified by Eq 15-4 and Fig 15-3 and the group-delay distortion shall fall within the limits specified by Eq 15-5 and Fig 15-5.

$$\text{PAD} = \begin{cases} \pm 0.1, & 0 \leq |f| \leq \frac{B}{8} \\ \pm 0.8 \frac{f}{B}, & \frac{B}{8} \leq |f| \leq \frac{B}{2} \end{cases} \quad (\text{Eq } 15\text{--}4)$$

where
- PAD denotes the maximum permissible amplitude distortion relative to the center of the signaling band, measured as a fraction of 1/B seconds
- f denotes frequency variation (Hz) relative to the center of the signaling band
- B denotes the bandwidth of the channel (Hz) (for example, 1.5 MHz, 6 MHz, or 12 MHz).

15.6.5 Signal to Noise (S/N) Level. It is recommended that the signal to noise level be at least +40 dB (V rms /(V rms)). In no case shall it be less than +30 dB (as measured at any station or remodulator).

TOKEN-PASSING BUS

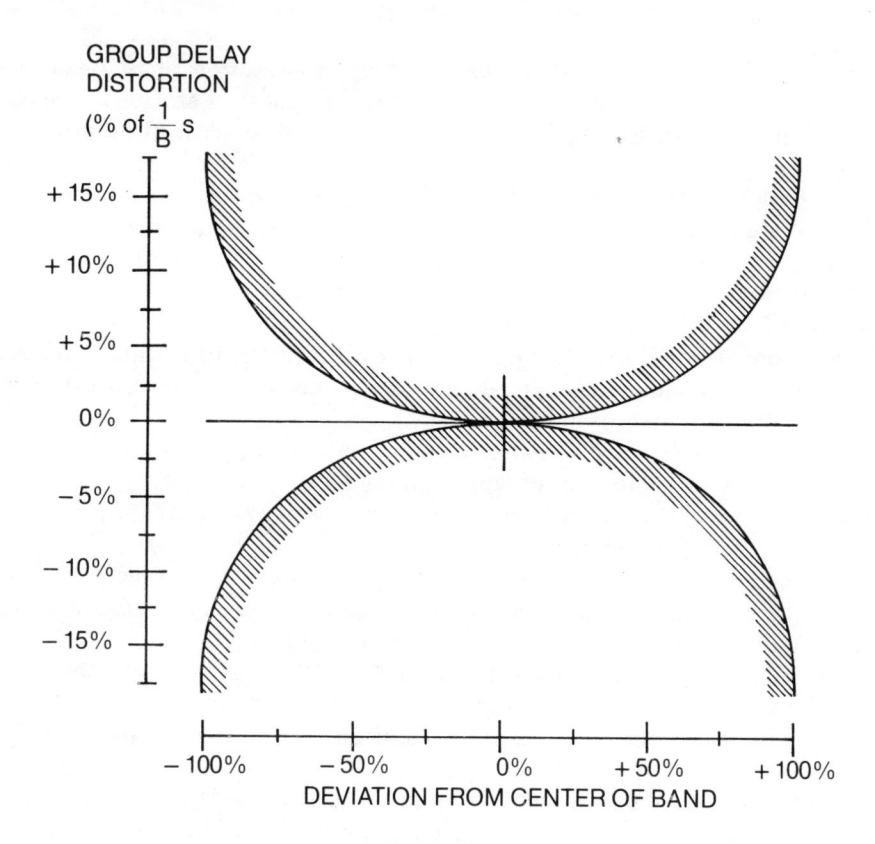

**Fig 15-4
Limits for Group-Delay Distortion**

$$PGD = \pm 10 \log_{10} \cos\left(\pi \frac{f}{B}\right), \quad |f| \leq \frac{B}{2} \qquad \text{(Eq 15-5)}$$

where
- PGD denotes the maximum permissible channel group delay distortion relative to the center of the signaling band, measured as a <u>percent</u> of 1/B seconds
- f denotes frequency variation (Hz) relative to the center of the signaling band
- B denotes the bandwidth of the channel (Hz).

15.6.6 Third-Order Distortion. The composite triple beat due to all the signals on the cable except those provided by this station shall be at most −57 dB (1 mV, 75 Ω) [dBmV] as measured at the point of station connection. This measurement should be performed in accordance with standard CATV practice.

15.6.7 Power Handling Capability. The 50 Hz or 60 Hz ac power commonly carried on broadband trunk cables shall not be carried on the (drop-cable) medium which connects directly to the station or remodulator. The total power over the entire cable spectrum, as presented to the station or remodulator, shall be less than 0.25 W.

15.6.8 Compatibility with the Stations and Head-End Remodulator. An embodiment of a broadband bus medium "layer" entity is deemed to support a specific broadband bus local area network if

(1) It provides a _forward_ channel of suitable bandwidth for the local area network and a _reverse_ channel of equal bandwidth

(2) The stations of that local area network can receive on that forward channel and transmit on that reverse channel

(3) The network has a remodulator connected closer to the cable system's head-end than all (other) stations, and that remodulator can transmit on that forward channel and receive on that reverse channel

(4) The requirements of 15.6.1 through 15.6.7 (inclusive) are met on the reverse channel when measured from the point of remodulator connection to the medium, independent of which point of station connection to the medium is chosen for test signal origination

(5) The requirements of 15.6.1 through 15.6.7 (inclusive) are met on the forward channel when measured from each point of station connection to the medium, with test signals originated at the point of remodulator connection to the medium.

15.6.9 Alternate Broadband Media. [OPTIONAL] Section 14 specifies the standard (preferred) broadband medium configuration as a single trunk cable and single drop cable, bidirectional by frequency, mid-split CATV-like configuration. Other configurations are possible which meet the intent of this standard, including mid-split, high-split, or dual-cable media, and redundant media.

15.6.10 Redundancy Considerations. As implied by 14.9.8 and 14.9.17, redundant broadband media are not precluded from this standard. Where redundant media are employed, the provisions of 15.6.1 to 15.6.8 shall apply separately and independently to each single nonredundant medium interface. Additionally, the forward channel frequency and bandwidth, and reverse channel frequency and bandwidth, for the local area network shall be the same on all of the redundant media.

15.6.11 Reliability. All active (powered) medium "layer" equipment should be designed so that the aggregate probability of that equipment causing a communication failure at more than one station connected to the medium is less than 10^{-4} per hour of continuous (or discontinuous) operation. Connectors and other passive components comprising the means of connecting the station to the coaxial cable medium shall be designed to minimize the probability of total network failure.

15.7 Environmental Specifications

{NOTE: Subsection 15.7 is not a part of the ISO standard. The subject of international standards in this area is under study by the International Electrotechnical Commission and other organizations.}

15.7.1 Safety Requirements. Recommendations and guidelines related to safety concerns are given in this subsection. The list is incomplete; neither does it address all possible safety concerns. The designer is urged to consult the relevant local, national, and international safety codes and regulations to ensure compliance with the appropriate codes and standards. EIA CB 8-1981[9] provides additional guidance on many relevant regulatory requirements.

Local area network cable systems as described in Section 15 are subject to at least four direct electrical safety hazards during their use, and designers of connecting equipment should be aware of these hazards. The hazards are

(1) Direct contact between local network components and power or lighting circuits

(2) Static charge buildup on local network cables and components

(3) High-energy transients coupled onto the local network cabling system

(4) Potential differences between safety grounds to which various network components are connected.

These electrical safety hazards, to which all similar cabling systems are subject, should be alleviated properly for a local area network to perform correctly. In addition to provisions for properly handling these faults in an operational system, special measures shall be taken to ensure that the intended safety features are not negated when attaching or detaching equipment from the local area network medium of an existing network.

15.7.1.1 Sound installation practice, as defined by ANSI/NFPA 70-1984[3], Article 820 and applicable local codes and regulations shall be followed in every instance in which such practice is applicable.

15.7.1.2 The shields of the trunk coaxial cable segments and the tap housings of all connected taps are connected in series in each branch of a properly installed broadband bus medium. This connected conductive path shall be effectively grounded at more than one point along the length of the trunk cable, and at every point where the cable enters or leaves a building structure. The suggested practice is to effectively ground each tap housing, and to effectively ground the cable shield at least once per hundred meters on long cable runs between tap housings, but where large differences in ground potential exist between grounding points, other practices may be necessary. Effectively grounded means—permanently connected to earth through a ground connection of sufficiently low impedance and having sufficient ampacity to prevent the buildup of voltages that may result in undue hazard to connected equipment or to persons.

15.7.1.3 The shields of all drop coaxial cable segments shall be effectively grounded to the tap housings to which they connect.

15.7.1.4 Where there is reason to believe that the ground potential of an exposed shield of a coaxial cable, or housing of a connector or tap differs from the ground potential in the vicinity of that component by more than a few volts, an insulating sleeve, boot, or cover should be affixed to that equipment in such a manner as to ensure that users (not installers) of the equipment will not inadvertently complete a circuit between the exposed shield or housing and the local ground through body contact.

15.7.1.5 Installation and Maintenance Guidelines. Installation and maintenance guidelines developed within the CATV industry for inter- and intra-facility installation of coaxial cable systems shall be followed where applicable. In addition the following caution shall be observed:

> **CAUTION:** At no time should the shield of any portion of the coaxial trunk cable be permitted to float without an effective ground. If a section of floating cable is to be added to an existing cable system, the installer shall take care not to com plete the circuit between the shield of the floating cable section and the grounded cable section through body contact.

15.7.1.6 The installation instructions for broadband coaxial cable networks shall contain language which familiarizes the installer with the caution and guidelines of 15.7.1 through 15.7.1.5.

15.7.2 Electromagnetic and Electric Environment. Sources of interference from the environment include electromagnetic fields, electrostatic discharge, transient voltages between earth connections, etc. Several sources of interference contribute to voltage buildup between the coaxial cable and the earth connection, if any, of the station.

The medium "layer" entity embodiment shall meet its specifications when operating in an ambient plane wave-field of
(1) 2 V/m from 10 kHz through 30 MHz
(2) 5 V/m from 30 MHz through 1 GHz.

15.7.3 Temperature and Humidity. Any embodiment of this standard is expected to operate over a reasonable range of environmental conditions related to temperature, humidity, and physical handling such as shock and vibration. Specific requirements and values for these parameters are considered to be beyond the scope of this standard. Manufacturers are requested to indicate in the literature associated with system components and equipment (and on the components if possible) the operating environment specifications to facilitate selection, installation, and maintenance of these components.

15.7.4 Regulatory Requirements. The following regulatory requirements may apply to local area network equipment and media:
ANSI/NFPA 70-1984[3], Articles 250, 800, and 820, ANSI/UL 94-1979[4], rated under V-0, ANSI/UL 114-1982[5], ANSI/UL 478-1979[6], CSA Standard C22.2 No 154-M 1983[8], FCC Docket 20780-1980 (Part 15, Subpart J and Part 76, Subpart K)[10], and IEC 716-1983[11].

TOKEN-PASSING BUS

IEEE
Std 802.4-1985

In particular, the FCC requirements for radiation from the coaxial cable medium and connected equipment (Part 15) do apply, and shall be considered in any embodiment of the medium "layer" entity specified in this standard.

NOTE: Equipment designed for CATV use must comply with the relevant FCC requirements (Part 76), which generally are more stringent than Part 15.

15.8 Transmission Path Delay Considerations. When specifying an embodiment of a medium "layer" which conforms to the specifications of this Section (15), a vendor shall state the Transmission Path Delay as the maximum delay which the broadband bus medium could be expected to induce on a transmission from any connected station through the head-end remodulator and back to that station. The delays induced by the transmitting and receiving stations themselves should not be included in the Transmission Path Delay.

For each potentially worst-case path through the medium, a path delay is computed as the sum of the medium-induced delay and head-end remodulator-induced delay in propagating a signal from one station to another. The Transmission Path Delay used for determining the network's slot_time (see 6.1.9) shall be the largest of these path delays for the cable system.

These path delay computations shall take into account all circuitry delays in the head-end remodulator and the medium "layer" amplifiers, taps, splitters, etc, and all signal propagation delays within the cable segments themselves. The head-end remodulator delays shall be determined as specified in 14.11 and 6.1.9.

The Transmission Path Delay shall be expressed in terms of the network's symbol signaling rate on the medium. When not an integral number of signaled symbols, it shall be rounded up to such an integral number. When uncertain of the exact value of the delay, vendors shall state an upper bound for the value.

15.9 Documentation. It is recommended that each vendor of an embodiment of a medium "layer" entity conformant to this standard provide to the user supporting documentation with at least these parameters

(1) Specific sections of the standards to which the embodiment conforms

(2) Configuration type—sub-split, mid-split, high-split, or dual-cable

(3) Upper limit of forward channel frequency spectrum (for example, 300 MHz, 400 MHz, 450 MHz)

(4) The transmission path delay, as specified in 15.8 and 6.1.9

(5) The proper range of transmitter output levels for head-end remodulators so that the signal-level requirements of 14.9.5.4, 14.9.9, and 14.9.19 are all met.

15.10 Network Sizing

15.10.1 Topology Considerations. Very small systems can be constructed using only flexible coaxial cable and passive impedance-matching networks. Larger systems require amplifiers and power supplies, together with semirigid trunk cable and flexible drop cables. Highly branched topologies are achieved easily in this medium using standard CATV-like components.

Each head-end remodulator shall be "upstream" from all of the (other) stations on its local area network, but need not actually be at the head-end of the entire cable system. It is only necessary that the head-end remodulator be closer to the "root" of the tree-shaped cable system than any of the other stations of its network. Thus in large systems (for example, campus-wide or city-wide), a large cable tree could have many subtrees, with a head-end remodulator at the root of each subtree controlling a local area network within that subtree, and with all the networks using the same pair of forward and reverse channels. Band-stop (notch) filters are needed in the cable segments which connect those subtrees to isolate the forward and reverse channels of each subtree's network to that subtree.

15.10.2 Signal Loss Budget Considerations. The placement of broadband amplifiers, and the placement of taps, choice of number of drops in each tap, and determination of the tap's insertion and drop losses shall take into account

(1) Each station's minimum transmit level and receive level specifications (see 14.9.5.4 and 14.9.9)

(2) The desired current and anticipated future placement of station's and head-end remodulator

(3) The presented signal level, signal to noise, and intermodulation distortion specifications of 15.6.

Appendix A

A Model Used for the Service Specification

(This Appendix is not a part of this standard but is included for information only.)

A1. Service Hierarchy. The services of a layer are the capabilities which it offers to a user in the next higher layer. To provide its service, a layer builds its functions on the services which it requires from the next lower layer. Fig A1 illustrates this notion of service hierarchy and shows the relationship of the two correspondent N-users and their associated N-layer peer protocol entities.

A2. N-layer Interface. Services are specified by describing the information flow at the interface between the N-user and the N-layer. This information flow is modeled by discrete, instantaneous interface events, which characterize the provision of a service. Each event consists of passing a service primitive from one layer to the other through an N-layer service access point associated with an N-user. Service primitives convey the information required in providing a particular service. These service primitives are an abstraction in that they specify only the service provided rather than the means by which the service is provided. This definition of service is independent of any particular interface implementation.

**Fig A1
Service Hierarchy Relationships**

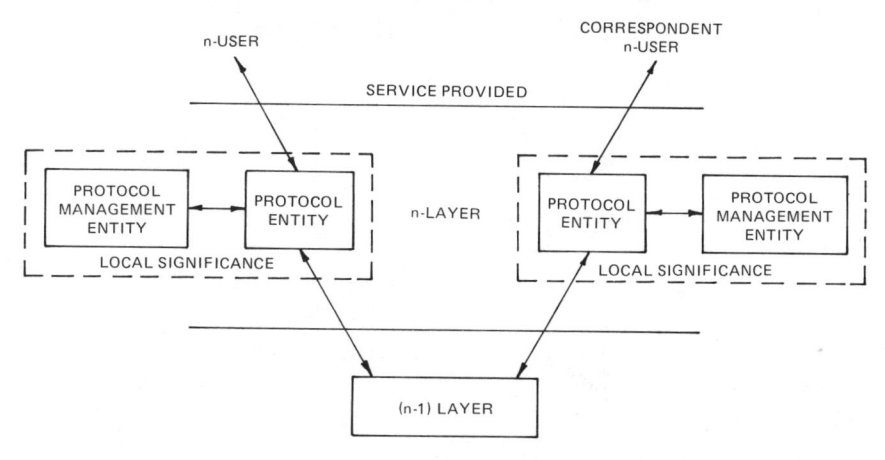

Specific implementations may also include provisions for interface interactions which have no direct end-to-end effects. Examples of such local interactions include interface flow control, status requests and indications, error notifications, and layer management.

A3. Specification of Services. Services are specified here by describing the service primitives and parameters which characterize each service. A service may have one or more related primitives which constitute the interface activity which is related to the particular service. Each service primitive may have zero or more parameters which convey the information required to provide the service.

A4. Classification of N-layer Service Primitives. Primitives are of three generic types.

A4.1. Request. The request primitive is passed from the N-layer to the (N-1)-layer to request that a service be initiated.

A4.2. Indication. The indication primitive is passed from the (N-1)-layer to the N-layer to indicate an internal (N-1)layer event which is significant to the N-layer. This event may be logically related to a remote service request, or may be caused by an event internal to the (N-1)-layer.

A4.3. Confirmation. The confirmation primitive is passed from the (N-1)-layer to the N-layer to convey the results of the associated previous service request.

A5. Interaction Behavior. Possible relationships among primitive types are illustrated by the time sequence diagrams shown in Fig A2. The figure also indicates the logical relationship of the primitive types. Primitive types which occur earlier in time and are connected by dotted lines in the diagrams are the logical antecedents of subsequent primitive types. Note that the logical and time relationship of the indication and the response primitive types are specified by the semantics of a particular service.

**Fig A2
Service Primitive Interactions**

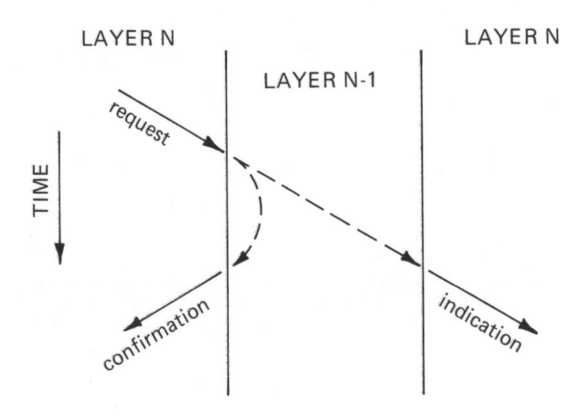

S. Aggarwal